Sex
On
Campus

ROBERT McGONIGLE

Sex
On
Campus

The Naked Truth
About the Real Sex Lives
of College Students

Leland Elliott
Cynthia Brantley

RANDOM HOUSE   NEW YORK

Library of Congress Cataloging-in-Publication Data

Elliott, Leland and Brantley, Cynthia.
Sex on Campus / Leland Elliott and Cynthia Brantley.—1st ed.
p.   cm.
ISBN 0-679-74630-7
I. Title.

Manufactured in the United States of America on acid-free paper

First Edition
U.S.

Table

of

Contents

Acknowledgments

The authors would like to thank the following for their initiative: Joe Dolce, who shared our enthusiasm for investigating the sex lives of college students; big thanks to Tim Moss for keeping the lines of communication open even while juggling his own monthly magazine deadlines; Chris Kensler for his excellent editorial work and guidance early in the project; Jon Karp and Sean Abbott at Random House for their sharp editorial senses and support; massive kudos to all the folks at Condé Nast Research and Willard & Schulman, who brought the massive survey project home safely; thanks also to Beth Gibson for overseeing the production, and a big hug and kiss to Amy Bryant, who remained calm in the storm and never dropped the ball.

We would especially like to thank everyone at SIECUS (Sexual Information and Education Council of the United States) and the Mary S. Caldrone Library, who let us use their incredible resources and reference tools. Without them, we never would have found the insights provided by the college sex surveys done before ours, which gave us direction and which we reference throughout this book. SIECUS is a unique and invaluable resource for anyone and everyone concerned about sexual health and sexuality in America. If you're ever in New York, look them up and pay them a visit.

Disclaimer

This book candidly explores various sexual activities. **Readers should not attempt any of the activities described in these pages without employing safe sex practices.** The authors provide basic health warnings in the appropriate chapters to remind readers of the health hazards involved, but these warnings should not be considered comprehensive. Neither the authors of this book nor its publishers assume any responsibility for the exercise or misuse of the practices described herein.

Foreword

For almost all of the important things the young have to learn in order to become responsible adults—everything from the 3 Rs, social etiquette, and the value of money, to using a computer and driving a car—society provides a multitude of resources. Among these are family and neighbors, schools and colleges, detailed books, tapes, and videos.

Sexuality, however, is the exception. Despite all the sexual titillation in our society, there is actually very little real information, especially on exactly how to go about having sex. To be sure, there has been some progress. Before Kinsey's studies were published half a century ago, not only wasn't there information on how to "do it," there also wasn't much material about what people were doing. It is all well and good for a parent, teacher, or therapist to tell someone "It doesn't make any difference what others are doing, you have to decide for yourself." But while this statement has a certain inherent truth, it is also naïve. Humans are social beings. What others are doing is extremely important to us. We need our reference points, we need to know what is normal or typical.

We have come a long way with this kind of knowledge. Numerous studies have informed us on the attitudes held by and the behaviors engaged in by other people. This is the kind of information taught so well in college sex courses. *Sex on Campus* makes its own contribution. It uses the largest sample of college students I'm aware of to inform us what students are thinking and doing. This is one of the things that makes this book helpful.

When we turn to teaching the actual how-to of sex, progress has been much slower. Most sex books are far less explicit than most cookbooks. High school and college sex courses are useful for teaching anatomy, physiology, and demographics—that is, who does what to whom and how often—but I have yet to hear of any such course that teaches exactly *how* to perform these activities. It was considered a giant step forward several years ago when many sex educators, in response to the AIDS crisis, started demonstrating how to put on a condom. However, I have not heard of a teacher who taught what to do after the condom is on.

One reason that our society has not made any formal arrangements to teach young people how to have sex is the prevalent notion that there's nothing to teach because the knowledge and skills are instinctive. But that is true in only one sense. The desire to have intercourse is programmed into us because it is necessary for the survival of the species. However, this says nothing about good sex, fun sex, and sex that treats each partner with respect and that leaves both of them satisfied and happy. There is no natural programming for this kind of sex. Good sex has to be learned, but we as a society have yet to acknowledge this.

This is tragic. Sex *is* important. Not only is it the basis of all life, but it is also fun and one of the primary bonds—the glue, if you will—that keeps couples together. Being misinformed and unskillful in sex leads to horrible and widespread problems: in personalities, in relationships, and, of course, in sex itself. Yet our society has left it to every individual, every couple, and every generation to bumble and stumble on their own, trying to figure out how to get sex right. A great many individuals and couples never do. We now have, of course, an army of marital and sex therapists to help with these problems, but that isn't enough.

A great deal of human suffering could be prevented if we just gave young people, those at the onset of their sexual activities, the information they need. It won't happen any time soon in an official way because the teaching of sex is a hot political issue. But those not in an official capacity can make a huge difference. I like *Sex on Campus* because it covers both sides of the information everyone needs to know about sex—what peers are doing and how they are doing it. The survey results are informative and sure to be of interest to most college students and those who care about and teach them.

The how-to sections are explicit, as they should be. They tell readers how to go about masturbation, oral sex, and other important behaviors, as well as providing suggestions for dealing with problems that may arise in these areas. And, yes, the authors are equally explicit about how to protect oneself and one's partner from the risks of sex.

This work represents a rational way of dealing with sex. No religion, no government, no one, and no thing has ever prevented young people from engaging in sex. For over 2,000 years, young people have been told to just say no or wait until they are married. It has never worked. Even the so-called Puritans were not as pure as we'd like to think. Records indicate that, in Colonial America, about a third of brides were pregnant before their weddings. What the negative teachings about sex have done is made people feel bad for what they are doing and created conditions that made their activities less pleasurable and less safe than they could have been. Young people will have sex. Why not provide the information and tools they need to make it as joyful, loving, and safe as possible? This is what *Sex on Campus* is all about.

This is a fun book, an informative book, and a very useful book. I wish it had been available when I was in college. I'm confident many of today's students will be happy to have it and will learn a great deal from it.

Bernie Zilbergeld, Ph.D.
Psychologist and sex therapist, Oakland, California
Former Codirector of Clinical Training, Human Sexuality Program,
University of California Medical School, San Francisco,
and Author of Male Sexuality *and* The New Male Sexuality

Part One

Introduction

Welcome to *Sex on Campus*—your one-stop source for the how-to, how-many, where, why, and *what?!* of college sexuality. This is a book exclusively for college students, put together by a couple of writers who were in college recently enough to know what's what. It is part guidepost, part reference manual.

The guidepost part comes from an unprecedented survey of college students conducted by *Details* magazine and Random House. In October 1996, *Details* sent out 20,000 surveys asking college students more than 150 questions about their sex lives. Nearly 2,000 (1,752, to be exact) complete, usable surveys were returned, making this one of the most comprehensive surveys of student sexuality to date. We use the results of the survey throughout this book as a part of our discussion on various topics. For quick reference, we have reprinted some of the survey results on pages 5 through 35. We hope this information will give students a better idea of what their peers are up to. Profit from their experience and learn from their mistakes—as you will see, there is plenty of both.

The reference manual part contains important information about sexual health, safe sex, birth control, and all-important sexual techniques gathered through months of research and interviews with counselors and professionals (and, yes, through personal experience, too, in case you were wondering). But *Sex on Campus* is no ordinary, general how-to manual for the masses. The information is tailored specifically to the needs of college students. We address such important, college-specific issues as:

- How to avoid making an ass of yourself at frat parties
- How to ask for a date after class without looking cheesy

■ How to get a one-night-stander out of your dorm room once you realize you've made a terrible, terrible mistake

And much, much more! Plus, we aren't going to talk to you in dry medical jargon and give you a bunch of unrealistic advice. You'll get the straight dope in terms you can understand from people who have been in the trenches and know what you are facing.

Speaking of jargon, make sure to check out the glossary at the end of the book. It is filled with sexual slang no college student's repertoire should lack.

We hope you find *Sex on Campus* as enjoyable and useful to read as we did to write. Useful to write, you ask? Imagine starting a conversation by saying, "I'm writing a book about sex. . . ." See what we mean?

Anyway, good luck and happy reading!

CHAPTER 1

Sex on Campus Survey

Here are the highlights of our findings. The numbers you see are percentages. For each question, we have given you the overall total and the breakdown by gender, status of virginity, and sexual preference.

PRELIMINARY QUESTIONS

						Sexual Orientation			
	Total	Male	Female	Virgin	Not a Virgin	Male Heterosexual	Male Gay/ Bisexual	Female Heterosexual	Female Gay/ Bisexual
Are you a virgin?									
Yes	20	20	19	NA		21	10	19	14
No	80	80	81		NA	79	90	81	86
Are you currently involved in a relationship?									
Yes	54	50	57	33	59	52	20	57	60
No	46	50	43	67	41	48	80	43	40
You consider yourself . . .									
Heterosexual	92	92	92	95	92	NA		NA	
Homosexual	2	3	1	0	3		44		19
Bisexual	5	4	6	4	5		56		81
Asexual	0	0	0	0	0				

IMAGE IS EVERYTHING

	Total	Male	Female	Virgin	Not a Virgin	Sexual Orientation			
						Male Heterosexual	Male Gay/Bisexual	Female Heterosexual	Female Gay/Bisexual

When you first take off your clothes with a new sex partner, you are more likely to feel ...

	Total	Male	Female	Virgin	Not a Virgin	Male Heterosexual	Male Gay/Bisexual	Female Heterosexual	Female Gay/Bisexual
Confident—keep the lights on if you feel like it	53	72	36	44	54	73	56	35	54
Embarrassed—rather turn 'em out	47	28	64	56	46	27	44	65	46

Your biggest obstacle to having sex is your ...

	Total	Male	Female	Virgin	Not a Virgin	Male Heterosexual	Male Gay/Bisexual	Female Heterosexual	Female Gay/Bisexual
Shyness	17	21	15	13	18	22	5	14	13
Performance anxiety	14	17	12	4	17	18	14	12	9
Body image	20	12	26	10	22	9	48	27	21
Lack of partner	22	28	17	22	23	28	33	16	27
Religious beliefs or personal value system	28	23	33	57	22	24	6	33	29

How often do you work out?

	Total	Male	Female	Virgin	Not a Virgin	Male Heterosexual	Male Gay/Bisexual	Female Heterosexual	Female Gay/Bisexual
Very rarely or never	24	22	27	22	25	21	35	27	29
Once a week	14	12	15	14	14	12	15	15	21
Twice a week	16	15	16	16	16	16	14	16	14
Three times a week	17	16	18	18	17	16	19	18	20
Four times a week	11	13	10	12	11	14	2	10	9
Five or more times a week	17	22	13	18	17	22	15	14	7
Average (mean)	2.5								

The primary reason I work out is ...

	Total	Male	Female	Virgin	Not a Virgin	Male Heterosexual	Male Gay/Bisexual	Female Heterosexual	Female Gay/Bisexual
For my health	29	34	25	31	28	34	22	24	31
To look better	42	36	46	39	42	36	38	47	33
To feel better	35	35	34	36	34	35	38	34	40
To enhance my sex life	2	2	1	0	2	2	9	1	3

Have you ever ...

	Total	Male	Female	Virgin	Not a Virgin	Male Heterosexual	Male Gay/Bisexual	Female Heterosexual	Female Gay/Bisexual
Taken steroids to bulk up	2	5	0		3	5	5	0	
Used weight-gaining powders	22	52	1	18	22	55	28	1	2
Used diet pills	25	10	35	21	26	9	16	34	41
Gone on a diet	82	59	96	83	81	57	74	97	94

	Total	Male	Female	Virgin	Not a Virgin	Sexual Orientation			
						Male Heterosexual	Male Gay/Bisexual	Female Heterosexual	Female Gay/Bisexual
Men: Please (honestly) estimate the size of your erect penis.									
4 inches	2	2		8	0	2	2		
5 inches	12	12		19	10	12	17		
6 inches	38	38		37	38	37	44		
7 inches	32	32		21	34	32	26		
8 inches	11	11		11	11	12	6		
9 inches	4	4		3	5	4	5		
10 inches or more	0	0		1	0	0			
Average (mean)	6.5								
Men: How do you rate the size of your penis?									
Below average	11	11		20	9	11	13		
About average	76	76		73	76	76	76		
Above average	13	13		7	15	13	11		
Men: Would you ever consider having an operation to enlarge it?									
Yes	12	12		7	14	12	20		
No	88	88		93	86	88	80		
Women: Please estimate the average size of a man's penis.									
4 inches									
5 inches									
6 inches	41		41		46			41	
7 inches	36		36	100	29			36	
8 inches	16		16		17			16	
9 inches	7		7		8			7	
10 inches or more									
Average (mean)	6.9								
Women and gay or bisexual men: If you could change it, would you rather your current (or most recent) partner had a larger penis?									
Absolutely	6	9	6	3	6		9	5	13
Sure, but no big deal	39	43	39	41	39		43	39	32
No	55	48	56	56	55		48	56	55
Women: How do you rate the size of your breasts?									
Below average	23		23	27	22			23	15
About average	56		56	48	58			57	49
Above average	21		21	24	21			20	36

	Total	Male	Female	Virgin	Not a Virgin	Sexual Orientation			
						Male Heterosexual	Male Gay/ Bisexual	Female Heterosexual	Female Gay/ Bisexual
Women: Would you ever consider having an operation to enlarge them?									
Yes	11		11	6	13			12	4
No	89		89	94	87			88	96
If you could instantly change your body, what would you change?									
Stomach	56	48	63	50	58	48	54	63	59
Weight	40	25	52	42	39	24	36	53	38
Muscularity	35	45	27	33	36	44	63	27	35
Butt	32	14	46	35	31	12	36	47	40
Chest/breasts	30	30	29	31	29	29	45	29	30
Legs	30	13	44	31	29	12	20	44	40
Waist	27	15	38	28	27	14	24	38	39
Height	24	24	25	24	25	24	26	25	22
Arms	21	23	20	22	21	22	30	20	20
Skin	20	17	23	25	19	17	12	23	23
Hair	17	15	18	17	17	16	10	18	19
Nose	12	10	13	15	11	10	14	13	12
Penis	6	14	0	9	6	13	22	0	
Lips	4	3	5	6	4	3	11	5	5
Chin	3	1	4	4	3	1	2	4	5
What's your opinion of cosmetic surgery for women?									
Why not—it makes you look and feel better.	40	39	41	31	42	38	52	41	36
Not a good idea—you should play with the hand you're dealt.	54	56	51	60	52	57	42	52	39
It's oppressive and all that is wrong with society.	7	6	8	9	7	5	9	7	26
What's your opinion of cosmetic surgery for men?									
Why not—it makes you look and feel better.	37	36	38	29	39	35	53	39	33
Not a good idea—you should play with the hand you're dealt.	55	59	53	63	54	60	43	54	39
It's oppressive and all that is wrong with society.	7	5	9	9	7	5	4	7	28
Using a scale of 1 (most important) to 12 (least important), please rank the qualities that you find attractive in a sexual partner.									
Power or success	8.9	9.7	8.1	8.9	8.9	9.8	8.6	8.1	9.0
Legs	8.8	7.6	9.9	9.1	8.8	7.5	8.7	10.0	9.3
Chest/breasts	8.6	7.8	8.8	8.8	8.5	7.8	8.4	9.3	9.1
Butt	8.4	7.8	8.8	8.8	8.2	7.8	7.9	8.8	9.4

	Total	Male	Female	Virgin	Not a Virgin	Sexual Orientation			
						Male Heterosexual	Male Gay/ Bisexual	Female Heterosexual	Female Gay/ Bisexual
Height	8.3	9.5	7.4	8.2	8.4	9.5	8.8	7.4	7.9
Eyes	6.7	6.9	6.4	6.8	6.6	7.0	6.2	6.4	6.5
Good body	5.9	5.3	6.3	6.2	5.8	5.3	5.9	6.3	7.0
Beauty	5.7	4.2	7.0	5.8	5.7	4.1	5.6	7.0	6.8
Sensitivity	4.9	5.9	4.1	4.6	5.0	5.9	5.3	4.1	3.4
Brains	4.6	4.9	4.3	4.2	4.7	5.0	3.9	4.4	3.8
Humor	4.4	5.0	3.9	4.3	4.4	5.0	4.3	3.9	3.6
Personality	2.4	2.8	2.0	2.1	2.4	2.8	2.9	2.0	1.9

Using the same scale (1 to 12), please rank the qualities that you believe potential sexual partners find attractive about your gender.

	Total	Male	Female	Virgin	Not a Virgin	Male Heterosexual	Male Gay/ Bisexual	Female Heterosexual	Female Gay/ Bisexual
Power or success	8.3	6.4	9.9	8.4	8.3	6.4	7.5	10.0	9.5
Height	7.9	7.1	8.6	8.0	7.9	7.1	7.2	8.6	9.5
Legs	7.7	9.5	6.1	7.7	7.7	9.6	8.6	6.1	6.5
Brains	7.5	6.7	8.2	7.5	7.5	6.8	6.5	8.3	6.9
Sensitivity	7.2	5.9	8.4	7.1	7.3	5.8	7.2	8.5	7.1
Eyes	7.2	7.1	7.3	7.3	7.2	7.2	6.4	7.3	7.0
Butt	6.3	6.7	6.0	6.9	6.2	6.8	5.7	5.9	7.0
Humor	6.2	5.3	6.9	6.2	6.2	5.3	5.8	7.0	6.3
Chest/breasts	5.9	8.0	4.2	5.8	6.0	8.2	6.4	4.1	4.7
Beauty	4.6	6.3	3.1	4.7	4.6	6.3	6.7	3.1	3.2
Personality	4.4	3.7	5.0	4.2	4.4	3.6	4.9	5.0	4.2
Good body	4.2	4.4	4.0	4.2	4.2	4.4	3.7	4.0	4.9

What's the reason you're least likely to go to bed with someone?

	Total	Male	Female	Virgin	Not a Virgin	Male Heterosexual	Male Gay/ Bisexual	Female Heterosexual	Female Gay/ Bisexual
They're ugly.	34	40	28	28	35	42	18	28	30
They're fat.	29	37	23	27	30	37	47	23	14
They're dumb.	26	14	35	32	24	13	26	34	54
They're of a different race or ethnicity.	10	7	12	9	10	7	10	13	6
They're poor.	3	3	3	4	3	3		3	0

How do you like the way you look?

	Total	Male	Female	Virgin	Not a Virgin	Male Heterosexual	Male Gay/ Bisexual	Female Heterosexual	Female Gay/ Bisexual
I don't, I think I'm ugly.	4	3	4	6	3	3	2	4	4
I'm passable—there's room for improvement.	52	48	55	56	50	47	55	56	48
I'm good-looking.	42	46	38	35	43	46	40	38	42
I'm a knockout.	3	3	3	3	3	3	3	3	6

Women: **I wish I looked more like this person:**

	Total	Male	Female	Virgin	Not a Virgin	Male Heterosexual	Male Gay/ Bisexual	Female Heterosexual	Female Gay/ Bisexual
Janet Jackson	18		18	13	19			18	17
Toni Braxton	9		9	7	10			9	11

	Total	Male	Female	Virgin	Not a Virgin	Sexual Orientation			
						*Male Heterosexual	Male Gay/ Bisexual	Female Heterosexual	Female Gay/ Bisexual
Tia Carrera	9		9	12	8			9	9
Gong Li	8		8	11	7			8	5
Drew Barrymore	7		7	7	7			7	7
Courtney Love	7		7	10	7			7	7
Uma Thurman	6		6	9	5			6	6
Claudia Schiffer	6		6	4	6			6	3
Jenny McCarthy	4		4	4	4			4	5
Alanis Morrisette	4		4	3	4			4	6
Jennifer Aniston	4		4	5	4			4	2
Pamela Anderson Lee	3		3	5	2			3	2
Cindy Crawford	2		2	2	3			2	4
Jodi Foster	2		2	1	2			2	2
Naomi Campbell	2		2		2			2	4
Tabitha Soren	1		1	1	1			2	
Mariah Carey	1		1	0	1			0	4
Jasmine Guy	0		0	1	0			0	1
Michelle Pfeiffer	0		0	0	0			0	2
Sandra Bullock	0		0	0	0			0	1
Courtney Cox	0		0	0				0	
All other models mentions	2		2	2	2			2	
All other female mentions	0		0	0	1			0	1

Men: I wish I looked more like this person:

	Total	Male	Female	Virgin	Not a Virgin	*Male Heterosexual	Male Gay/ Bisexual	Female Heterosexual	Female Gay/ Bisexual
George Stephanopoulos	17	17		13	18	19			
Will Smith	16	16		24	15	16	19		
Ethan Hawke	13	13		13	13	13	14		
Trent Reznor	13	13		7	14	14			
Fabio	8	8		18	6	9			
Keanu Reeves	7	7		7	7	8			
Don Johnson	7	7			8	6	12		
Richard Gere	6	6			8	7			
Lorenzo Lamas	5	5			7	6			
Johnny Depp	3	3		17			32		
Mel Gibson	2	2			3		22		
Sean Connery	1	1			2				

About how often do you think about sex?

	Total	Male	Female	Virgin	Not a Virgin	*Male Heterosexual	Male Gay/ Bisexual	Female Heterosexual	Female Gay/ Bisexual
Every 10 minutes	10	17	5	8	11	17	17	4	7
Every 30 minutes	13	20	6	10	13	21	19	6	7

	Total	Male	Female	Virgin	Not a Virgin	Sexual Orientation			
						Male Heterosexual	Male Gay/ Bisexual	Female Heterosexual	Female Gay/ Bisexual
Every 60 minutes	10	12	9	12	10	13	7	8	16
Every few hours	30	32	28	26	31	32	38	27	31
Once a day	21	13	28	19	21	13	15	28	23
Every few days	10	4	16	11	10	3	4	16	12
Once a week	4	2	5	6	3	2		6	3
Less	2	0	4	8	0	0		4	

⍰ My ideal image of masculinity is . . .

	Total	Male	Female	Virgin	Not a Virgin	Male Heterosexual	Male Gay/ Bisexual	Female Heterosexual	Female Gay/ Bisexual
Jean-Claude Van Damme	22	30	16	21	23	31	15	17	6
George Clooney	19	16	22	18	20	16	22	22	21
Michael Jordan	15	18	13	12	16	18	13	13	7
Keanu Reeves	13	9	16	14	13	8	27	17	12
Ethan Hawke	9	4	13	7	9	3	11	12	26
Hugh Grant	7	5	8	10	6	5	7	8	7
Will Smith	5	5	6	4	6	5	4	6	3
Trent Reznor	2	2	3	3	2	2	2	2	8
George Stephanopoulos	1	2	0	0	1	2		0	3
Fabio	0	1	0	0	0	1		0	2

⍰ My ideal image of femininity is . . .

	Total	Male	Female	Virgin	Not a Virgin	Male Heterosexual	Male Gay/ Bisexual	Female Heterosexual	Female Gay/ Bisexual
Michelle Pfeiffer	29	23	34	27	29	23	18	35	20
Jodie Foster	14	10	18	16	14	9	22	17	30
Elisabeth Shue	10	13	8	10	10	14	4	8	6
Pamela Anderson Lee	9	13	5	8	9	14	5	5	6
Gabrielle Reece	9	9	8	13	7	9	5	9	5
Uma Thurman	8	9	8	8	8	9	13	7	12
Drew Barrymore	8	9	7	7	8	9	13	6	16
Naomi Campbell	6	5	7	3	7	5	11	7	3
Courtney Love	2	2	1	2	2	3		1	
Tabitha Soren	1	2	0	0	1	1	6	0	1

⍰ Now that men are being depicted as sex objects (in underwear ads, etc.), do you think . . .

	Total	Male	Female	Virgin	Not a Virgin	Male Heterosexual	Male Gay/ Bisexual	Female Heterosexual	Female Gay/ Bisexual
It's a sign of more equal footing between the sexes.	46	47	45	37	48	48	38	47	30
It's emasculating to most men.	5	6	3	4	5	6	12	3	5
It puts more pressure on men to look good.	31	36	27	32	31	35	46	28	19
It sucks—no one should be depicted as a sex object.	18	11	25	27	17	11	7	23	48

| | | | | | Sexual Orientation | | | |
| | | | | | | Male | | Female |
	Total	Male	Female	Virgin	Not a Virgin	Male Heterosexual	Gay/ Bisexual	Female Heterosexual	Gay/ Bisexual
Compared to the sex you see on television, in movies, and in magazines, your own sex life is . . .									
Better	24	21	27	7	27	20	30	25	50
About as good	32	29	35	10	35	30	21	36	24
Not as good	44	50	38	84	38	50	49	39	26
Overall, the sexual imagery in popular culture is . . .									
A turn-on	39	48	31	32	41	48	54	32	17
Exploitative	40	35	44	42	39	36	22	44	41
A turnoff	7	5	9	9	7	4	14	8	16
Numbing	14	12	16	18	13	12	11	16	25
Compared to other people your age, your sex life is . . .									
Better than most	36	34	37	5	41	35	33	36	47
About average	39	37	41	27	41	38	28	41	42
Not as good	25	28	22	68	18	27	39	23	11
In your experience, sex generally . . .									
Falls short of your expectations	21	16	26		21	15	25	26	25
Meets your expectations	60	65	55		60	67	53	56	51
Surpasses your expectations	19	19	19		19	19	22	18	24
In your life so far, rate your overall satisfaction with your sex life.									
Very satisfied	42	38	45	24	44	39	22	46	45
Somewhat satisfied	42	45	40	30	44	45	52	40	43
Not very satisfied	16	17	15	46	12	17	26	14	12

EYES ON THE PRIZE

| | | | | | Sexual Orientation | | | |
| | | | | | | Male | | Female |
	Total	Male	Female	Virgin	Not a Virgin	Male Heterosexual	Gay/ Bisexual	Female Heterosexual	Gay/ Bisexual
If you are a virgin, are you . . .									
Waiting for marriage before you have sex	33	31	35	33		33		37	14
Waiting for someone you love	39	37	41	39		37	43	39	65
Waiting till it feels right	25	28	23	25		27	57	23	20
Too anxious to bother right now	2	3	1	2		4		2	

	Total	Male	Female	Virgin	Not a Virgin	Sexual Orientation			
						Male Heterosexual	Male Gay/ Bisexual	Female Heterosexual	Female Gay/ Bisexual
If not, did you lose your virginity . . .									
Before junior high school	2	3	2		2	3	7	1	5
While in junior high school	9	12	6		9	12	16	6	13
While in high school	63	63	63		63	64	54	64	50
While in college	26	22	29		26	21	23	29	32
How did you feel when you lost your virginity?									
Thrilled	36	50	23		36	51	47	23	26
Confused	24	18	29		24	18	26	30	19
Bad	14	7	20		14	7	8	20	17
No different	28	26	29		28	26	19	28	40
Have you ever met a sexual partner . . .									
Online	5	6	4		5	4	27	3	9
On a phone sex or party line	1	2	1		1	1	10	0	4
Through a personal ad	2	3	1		2	2	18	0	7
Which of the following have you done to prepare for a date?									
Gotten a haircut or had your hair styled	39	51	30	35	40	51	52	30	30
Bought clothing	51	40	59	40	53	39	53	61	44
Wore special underwear or lingerie	62	43	78	41	67	41	62	78	85
Applied a fragrance	84	79	88	71	87	79	88	88	80
Bought condoms or other birth control	38	50	27	6	45	50	47	26	44
Rehearsed dialogue	17	18	16	23	16	18	14	16	17
Cleaned up your bedroom, house, or apartment	70	69	72	59	73	69	61	72	74
Changed the sheets on your bed	24	30	20	13	27	30	34	19	25
Hid incriminating items from sight	41	43	40	31	44	43	37	40	40
In general, who asks who for a date?									
You ask	44	77	16	46	43	79	64	14	34
You get asked	56	23	84	54	57	21	36	86	66

	Total	Male	Female	Virgin	Not a Virgin	Sexual Orientation			
						Male Heterosexual	Male Gay/ Bisexual	Female Heterosexual	Female Gay/ Bisexual
During an average week, which do you think about most?									
Schoolwork	42	36	48	54	40	36	33	48	42
Love	29	23	34	28	29	23	24	35	31
Sex	16	25	8	12	17	25	25	7	14
Money	11	13	10	6	13	12	16	10	11
Career	6	8	5	7	6	8	6	5	8
Generally, you go out with . . .									
Several people at once	24	25	24	25	24	24	33	23	29
One person at a time	76	75	76	75	76	76	67	77	71
If you like the person, how far do you generally go on the first date?									
Nowhere—I'll save it for next time	22	24	22	36	19	24	17	22	11
Kissing	46	34	56	44	46	35	19	56	58
Fondling the breasts or butt	11	9	13	13	11	9	2	13	14
Genital fondling	4	4	4	2	5	3	16	4	7
Oral sex	1	2	1	0	2	1	4	1	2
Intercourse	1	1	1	0	1	0	6	1	1
As far as the other person will let me	16	28	5	6	18	28	37	5	11
Please fill out the following chart: I have . . .									
Lied about myself to get someone in bed									
I've done it.	21	29	14	10	24	29	28	14	15
I'd do it again.	4	7	2	0	5	7	7	2	2
I wouldn't do it again.	10	12	9	7	11	12	15	9	12
Tried to get someone drunk or high to get them in bed									
I've done it.	21	30	14	11	24	30	33	13	19
I'd do it again.	5	6	3	1	6	6	11	3	5
I wouldn't do it again.	10	13	8	7	11	14	7	7	8
Slept with someone knowing I would never call again									
I've done it.	32	41	25	9	38	39	64	25	33
I'd do it again.	8	12	5	2	10	11	25	5	4
I wouldn't do it again.	12	12	12	6	13	11	22	11	17

		Total	Male	Female	Virgin	Not a Virgin	Sexual Orientation			
							Male Heterosexual	Male Gay/ Bisexual	Female Heterosexual	Female Gay/ Bisexual
Had a one-night stand										
	I've done it.	46	51	42	12	54	49	70	42	44
	I'd do it again.	13	18	9	2	16	17	38	9	15
	I wouldn't do it again.	16	13	19	6	18	12	13	19	15
Cheated on a steady partner										
	I've done it.	43	45	42	15	50	44	46	41	57
	I'd do it again.	6	6	5	1	7	5	9	5	10
	I wouldn't do it again.	23	24	23	9	27	24	28	23	25

❓ Answer the following statements.

		Total	Male	Female	Virgin	Not a Virgin	Male Heterosexual	Male Gay/ Bisexual	Female Heterosexual	Female Gay/ Bisexual
People should be in love if they have sex.										
	True	53	45	60	71	49	47	18	61	44
	False	45	52	38	24	50	50	82	37	53
It's fine for men to have multiple sex partners.										
	True	20	27	13	11	22	26	43	12	31
	False	77	69	85	85	76	71	55	86	66
It's fine for women to have multiple sex partners.										
	True	18	22	14	10	20	21	40	12	42
	False	79	74	83	84	78	75	58	85	56
I consider myself promiscuous.										
	True	17	23	11	8	19	22	27	10	19
	False	79	70	86	83	78	71	71	86	80

ALL THE WAY

		Total	Male	Female	Virgin	Not a Virgin	Sexual Orientation			
							Male Heterosexual	Male Gay/ Bisexual	Female Heterosexual	Female Gay/ Bisexual
❓ How often do you have sex?										
	Every day	7	6	8		7	6		8	7
	Two or three times a week	31	25	36		31	26	20	35	52
	Once a week	13	12	13		13	12	3	13	16
	Twice a month	14	17	11		14	17	15	12	1
	Once a month	7	8	5		7	8	11	5	1
	Less than once a month	13	15	11		13	14	30	11	12

	Total	Male	Female	Virgin	Not a Virgin	Sexual Orientation			
						Male Heterosexual	Male Gay/ Bisexual	Female Heterosexual	Female Gay/ Bisexual
Less than every six months	9	9	8		9	9	12	8	9
Less than once a year	7	7	8		7	7	9	8	3

Which adjective best describes your attitude toward sex?

	Total	Male	Female	Virgin	Not a Virgin	Male Heterosexual	Male Gay/ Bisexual	Female Heterosexual	Female Gay/ Bisexual
Adventurous	35	37	32	12	40	37	41	32	41
Self-confident	23	23	22	9	26	23	28	22	19
Cautious	22	20	24	34	19	20	11	24	19
Kinky	8	9	7	2	9	9	8	7	13
Confused	5	3	6	8	4	3	5	5	8
Uncomfortable	4	2	5	8	3	2	5	5	0

I often feel unsure about how to satisfy sexual partners.

	Total	Male	Female	Virgin	Not a Virgin	Male Heterosexual	Male Gay/ Bisexual	Female Heterosexual	Female Gay/ Bisexual
True	35	33	37		35	33	29	38	27
False	65	67	63		65	67	71	62	73

What's the longest you've gone without having sex?

	Total	Male	Female	Virgin	Not a Virgin	Male Heterosexual	Male Gay/ Bisexual	Female Heterosexual	Female Gay/ Bisexual
A few days	0	1	0		0	0	5	0	1
A week	2	1	2		2	1		2	3
Two or three weeks	7	6	8		7	6	2	7	13
A month	11	11	11		11	12		12	5
Three months	23	24	21		23	24	25	21	21
Six months	23	23	24		23	22	32	24	15
A year or more	34	34	34		34	34	36	33	40

If you have ever decided to abstain from sex for a long period of time, was it because . . .

	Total	Male	Female	Virgin	Not a Virgin	Male Heterosexual	Male Gay/ Bisexual	Female Heterosexual	Female Gay/ Bisexual
A bad relationship soured you on sex for a while.	36	32	39		36	34	24	39	28
You just wanted a break from the pressures of dating and sex.	41	46	37		41	47	38	37	38
You felt there is too much emphasis placed on sex these days.	15	13	15		15	12	27	15	18
You felt sex itself is overrated.	8	8	7		8	8	9	6	16
You were unhappy with your performance.	2	1	2		2	1	2	2	3

Are you satisfied with the amount of sex you're having?

	Total	Male	Female	Virgin	Not a Virgin	Male Heterosexual	Male Gay/ Bisexual	Female Heterosexual	Female Gay/ Bisexual
Yes	56	46	64		56	47	36	65	65
No	44	54	36		44	53	64	35	35

	Total	Male	Female	Virgin	Not a Virgin	Sexual Orientation			
						Male Heterosexual	Male Gay/ Bisexual	Female Heterosexual	Female Gay/ Bisexual

If not what's preventing you from having more?

	Total	Male	Female	Virgin	Not a Virgin	Male Heterosexual	Male Gay/Bisexual	Female Heterosexual	Female Gay/Bisexual
An unwilling partner	12	15	8	12	16	3	8	14
Shyness	11	15	6	11	15	14	5	3
Laziness	2	3	0	2	4		0	
I'm too busy	23·	21	26	23	21	26	24	42
No one wants me	9	11	8	9	9	27	7	11
No partner	47	41	54	47	41	49	56	45
Fear of disease	9	7	13	9	7	3	14	6

How many sex partners have you had in your life?

	Total	Male	Female	Virgin	Not a Virgin	Male Heterosexual	Male Gay/Bisexual	Female Heterosexual	Female Gay/Bisexual
1	23	21	25		23	23	5	25	18
2	19	19	19		19	20	11	19	12
3	13	13	12		13	13	13	12	19
4	8	7	9		8	7	14	9	5
5	8	8	8		8	8	9	7	12
6–9	14	14	14		14	15	9	14	16
10–14	7	7	7		7	6	17	7	5
15–19	4	4	3		4	4	8	3	4
20–24	1	1	1		1	1	3	1	2
25 or more	3	4	2		3	4	13	2	6
Average	6.4	7.2	5.7		6.4	6.5	14.4	5.5	8.0

Have you ever had sex with someone you didn't like?

	Total	Male	Female	Virgin	Not a Virgin	Male Heterosexual	Male Gay/Bisexual	Female Heterosexual	Female Gay/Bisexual
Yes	36	41	32		36	39	60	30	50
No	64	59	68		64	61	40	70	50

If so, why?

	Total	Male	Female	Virgin	Not a Virgin	Male Heterosexual	Male Gay/Bisexual	Female Heterosexual	Female Gay/Bisexual
It just happened.	47	45	48		47	43	58	51	30
I wanted to be nice.	8	5	11		8	5	6	9	27
I was desperate.	10	14	6		10	12	30	5	17
I was drunk or high.	40	39	42		40	44	7	42	38

Under what circumstances will you have sex?

	Total	Male	Female	Virgin	Not a Virgin	Male Heterosexual	Male Gay/Bisexual	Female Heterosexual	Female Gay/Bisexual
Whenever possible	10	19	3		10	17	33	3	5
Only if I'm really attracted to someone	25	33	18		25	34	34	17	23
Only if I really like the person	28	25	31		28	24	30	31	35
Only in a steady relationship	39	24	52		39	26	3	53	41

	Total	Male	Female	Virgin	Not a Virgin	Sexual Orientation			
						Male Heterosexual	Male Gay/ Bisexual	Female Heterosexual	Female Gay/ Bisexual
What's your favorite sexual position?									
Missionary (man on top)	38	25	48	38	25	26	49	39
Woman on top	39	45	33	39	47	18	33	33
Doggie style	19	25	15	19	24	27	15	11
The spoon	4	4	5	4	3	12	5	3
Other	6	7	6	6	6	20	4	21
During intercourse, have you ever fantasized that you were having sex with ...									
A friend or acquaintance	22	27	18	22	25	55	17	34
Another lover	19	21	17	19	20	30	15	36
An ex	16	17	16	16	17	18	14	28
A celebrity	12	19	7	12	18	25	7	11
A stranger	8	10	5	8	8	34	5	8
A made-up person	7	8	6	7	7	15	5	11
A relative	1	2	0	1	1	7	0	
None of the above	58	55	61	58	57	34	63	36
If a celebrity, which ones?									
Male (net)	55	49	70	55	48	54	75	16
Female (net)	45	51	30	45	52	46	25	84
Elizabeth Shue	21	25	9	21	27	12	8	23
Other male mentions	13	9	24	13	8	15	27	
Brad Pitt	11	11	14	11	9	24	12	16
Other specific male sports figures	10	8	16	10	9		18	
Tom Cruise	10	10	12	10	9	16	13	
Bruce Willis	8	9	4	8	10		5	
Christie Brinkley	7	8	5	7	8	9	3	16
Teri Hatcher	4	4	6	4	4		5	16
Pamela Anderson Lee	2	2	3	2	2			29
Jennifer Aniston	2	3		2	3			
Sean Connery	1	1		1	2			
Robert Redford	0	1		0	1			
Tabitha Soren	0	0		0		8		
Mariah Carey	0		2	0			2	
How many friends have you had sex with?									
None	37	32	41	37	34	14	43	22
One	31	32	31	31	32	28	30	40

	Total	Male	Female	Virgin	Not a Virgin	Sexual Orientation			
						Male Heterosexual	Male Gay/ Bisexual	Female Heterosexual	Female Gay/ Bisexual
Two or three	23	26	20		23	25	32	19	26
Four or more	6	6	5		6	6	16	5	7
Many	3	4	3		3	3	10	2	5

In general, it . . .

	Total	Male	Female	Virgin	Not a Virgin	Male Heterosexual	Male Gay/ Bisexual	Female Heterosexual	Female Gay/ Bisexual
Made you closer	17	17	18		17	15	27	14	30
Ruined the friendship	22	20	30		22	21	21	26	39
Developed into a romance	13	14	10		13	18		14	
Had no effect	47	49	42		47	46	53	46	30

Which of the following, if any, have you used during sex, and how did they affect your experience?

	Total	Male	Female	Virgin	Not a Virgin	Male Heterosexual	Male Gay/ Bisexual	Female Heterosexual	Female Gay/ Bisexual
Pot	28	25	30		28	25	31	28	48
Enhanced it	63	63	64		63	64	72	64	68
Made it worse	16	16	17		16	16	18	17	13
Had no effect	19	18	20		19	18	9	19	19
LSD	6	7	5		6	6	16	4	14
Enhanced it	64	56	75		64	58	52	76	86
Made it worse	17	20	14		17	19	27	12	14
Had no effect	13	15	10		13	16		9	
Heroin	1	1	1		1	1	2	0	4
Enhanced it	13		25		13			23	49
Made it worse	3		7		3				
Had no effect	48	78	19		48	86		12	
Ecstasy	5	6	4		5	5	16	3	13
Enhanced it	83	79	87		83	82	68	88	85
Made it worse	8	12	2		8	7	32	3	
Had no effect	8	9	7		8	11		9	
Crystal meth	2	2	1		2	2		0	4
Enhanced it	52	44	63		52	40		74	29
Made it worse	28	30	24		28	33		9	71
Had no effect	20	25	12		20	27		16	
Alcohol	68	68	69		68	67	77	68	78
Enhanced it	53	51	54		53	52	38	56	37
Made it worse	26	25	27		26	24	42	26	35
Had no effect	20	22	18		20	22	20	17	28
Cocaine	3	4	3		3	5		3	4
Enhanced it	59	66	50		59	65		50	53
Made it worse	18	22	14		18	22		9	47
Had no effect	19	13	28		19	13		31	

	Total	Male	Female	Virgin	Not a Virgin	Male Heterosexual	Male Gay/ Bisexual	Female Heterosexual	Female Gay/ Bisexual
						Sexual Orientation			
Barbiturates	2	2	1		2	2		0	8
Enhanced it	31	23	41		31	16		44	38
Made it worse	43	43	44		43	46		44	43
Had no effect	26	34	15		26	37		12	19
Other	3	4	2		3	3	10	2	4
Enhanced it	82	85	77		82	86	80	78	100
Made it worse	7	8	5		7	5	20	6	
Had no effect	11	7	18		11	8		15	

Where have you had sex?

	Total	Male	Female	Virgin	Not a Virgin	Male Heterosexual	Male Gay/ Bisexual	Female Heterosexual	Female Gay/ Bisexual
In a car	70	73	68		70	72	78	68	71
At the office	9	8	10		9	7	16	10	18
On a waterbed	48	51	46		48	50	53	46	49
Outdoors	65	66	65		65	66	59	64	75
In a library	3	4	3		3	4	5	2	7
In a nightclub	4	5	3		4	4	16	2	12
In a sex club	0	1	0		0	0	10	0	1
In a plane	2	2	1		2	2	3	0	3
In a train	2	3	0		2	2	10	0	6
In a bus	4	6	3		4	5	9	3	8
In your parents' bed	41	45	36		41	47	30	36	38
In other public buildings	28	30	26		28	28	48	25	35
Online	10	11	9		10	8	41	8	17

Please fill in the chart below: WHAT I HAVE DONE.

	Total	Male	Female	Virgin	Not a Virgin	Male Heterosexual	Male Gay/ Bisexual	Female Heterosexual	Female Gay/ Bisexual
Talked dirty	64	65	63		64	65	70	62	76
Spanking	27	30	24		27	30	24	24	33
Bondage	26	27	26		26	26	34	24	48
Sex with much older partner	16	17	16		16	16	26	14	36
Taken photographs	13	13	13		13	12	22	13	22
Role-played	12	11	14		12	9	26	13	28
A threesome	11	13	10		11	11	42	7	40
Online sex	10	12	10		10	8	47	8	24
Phone-sex lines	10	13	7		10	12	26	7	9
Golden shower	9	10	9		9	10	9	9	9
Sex with violence	6	5	7		6	5	9	6	18
S/M	6	6	6		6	6	5	5	21
Same-sex sex (if hetero)	5	4	6		5	3	13	3	38
Used a video camera	5	6	4		5	6	7	4	6

	Total	Male	Female	Virgin	Not a Virgin	Male Heterosexual	Male Gay/ Bisexual	Female Heterosexual	Female Gay/ Bisexual
						Sexual Orientation			
An orgy	4	5	3		4	4	13	2	14
Cross-dressed	4	5	3		4	3	20	2	15
Rape	3	2	5		3	1	5	4	10
Opposite sex sex (if gay)	2	2	2		2		29		30
Sex with an animal	1	1	1		1	1	2	0	7
Other	4	5	3		4	5		3	6

Please fill in the chart below: WHAT I'VE FANTASIZED ABOUT

	Total	Male	Female	Virgin	Not a Virgin	Male Heterosexual	Male Gay/ Bisexual	Female Heterosexual	Female Gay/ Bisexual
A threesome	40	55	27		40 .	54	56	26	44
Used a video camera	28	35	22		28	35	30	22	24
Bondage	24	23	25		24	21	40	24	32
An orgy	22	32	15		22	30	51	13	33
Taken photographs	22	25	19		22	26	24	18	28
Sex with much older partner	22	29	16		22	29	27	15	24
Talked dirty	13	14	13		13	14	16	12	20
Role-played	13	14	13		13	13	19	12	16
S/M	11	11	11		11	11	15	9	21
Sex with violence	11	10	11		11	9	16	11	16
Spanking	10	12	9		10	12	13	8	16
Same-sex sex (if hetero)	10	4	15		10	4	10	14	23
Rape	7	7	8		7	6	15	7	17
Golden shower	5	7	4		5	8	2	4	2
Phone-sex lines	5	6	4		5	6	4	4	4
Online sex	3	4	2		3	4	2	2	3
Cross-dressed	2	3	2		2	3	8	1	6
Sex with an animal	2	3	2		2	2	12	2	8
Opposite sex sex (if gay)	0	1	0		0		13		9
Other	3	3	3		3	3	5	3	3

Has there ever been anything that someone wanted you to do that you wouldn't do?

	Total	Male	Female	Virgin	Not a Virgin	Male Heterosexual	Male Gay/ Bisexual	Female Heterosexual	Female Gay/ Bisexual
Yes	52	30	70		52	28	49	70	70
No	48	70	30		48	72	51	30	30

In general, what has held you back from acting on the things you've only fantasized about?

	Total	Male	Female	Virgin	Not a Virgin	Male Heterosexual	Male Gay/ Bisexual	Female Heterosexual	Female Gay/ Bisexual
They're too scary to try.	16	9	22		16	8	19	21	25
I've been too embarrassed to bring them up.	57	49	65		57	49	45	67	47
I had an unwilling partner.	28	43	14		28	44	39	13	34

	Total	Male	Female	Virgin	Not a Virgin	Sexual Orientation			
						Male Heterosexual	Male Gay/ Bisexual	Female Heterosexual	Female Gay/ Bisexual
Which of the following has been up your butt?									
A finger	37	30	42		37	25	87	40	69
A tongue	17	15	18		17	12	49	18	28
A dildo	4	4	3		4	2	30	2	14
A penis	20	6	31		20	1	61	30	45
None of the above	57	67	48		57	73	11	50	28

THE BIG O

	Total	Male	Female	Virgin	Not a Virgin	Sexual Orientation			
						Male Heterosexual	Male Gay/ Bisexual	Female Heterosexual	Female Gay/ Bisexual
Have you ever had an orgasm?									
Yes	90	94	87	68	95	94	100	86	97
No	10	6	13	32	5	6		14	3
If so, let's count the ways.									
Masturbation	70	86	55	79	68	86	93	52	80
Oral sex	72	74	70	35	77	73	84	69	80
Manual stimulation by a partner	74	76	72	50	78	75	84	71	79
Intercourse	77	80	74		88	80	73	75	61
Other	6	7	4	5	6	8	2	3	16
Have you ever faked an orgasm?									
Yes	41	18	61	13	47	17	27	60	71
No	59	82	39	87	53	83	73	40	29
Have you ever had multiple orgasms?									
Yes	55	47	63	37	58	46	55	63	71
No	45	53	37	63	42	54	45	37	29
How important is it that both you and your partner have orgasms during sex?									
It's essential.	24	33	16		24	33	32	16	16
It's very important.	46	48	44		46	49	44	44	43
It's not that important.	23	14	31		23	13	18	30	33
It doesn't matter.	8	5	10		8	5	7	10	8

					Sexual Orientation			
	Total	Male	Female	Virgin	Not a Virgin	Male Heterosexual	Male Gay/ Bisexual	Female Heterosexual	Female Gay/ Bisexual

How often do you achieve orgasm during sex?

	Total	Male	Female	Virgin	Not a Virgin	Male Heterosexual	Male Gay/Bisexual	Female Heterosexual	Female Gay/Bisexual
Always	33	56	13		33	57	48	12	18
Most of the time	38	35	40		38	34	39	40	48
Half the time	12	5	18		12	5	7	19	6
Rarely	9	3	14		9	2	5	14	13
Never	9	1	15		9	1		15	15

When your partner does not achieve orgasm, whose fault is it?

	Total	Male	Female	Virgin	Not a Virgin	Male Heterosexual	Male Gay/Bisexual	Female Heterosexual	Female Gay/Bisexual
Mostly yours	57	73	44		57	75	56	45	31
Mostly theirs	43	27	56		43	25	44	55	69

Have you ever had trouble getting or staying aroused during sex?

	Total	Male	Female	Virgin	Not a Virgin	Male Heterosexual	Male Gay/Bisexual	Female Heterosexual	Female Gay/Bisexual
Yes	57	50	62		57	49	59	61	71
No	43	50	38		43	51	41	39	29

If so, what do you think was the reason?

	Total	Male	Female	Virgin	Not a Virgin	Male Heterosexual	Male Gay/Bisexual	Female Heterosexual	Female Gay/Bisexual
Not attracted to partner	19	17	21		19	17	18	19	33
Too much on my mind	53	42	61		53	40	60	60	65
Too tired	57	51	62		57	49	69	62	62
Too anxious	23	27	20		23	26	26	20	21
Too drunk or too high	31	39	25		31	41	20	25	23
Switching positions distracted me	26	21	30		26	20	25	31	21
Other	13	15	12		13	15	6	12	16

THE ORAL GROOVE

						Sexual Orientation			
	Total	Male	Female	Virgin	Not a Virgin	Male Heterosexual	Male Gay/ Bisexual	Female Heterosexual	Female Gay/ Bisexual

Have you ever . . .

	Total	Male	Female	Virgin	Not a Virgin	Male Heterosexual	Male Gay/Bisexual	Female Heterosexual	Female Gay/Bisexual
Performed oral sex	81	82	80	33	91	81	94	79	91
Received oral sex	84	83	85	38	94	82	90	84	95
Neither	13	13	13	58	3	13	6	13	5

	Total	Male	Female	Virgin	Not a Virgin	Sexual Orientation			
						Male Heterosexual	Male Gay/Bisexual	Female Heterosexual	Female Gay/Bisexual
How do you feel about performing oral sex?									
I love it.	47	61	34	28	50	60	79	32	58
I don't care either way.	25	20	29	32	24	21	6	30	16
You have to give some to get some.	16	13	19	16	16	13	15	18	22
I can't stand it.	12	6	18	24	10	6		19	4
If you hate it, why?									
I don't like the smell or taste.	43	62	38	35	46	61		37	100
I feel incompetent.	12	2	15	13	12	2		14	33
I feel uncomfortable.	45	26	50	53	43	27		51	33
It feels demeaning to me.	33	9	40	34	32	9		39	57
It demeans my partner.	4	6	4	13	2	6		4	
It doesn't feel good.	19	12	21	17	19	12		21	33
***Women and gay or bisexual men:* When performing fellatio, you . . .**									
Pull your mouth away and use your hands for the climax	49	52	49	64	48		52	50	35
Swallow the semen	41	40	41	32	42		40	41	50
Spit out the semen	18	10	18	12	18		10	18	24
Under what conditions will you engage in oral sex?									
Whenever possible	13	23	5	10	14	22	34	5	9
Only if I'm really attracted to someone	21	26	17	16	22	26	32	17	19
Only if I really like the person	22	19	24	17	22	18	29	24	25
Only in a steady relationship	46	34	57	58	44	36	5	58	54
How satisfied are you with the amount of oral sex you're getting?									
Very	39	28	49	33	40	27	29	50	41
Somewhat	35	40	31	23	37	40	46	31	33
Not at all	26	32	20	44	23	33	25	19	27

	Total	Male	Female	Virgin	Not a Virgin	Sexual Orientation			
						Male Heterosexual	Male Gay/ Bisexual	Female Heterosexual	Female Gay/ Bisexual

How often would you say you and your current (or most recent) partner use birth control?

	Total	Male	Female	Virgin	Not a Virgin	Male Heterosexual	Male Gay/Bisexual	Female Heterosexual	Female Gay/Bisexual
Always	63	62	64		63	63	46	64	63
Most of the time	19	20	18		19	20	11	19	9
Sometimes	6	7	5		6	7	10	4	6
Rarely	5	5	5		5	4	9	6	1
Never	8	7	8		8	5	24	7	21

PLAYING IT SAFE

	Total	Male	Female	Virgin	Not a Virgin	Sexual Orientation			
						Male Heterosexual	Male Gay/ Bisexual	Female Heterosexual	Female Gay/ Bisexual

What method of birth control do you usually use with your partner?

	Total	Male	Female	Virgin	Not a Virgin	Male Heterosexual	Male Gay/Bisexual	Female Heterosexual	Female Gay/Bisexual
Condom	68	73	63		68	73	77	63	61
Birth control pills	40	38	42		40	40	12	43	35
Withdrawal method	19	19	19		19	20	16	20	9
Spermicidal jelly/cream/foam/suppositories	6	8	5		6	7	13	5	13
Rhythm method	5	5	6		5	4	6	6	5
Depo-Provera	2	1	3		2	2		3	
Diaphragm	1	2	0		1	2		0	6
Contraceptive implant (Norplant)	0	0	0		0	0	3	0	
Female condom	0	0	0		0	0	4	0	
IUD	0	0			0	0			
Cervical cap									

Which is your favorite?

	Total	Male	Female	Virgin	Not a Virgin	Male Heterosexual	Male Gay/Bisexual	Female Heterosexual	Female Gay/Bisexual
Birth control pills	42	39	44		42	41	16	46	32
Condom	33	32	33		33	31	48	33	30
Withdrawal method	8	9	7		8	9	9	7	2
Rhythm method	3	3	3		3	3	3	3	
Depo-Provera	3	2	3		3	2		4	
Spermicidal jelly/cream/foam/suppositories	2	2	1		2	2	5	1	2
Contraceptive implant (Norplant)	0	2	0		0	2	3	0	
Diaphragm	0	0	0		0	0		0	

	Total	Male	Female	Virgin	Not a Virgin	Sexual Orientation			
						Male Heterosexual	Male Gay/ Bisexual	Female Heterosexual	Female Gay/ Bisexual
Female condom	0	0	0		0	0	2	0	
IUD	0	0	0		0	0		0	
Cervical cap									

What percentage of the time would you estimate you have safe sex?

	Total	Male	Female	Virgin	Not a Virgin	Male Heterosexual	Male Gay/ Bisexual	Female Heterosexual	Female Gay/ Bisexual
Always	45	48	43		45	49	35	43	46
Most of the time	34	34	34		34	33	40	35	25
Sometimes	10	9	10		10	8	15	10	13
Rarely	7	6	8		7	6	9	8	1
Never	4	3	5		4	3	2	4	14

Have you had sex in the last two years without using a condom because

	Total	Male	Female	Virgin	Not a Virgin	Male Heterosexual	Male Gay/ Bisexual	Female Heterosexual	Female Gay/ Bisexual
I knew that my partner was disease free.	39	37	40		39	37	39	42	23
I didn't care.	21	19	23		21	19	18	24	18
I was drunk or high.	18	17	19		18	17	11	19	19
I didn't want to spoil the mood.	16	16	16		16	16	19	16	10
My partner was just too hot.	14	17	12		14	17	10	11	12
I thought my partner was most likely disease free.	13	13	13		13	12	21	13	14
I was lazy.	13	14	12		13	14	18	12	9
My partner refused.	5	6	5		5	6	5	5	5
I was worried about my partner's response.	4	2	5		4	2	10	5	10

How often do you use a condom during oral sex?

	Total	Male	Female	Virgin	Not a Virgin	Male Heterosexual	Male Gay/ Bisexual	Female Heterosexual	Female Gay/ Bisexual
Always	2	3	2	1	2	3	2	2	
Usually	2	2	1		2	1	7	1	2
Sometimes	3	3	2	0	3	2	14	2	2
Never	77	78	75	30	88	79	67	75	88

How often do you use a dental dam during oral sex?

	Total	Male	Female	Virgin	Not a Virgin	Male Heterosexual	Male Gay/ Bisexual	Female Heterosexual	Female Gay/ Bisexual
Always	0	0	0	0	0	0		0	
Usually	0	0	0	0	0	0		0	
Sometimes	2	2	2	0	2	2	2	0	12
Never	76	78	75	29	88	77	84	75	78

Who usually buys the birth control?

	Total	Male	Female	Virgin	Not a Virgin	Male Heterosexual	Male Gay/ Bisexual	Female Heterosexual	Female Gay/ Bisexual
You	39	44	35		39	46	23	35	32
Your partner	22	19	25		22	20	11	25	18
You share	39	37	41		39	34	66	40	50

	Total	Male	Female	Virgin	Not a Virgin	Sexual Orientation			
						Male Heterosexual	Male Gay/ Bisexual	Female Heterosexual	Female Gay/ Bisexual

? Have you and a partner ever experienced an unplanned pregnancy?

	Total	Male	Female	Virgin	Not a Virgin	Male Heterosexual	Male Gay/ Bisexual	Female Heterosexual	Female Gay/ Bisexual
Yes	12	12	11		12	13	6	12	7
No	88	88	89		88	87	94	88	93

? If so, how many times?

	Total	Male	Female	Virgin	Not a Virgin	Male Heterosexual	Male Gay/ Bisexual	Female Heterosexual	Female Gay/ Bisexual
One	80	81	80		80	83	36	83	31
Two	12	12	12		12	10	64	11	28
Three	6	5	6		6	5		6	
Four or more	2	1	3		2	1			42

? If so, what happened?

	Total	Male	Female	Virgin	Not a Virgin	Male Heterosexual	Male Gay/ Bisexual	Female Heterosexual	Female Gay/ Bisexual
Had the child and kept it	19	24	14		19	25		14	
Had the child and gave it up for adoption	3	4	2		3	4		1	15
Had an abortion	53	43	61		53	43	100	63	42
Had a miscarriage	26	29	23		26	29		23	43

? Have you ever bean diagnosed with a sexually transmitted disease?

	Total	Male	Female	Virgin	Not a Virgin	Male Heterosexual	Male Gay/ Bisexual	Female Heterosexual	Female Gay/ Bisexual
Yes	7	4	9		7	3	12	9	13
No	93	96	91		93	97	88	91	87

? If so, which ones?

	Total	Male	Female	Virgin	Not a Virgin	Male Heterosexual	Male Gay/ Bisexual	Female Heterosexual	Female Gay/ Bisexual
Herpes	15	10	17		15	14		12	51
Gonorrhea	17	20	15		17	13	29	15	14
Syphilis	3	7	2		3		29	1	8
Crabs (pubic lice)	31	54	22		31	37	100	21	30
HIV									
Chlamydia	23	13	27		23	17		28	22
NSU (nonspecific urethritis)	4	4	3		4	6		2	14
Hepatitis B									
Genital warts (human papillomavirus)	31	14	38		31	20		39	33
Trichomoniasis	7	9	6		7	12		7	

GOING SOLO

	Total	Male	Female	Virgin	Not a Virgin	Sexual Orientation			
						Male Heterosexual	Male Gay/ Bisexual	Female Heterosexual	Female Gay/ Bisexual
How often do you masturbate?									
Once a day or more	10	17	4	10	10	15	38	4	9
Two or three times a week	22	33	12	21	22	33	38	10	32
Once a week	13	14	11	15	12	14	11	10	22
Every few weeks	11	10	11	9	11	11	3	11	11
Once a month	4	3	4	4	4	3		4	2
Less than once a month	14	10	17	10	15	10	5	18	13
Never	27	12	40	32	26	13	5	42	11
Masturbation is . . .									
Wrong or sinful	6	5	7	15	4	6		8	3
Perverted	15	9	19	18	14	10	2	20	6
Healthy and/or necessary	79	86	74	67	82	85	98	72	91
Who do you usually fantasize about when you masturbate?									
Your current partner	33	29	37	18	36	30	21	38	29
A celebrity	22	31	12	20	22	30	38	12	13
Someone you know	36	46	25	48	34	45	57	23	39
A stranger	5	7	3	4	6	7	14	3	1
A made-up person	10	9	12	12	10	8	10	12	14
No one	16	8	25	17	16	8	5	25	24
If you've ever fantasized about a celebrity, which one?									
Jennifer Aniston	26	23	32	55	21	25	13	35	8
Drew Barrymore	27	31	16	26	27	29	49	17	8
Pamela Anderson Lee	20	18	28	8	22	19		29	17
Gong Li	27	28	24	10	30	27	38	19	67
Have you ever used any of these items to enhance masturbation?									
Pornographic magazine	38	67	13	28	41	66	81	12	27
Porn video	34	60	12	23	37	58	73	12	18
Lubricants	26	45	11	17	29	43	73	9	31
Nonpornographic magazine	15	28	4	14	15	27	38	4	10
Advertisement	11	19	3	9	11	17	39	3	7

	Total	Male	Female	Virgin	Not a Virgin	Sexual Orientation			
						Male Heterosexual	Male Gay/ Bisexual	Female Heterosexual	Female Gay/ Bisexual
Vibrator	10	6	13	4	11	4	28	11	39
Lingerie or clothing	9	11	8	8	10	10	21	8	11
Clothing	7	10	5	8	7	9	26	4	21
Household items	6	3	9	2	7	2	19	8	27
Dildo	5	3	7	1	6	0	27	5	28
Food	4	4	4	3	5	3	22	4	13
Other	4	3	5	3	4	2	15	5	11
Cock ring	1	3	0		2	1	19	0	

Have you ever . . .

Manually stimulated another person to orgasm

	Total	Male	Female	Virgin	Not a Virgin	Male Heterosexual	Male Gay/ Bisexual	Female Heterosexual	Female Gay/ Bisexual
	72	74	70	35	81	73	87	69	83

Been manually stimulated to orgasm by another person

	67	71	64	34	75	71	79	63	81
Neither	19	16	21	53	10	16	9	22	9

Have you ever masturbated while another person watched?

Yes	35	38	32	8	40	36	69	30	58
No	65	62	68	92	60	64	31	70	42

What statement best describes your feelings about masturbation?

It's a poor substitute for sex.

	33	30	36	26	34	31	11	37	13
I always enjoy it.	22	23	21	16	23	22	41	18	52

It makes me feel lonely and depressed.

	6	5	6	10	5	6	5	6	2

It's the best way to reduce anxiety and frustration.

	29	36	23	24	31	36	43	23	29

ALTERNATIVE NATION

	Total	Male	Female	Virgin	Not a Virgin	Sexual Orientation			
						Male Heterosexual	Male Gay/ Bisexual	Female Heterosexual	Female Gay/ Bisexual

Did you initiate your sex life with

A partner of the same sex

	9	10	7		9	6	53	6	23

A partner of the opposite sex

	88	86	89		88	89	47	91	74
No answer	4	4	3		4	5		3	4

	Total	Male	Female	Virgin	Not a Virgin	Male Heterosexual	Male Gay/ Bisexual	Female Heterosexual	Female Gay/ Bisexual
						Sexual Orientation			

Which of the following have you experienced with a person of your own gender?

	Total	Male	Female	Virgin	Not a Virgin	Male Heterosexual	Male Gay/ Bisexual	Female Heterosexual	Female Gay/ Bisexual
Kissing	19	18	20	15	20	12	96	14	84
Caressing	16	15	17	9	17	8	94	11	79
Manual genital stimulation	11	13	10	5	13	7	86	5	67
Manual anal stimulation	4	6	2	1	5	2	61	1	15
Oral sex	10	13	8	4	12	7	85	4	60
Penetration	6	8	4		8	4	60	2	33
None	77	78	77	84	76	84	2	83	12

How did you feel about it?

	Total	Male	Female	Virgin	Not a Virgin	Male Heterosexual	Male Gay/ Bisexual	Female Heterosexual	Female Gay/ Bisexual
Great—can't wait for next time	44	42	46	48	44	22	84	25	93
Nothing special—could take it or leave it	30	29	30	27	30	38	13	41	7
Definitely not for me	17	22	13	16	17	33		19	
Ashamed	10	8	12	9	11	11	4	17	

If you haven't done so already, would you ever consider having sex with a person of your own gender?

	Total	Male	Female	Virgin	Not a Virgin	Male Heterosexual	Male Gay/ Bisexual	Female Heterosexual	Female Gay/ Bisexual
Absolutely	2	0	3	0	2	0		2	51
Maybe	13	4	21	12	13	4		21	19
Never	85	95	77	87	85	96		77	30

Do you consider yourself openly gay or bisexual?

	Total	Male	Female	Virgin	Not a Virgin	Male Heterosexual	Male Gay/ Bisexual	Female Heterosexual	Female Gay/ Bisexual
Yes	65	60	69	16	71		60		69
No	35	40	31	84	29		40		31

Do your parents know you are gay or bi?

	Total	Male	Female	Virgin	Not a Virgin	Male Heterosexual	Male Gay/ Bisexual	Female Heterosexual	Female Gay/ Bisexual
Yes	31	26	35	8	35		26		35
No	69	74	65	92	65		74		65

When did you become aware of your sexual orientation?

	Total	Male	Female	Virgin	Not a Virgin	Male Heterosexual	Male Gay/ Bisexual	Female Heterosexual	Female Gay/ Bisexual
College	26	13	37	20	27		13		37
High school	48	50	46	50	47		50		46
Junior high	13	20	6	17	12		20		6
Grade school	14	17	11	13	14		17		11

When did you have your first homosexual encounter?

	Total	Male	Female	Virgin	Not a Virgin	Male Heterosexual	Male Gay/ Bisexual	Female Heterosexual	Female Gay/ Bisexual
College	44	30	55	47	43		30		55
High school	40	53	29	47	40		53		29
Junior high	5	7	3		6		7		3
Grade school	11	9	12	6	11		9		12

	Total	Male	Female	Virgin	Not a Virgin	Sexual Orientation			
						Male Heterosexual	Male Gay/ Bisexual	Female Heterosexual	Female Gay/ Bisexual

Have you ever been teased, harassed, or attacked because of your sexual orientation?

Yes	52	62	43	41	53		62		43
No	48	38	57	59	47		38		57

If you have had anal sex, how often have you used a condom?

Every time	17	20	15		17	17	30	12	48
Most of the time	7	9	6		7	6	25	6	4
Sometimes	5	7	4		5	4	20	4	5
Rarely	5	5	6		5	5	5	6	7
Never	65	60	69		65	68	20	72	37

How do you feel about homosexuality?

It's great—whatever turns you on.	30	23	36	26	31	18	87	31	88
It's a little weird, but whatever.	44	43	45	43	45	46	11	48	10
It's wrong or sinful, whatever the reason.	26	34	19	31	24	36	2	20	2

Is there a strong community of gay and lesbian students at your school?

Yes	42	38	45	45	41	37	51	43	69
No	28	32	26	26	29	31	35	27	14
Don't know	30	31	29	29	30	32	14	30	16

Do you find the idea of sex between women alluring or sexy?

Yes	51	79	29	41	54	80	53	23	95
No	49	21	71	59	46	20	47	77	5

Do you find the idea of sex between men alluring or sexy?

Yes	12	11	12	7	13	5	94	10	43
No	88	89	88	93	87	95	6	90	57

Do you think gay people should have the legal right to marry?

Yes	64	55	72	63	64	52	91	70	95
No	36	45	28	37	36	48	9	30	5

In your opinion, making a distinction between gay and straight is . . .

An accurate description of the way things are	62	67	57	60	62	71	28	61	16
An outmoded distinction in an increasingly omnisexual world	38	33	43	40	38	29	72	39	84

OBSESSION CONFESSIONS

	Total	Male	Female	Virgin	Not a Virgin	Sexual Orientation			
						Male Heterosexual	Male Gay/ Bisexual	Female Heterosexual	Female Gay/ Bisexual
Have you ever been stalked or harassed with obscene phone calls?									
Yes	36	25	45	29	37	24	27	45	47
No	64	75	55	71	63	76	73	55	53
Have you ever followed, spied on, or made unwelcome phone calls to an ex- or current lover?									
Yes	23	19	27	11	26	20	16	27	28
No	77	81	73	89	74	80	84	73	72
Has a date, sexual partner, or friend ever physically forced you into a sexual act?									
Yes	21	11	29	7	24	10	21	28	40
No	79	89	71	93	76	90	79	72	60
Did you consider it rape?									
Yes	41	11	51	26	42	5	38	52	42
No	59	89	49	74	58	95	62	48	58
Have you ever been the victim of a forcible rape by a stranger?									
Yes	2	0	3	0	2	0	4	2	9
No	98	99	97	99	98	99	96	98	91
If so, who did you seek help from?									
Parents	63	32	74		70	39	46	79	36
Professional counselor	53	65	49	51	53	100		47	64
College or other health center	53	35	60	49	54	39	54	60	64
Church	5		7		5			8	
Police	4		5		4			6	
Rape crisis center	34	25	38	51	32	61		34	64
Support group	10		13		11			8	64
Other	17		23		19			21	36
Have you ever had sex with someone who was drunk or high?									
Yes	76	73	77		76	73	83	77	83
No	24	27	23		24	27	17	23	17
Have you ever had sex with an incoherently drunk or unconscious partner?									
Yes	5	7	3		5	7	9	3	3
No	95	93	97		95	93	91	97	97

	Total	Male	Female	Virgin	Not a Virgin	Sexual Orientation			
						Male Heterosexual	Male Gay/ Bisexual	Female Heterosexual	Female Gay/ Bisexual
Has a partner ever physically resisted your attempts to have sex with them?									
Yes	13	17	9	4	14	17	16	9	16
No	87	83	91	96	86	83	84	91	84
If so, what happened?									
You went through with it anyway.	44	47	39		42	43	89	39	37
You didn't go through with it.	56	53	61		58	57	11	61	63
In your opinion, if two people are having intercourse and one asks the other to stop and the person doesn't stop, is that rape?									
Yes	67	58	74	70	66	58	64	73	87
No	9	11	6	9	9	12	8	7	
Unclear	25	30	20	22	25	30	28	20	13
Have you ever said no to someone's advances?									
Yes	81	68	92	77	82	67	76	92	81
No	19	32	8	23	18	33	24	8	19

THE BIG PICTURE

	Total	Male	Female	Virgin	Not a Virgin	Sexual Orientation			
						Male Heterosexual	Male Gay/ Bisexual	Female Heterosexual	Female Gay/ Bisexual
What is your opinion of divorce?									
It's a tragedy.	41	42	41	50	39	43	27	43	18
It's a drag, but it happens.	56	56	56	47	58	55	65	54	75
It's inevitable.	3	3	3	2	3	3	8	3	8
What do you think of the idea of marrying one person for your whole life?									
Love it—I'll take the plunge someday.	70	69	70	76	68	71	40	73	43
Pretty hard to pull off, but definitely worth a try.	26	28	25	20	28	27	43	24	36
It's unrealistic—I'll probably have multiple marriages.	2	2	2	1	2	1	7	1	5
Marriage is simply an outmoded institution.	3	2	3	2	3	1	9	2	15

	Total	Male	Female	Virgin	Not a Virgin	Sexual Orientation			
						Male Heterosexual	Male Gay/ Bisexual	Female Heterosexual	Female Gay/ Bisexual
In general, when I hear the word "feminist" . . .									
I am sympathetic to the cause.									
	37	25	47	44	36	23	47	45	72
I am reminded of an older group of women.									
	18	13	23	17	19	14	8	23	11
I think of an outmoded cause—men and women today are basically equal.									
	34	44	26	30	35	44	35	27	15
I get angry—it's men who need a cause these days.									
	11	18	4	10	11	19	10	4	1
Twenty years ago, people my age had more sex.									
True	33	37	29	34	33	38	35	29	39
False	67	63	71	66	67	62	65	71	61
What is the most important ingredient to a good sex life?									
Love	54	49	58	66	51	50	28	59	50
Physical attraction	14	16	12	11	15	16	20	12	14
Good communication									
	19	16	22	18	20	16	19	22	28
Compatibility	11	10	11	10	11	10	6	11	14
Self-confidence	7	6	7	5	7	5	12	7	11
Having a partner with a nice body									
	3	4	2	3	3	3	8	2	2
Having a nice body yourself									
	2	1	2	2	2	1	3	2	0
Openness to experimentation									
	10	11	9	6	11	11	17	9	15
A good imagination	6	7	5	4	6	7	10	5	6
You're involved in a long-term relationship and the frequency of sex has begun to decline.									
Bail out—it's the beginning of the end.									
	3	4	2	1	3	4	5	2	4
Make do—there's more to a relationship than sex.									
	31	32	30	34	30	32	32	30	20
Confront it—keeping the fire alive takes work.									
	67	64	68	65	67	65	63	68	75
Which is more important to you?									
Sexual relationships	8	13	4	6	9	13	11	4	5
Friendships	92	87	96	94	91	87	89	96	95

	Total	Male	Female	Virgin	Not a Virgin	Sexual Orientation			
						Male Heterosexual	Male Gay/Bisexual	Female Heterosexual	Female Gay/Bisexual

In general, how do your romantic relationships and those of your friends compare to those of your parents' generation?

	Total	Male	Female	Virgin	Not a Virgin	Male Heterosexual	Male Gay/Bisexual	Female Heterosexual	Female Gay/Bisexual
They're better.	36	36	36	28	38	36	43	36	45
They're about the same.	43	46	40	47	42	46	44	40	37
They're worse.	21	18	24	25	20	18	14	24	18

If they're better, why?

	Total	Male	Female	Virgin	Not a Virgin	Male Heterosexual	Male Gay/Bisexual	Female Heterosexual	Female Gay/Bisexual
There's more intimacy or communication between partners.	50	49	52	55	50	52	18	51	60
There's more equality between the sexes.	18	17	19	18	18	17	6	18	26
There's more room for individuality in relationships.	29	24	32	30	28	23	45	32	33
There are fewer hang-ups about sex.	16	22	12	9	18	20	38	11	24

If they're worse, why?

	Total	Male	Female	Virgin	Not a Virgin	Male Heterosexual	Male Gay/Bisexual	Female Heterosexual	Female Gay/Bisexual
There's too much confusion about sex roles today.	12	15	9	15	11	15	15	10	
There's not enough commitment these days.	47	50	45	48	47	50	43	45	40
There's too much emphasis on career and money.	13	16	11	18	11	16	13	10	34
There's too much emphasis on sex and not enough on relationships.	37	28	43	36	38	28	28	43	32

Is there such a thing as perfect sex?

	Total	Male	Female	Virgin	Not a Virgin	Male Heterosexual	Male Gay/Bisexual	Female Heterosexual	Female Gay/Bisexual
Yes—I've experienced it.	28	27	29	3	34	27	34	29	40
Yes—I hope to experience it.	56	59	54	82	50	60	52	55	40
No—there's no such thing.	15	14	17	15	16	14	14	17	20

CHAPTER 2

Dating

MEETING YOUR MATCH

Ah, the College Experience

You can study whatever you want to, and use athletic facilities for free, and commiserate with others about how bad the food is, but with all these young, curious, diverse people around—all of whom now have the trivialities of high school behind them—you are probably thinking, "What a great opportunity to get laid!" And you know what? *It is*. It is also a great opportunity to get involved in a mature relationship and, dare we say, even to fall in love. It is unlikely that you will ever be around so many people in your immediate age group again. For many people, college is the first chance to explore their sexuality openly, to experiment freely without the burdens of parents, curfews, and easily assigned labels.

You Sexy Thing, You

Peacocks have it easy. They just show their plumes and they're marvelous to look at and they drive each other crazy. People are a little more sophisticated (at least we would like to think so) and, while having great hair, a great body, and perfect teeth never hurts, there are other things you should be aware of, too. Who you are is very important. So let's cut through some popular misconceptions.

Golden Reed frogs on a typical date. CAROL HUGHES; ABPL/CORBIS

Myth: Men are dogs who only want sex and aren't interested in relationships.
Reality: Men are dogs who definitely do want sex, but it isn't the only thing they want. They are also interested in relationships. They, too, have feelings, although a number have been socialized to believe that they should hide them. Deep down, everyone wants someone to cuddle with and laugh with, someone to hold hands with. Gosh, it really is true. Most men want someone they can depend on and whom they can share their feelings with, someone whom they want to spend the rest of their lives with, just as much as any woman does.

Myth: Men are interested only in beautiful women.
Reality: Well, men do put a higher value on the physical attractiveness of their mates than women do. But men will go to much more extreme lengths to woo women they really like than those they simply find gorgeous.

Myth: Women aren't as horny as men.
Reality: Women are subject to the same urges and desires as men, and they can be every bit as horny as men are.

Myth: Pretty girls date only handsome boys (or old guys with money).
Reality: Complete nonsense. Claudia Schiffer dates aging, cheesy illusionist David Copperfield. Rachel Hunter is married to Rod Stewart, who kind of resembles a rooster and is old enough to be her father. Christie Brinkley married Billy Joel. Voluptuous former *Playboy* model Anna Nicole Smith married an 86-year-old mummy. . . . Well, maybe that's not the best example, considering his net worth. The point is that pretty girls are interested in a lot more than having a nice ornament on their arm in the form of a football stud or Calvin Klein model. A guy who is smart, shy, short, or otherwise deviates from the Matthew McConaughey mold is not out of the running (not to say that McConaughey

REUTERS/CORBIS-BETTMANN

isn't smart, but you get the point). *Hint:* a guy who can make a girl laugh already has one up on the competition, despite his looks.

Myth: You must be in perfect shape to be attractive.
Reality: Oh, come on. Just look around. If that were true, the human species would have disappeared a long time ago. But people still fall for this myth—

Prime candidate for a date or a rupture? NIK WHEELER/CORBIS

particularly women. Then again, thanks to the cosmetics industry, magazines, television, and movies, there is a lot more pressure on women to have buns of steel and be able to fill a dress with the perfect configuration of curves and cleavage. Remember, a girl who can make a guy laugh and feel comfortable is already ahead of the competition, even if she hasn't touched her Ab-Roller in months.

In *Annie Hall*, Woody Allen, whose character is named Alvy Singer, stops a perfect-looking couple on the street and, to discover the secret of their mutual bliss, asks them how they manage to look so happy together. Here's what he discovers:

ALVY SINGER: You look like a really happy couple. Are you?
WOMAN: Yeah.
ALVY SINGER: Yeah? So how do you account for it?
WOMAN: Uh, I'm very shallow and empty, and I have no ideas and nothing interesting to say.
MAN: And I'm exactly the same way.

Notice a common theme here? The problem most students encounter is that they believe outward appearances are all that matter. Let's not be blindly idealistic, though. The simple fact is that looks do matter, and people blessed with natural beauty have one check in their plus column. But even if you're not Miss America or that guy in the Calvin Klein underwear ad, you can be very, very sexy—yes, maybe even sexier than a super-model.

The Covetous & the Shallow vs. the Loving & the Thoughtful, Part I

The top ten qualities college men find attractive in a sexual partner:

10. Nice butt
 9. Breasts/chests
 8. Good legs
 7. Pretty eyes
 6. Sensitivity
 5. Good body
 4. Sense of humor
 3. Brains
 2. Overall beauty
 1. Personality

The top ten qualities college *women be-lieve* potential sex partners find attractive about them:

10. Sensitivity
 9. Brains
 8. Pretty eyes
 7. Sense of humor
 6. Good legs
 5. Nice butt
 4. Personality
 3. Breasts
 2. Good body
 1. Overall beauty

Is anybody talking to anyone else out there, or are they learning about each other by watching relationships on *Baywatch* and *Melrose Place*? No wonder people are so confused.

Here are five tips you can use to help you get your bearings in any strange environment. They really work! Try them next time you go out:

1. **Smile.** Smiling immediately puts other people at ease and lets them know you are happy and relaxed.

2. **Stand up straight, shoulders back.** Slouching is a posture of insecurity, a kind of folding in on yourself. Standing up straight shows you are an open, welcoming person.

3. **Don't cross your arms.** Let them hang at your sides or use them to illustrate what you're talking about. Crossed arms is the stance of people who are on their guard or closing themselves off from their surroundings (ask any psychology major). If you are at a party and you need that physical guard, simply hold a beer in front of you. Everyone else will be holding a beer; it accomplishes the same type of security, and no one will notice anything strange.

4. **Introduce yourself to someone within five minutes of arrival.** If you arrive at your first intramural softball game, or a party, or a club meeting, standing by yourself in a corner is probably the thing you fear most. You will feel much more relaxed if you just walk in, quickly find someone (male or female) who looks friendly, and say, "Hey, I'm Bob. How's it going?" And remember tip #2.

5. **Make eye contact.** Nervous, insecure people often stare at the floor or shift their eyes away from the face of the person they are speaking with. This makes people uncomfortable. Making and keeping a comfortable amount of eye contact (you don't have to stare) shows you are listening.

The way in which you handle yourself in social situations can make you sexy, and you already may have figured out what works for you. Just relax. Simply by being relaxed you will attract people to you.

The Initial Approach and First Encounter

Meeting people is a tricky business, but it isn't rocket science. There you are, surrounded by hundreds or thousands of people your age with pursuits at least generally similar to yours (that is, they are going to college, too). You see them everyday. They're all around you.

But that initial hurdle often seems way too high to jump. The problem is, people worry too much. Even if your attempt fails, don't stress too much. No one will hold it against you and usually the only one who thinks you've been a moron is yourself. Here are a few common scenes.

At a Huge Party

At the typical college party, there's loud music, drinking, and general revelry. If people catch your interest at a party, it's unlikely you'll be able to engage them in deep conversation or impress them with any type of smooth introduction, simply because it is too loud for them to catch your subtle intonations. Also, people at most college parties are there to go a little nuts and have some mindless fun, so walking up to someone and saying, "The comments you made in class about Kierkegaard's political aspirations were intriguing. Could you elaborate on them for me?" will probably not go over well. You have to adapt to your situation. For instance, at a formal function you wouldn't go up to someone and say, "Hey, where's the pisser?," whereas, at a rowdy party, you just might indeed.

At a beer bash, these are always safe openers:

Big parties can be big fun.
HENRY DILTZ/CORBIS

- "Aren't you in my English class?"
- "Wanna dance?"
- "Do you want a beer?"
- "Can you show me where the beer is?"
- "What's your name?"
- "Does this band suck, or what?"
- "Hey, I'm _____. How's it going?" (always an effective intro)

If you're feeling more creative, don't be afraid to try something a little less conservative, like these:

- "Do you smell that?"
- "You know, I used to have a dress just like that."
- "I'd love to dance with you, but I think my shoes are stuck to the mung on the floor."
- "This reminds me of growing up."

If you can break the ice by making the person you want to talk to laugh, you've already scored some points. Also, at many college parties there are games going on—both drinking games and nondrinking games. It's not a bad idea to go up to someone and ask if he or she wants to be your partner in something. Of course, depending on where you are, every game might be a drinking game, so be careful whom you ask to do what.

Then there's always just making weird faces at people. If someone makes one back, you might have found a soul mate. No kidding. You see, as nerve racking as it all might seem, the game of meeting people can be a lot of fun if you approach it openly and with a sense of humor and adventure.

At a Bar

Bars have many different atmospheres. Dance clubs can strongly resemble huge campus parties in terms of noise and overall character, so try the same approach in both. In a smaller, publike environment, eloquence becomes more important. People usually go to bars in pairs or groups, so approaching someone can feel like putting on a performance for their friends as well. A little planning can help you get around this problem, and having a friend with you helps, too.

The Covetous & the Shallow vs. the Loving & the Thoughtful, Part II

The top ten qualities college women find attractive in a sexual partner:	The top ten qualities college *men believe* potential sex partners find attractive about them:
10. Nice butt	10. Nice eyes
9. Power and success	9. Height
8. Height	8. Nice butt
7. Overall beauty	7. Brains
6. Nice eyes	6. Power and success
5. Good body	5. Overall beauty
4. Brains	4. Sensitivity
3. Sensitivity	3. Sense of humor
2. Sense of humor	2. Good body
1. Personality	1. Personality

First of all, if you're interested in meeting someone, stand or sit at the bar; don't sit at a table. You are much less mobile at a table. If you can, position yourself in an area of relatively high traffic, such as the route to the bathroom. (OK, we know it sounds cheesy, but that's the best way to catch some-one alone. They aren't going to take all their friends to the bathroom with them, are they? Well, women do seem to go in groups, but . . .) This way, if you see someone who interests you, you can wait for the person to pass by. Here's when a friend comes in handy. When that person comes by, you will have just a second to grab his or her attention. What you choose to say should start a conversation of some sort, so "What's up?" is probably not going to be effective. Too vague. Try something like this instead:

- "Hey, could you settle an argument for us? Sam here believes that *Street Fighter* was the best family action epic of 1995, but I think it was definitely *Mortal Kombat*. What do you think?" (Obviously, you don't have to use these exact words. Just invite the person to join your discussion.)
- "We've been taking a poll. If you could order the summary execution of any three people, who would they be and why?" (If that sounds too creepy, ask: "If you had to be locked in a Motel 6 bathroom for the weekend with any three people, who would they be and why?")
- "Have you ever ordered anything to eat here? What's good? If we ordered a pizza, would you help us eat it?"

You get the idea.

Before or After Class

If you have a class with someone you find interesting, it's very easy to make his or her acquaintance. After all, you already know you have some-thing in common. Trying the old "Can I borrow your notes?" routine is kind of obvious, though. Instead, plan your approach more smoothly. Does the person you like arrive a few minutes early to class? If so, you have a small window of opportunity. Try asking the person a simple question, such as:

- "What did the professor talk about last time? I missed class."
- "Do you know when our next exam is?"
- "What are you writing your paper on?"
- "If I fall asleep and start to snore or drool, will you please kick me?"
- "Do you think the professor was drunk last time, or what?"

If the person never shows up early, after class you can still do any of the same things and, better yet, you can then ask where the person's headed and say

Haven't I Seen You Somewhere Before?

Should you ever use a pickup line? This depends entirely on your goals and the situation. Lines tend to come off as sounding insincere because they usually are. If you plan on actually getting to know someone, starting off your acquaintance with a tired old line isn't the most auspicious beginning. On the other hand, sometimes you're just looking for, to put it delicately, a short-term companion. The trick is, the person you try to pick up must feel like being a short-term companion, otherwise your approach probably won't work very well. If you decide to try a line on someone (or several someones in rapid succession) be prepared for a high failure rate. To improve your effectiveness, try being at least a little funny or original. Most standard lines are designed for use by men, but you women should feel free to experiment if you're interested.

Lines so old they're moldy—to be avoided at all costs:

- "Are you a model?" (Or the modern variation, "Are you an aerobics instructor?")
- "Live around here? Come here often?" (Clichéd openers.)
- "What's a nice girl like you doing in a place like this?"
- "I think I've just fallen in love!"
- "If I said you had a beautiful body, would you hold it against me?" (Ha ha, right?)
- "Your father must be a thief . . . because he took the stars from the skies and put them in your eyes." (Yes, people have actually said this.)
- "My wife doesn't understand me." (Not much of a line, but if a man ever says this to you, run screaming.)

Venerable lines that sound good only when delivered by old blues musicians:

- "Honey, I'd drink your bathwater."
- "You could make a blind man see."
- "Lord, have mercy."

Some of the funnier lines we've heard:

- "Baby, when I look at you my socks don't match."
- "You move me in strange places." (Then point to your elbow or something.)
- "If you don't mind, I'd like to be your future ex-husband."

Always a good option:

- Hey, I'm _____. How's it going?

you're going the same way—whether it's true or not. Now you have plenty of time to start a conversation and maybe even get a cup of coffee, if things are going well.

Cultural, Athletic, or Political Events and Outings

Art gallery openings have a lot in common with political rallies and football games. The people at these events have strong interests and opinions on certain things (such as art or politics or the rotten officiating). We hope you attend these functions because you share these interests. We say this because some of the more mercenary men and women of the world often take part in demonstrations or museum parties or what have you because they find it incredibly easy to pick up people by pretending to share their interests. We're thinking mainly here of men who participate in women's rights marches, happily joining such chants as "Hey hey, ho ho, this patriarchy has to go," all the while hoping to seduce the woman with the megaphone. Of course, countless women who don't know the difference between a field goal and a flea-flicker grace the stands of college stadiums each year for the sole purpose of being where the boys are, so maybe it all evens out.

Does this look like a good place to find a date? UPI/Corbis-Bettmann

---

Funny Meeting You Here . . .

College men who have met a sexual partner online: 6 percent.

College women who have done so: 4 percent.

College men who have met a sexual partner on a phone-sex or party line: 2 percent.

College women who have done so: 1 percent.

College men who have met a sexual partner through a personal ad: 3 percent.

College women who have done so: 1 percent

The truth is, it is very easy to meet someone in a context that focuses attention on a particular issue or interest. At an art gallery or museum, it's just a matter of saying "What do you think of this painting/sculpture?" At a football or basketball game, just ask "What down is this?" or "What was he called for?" At a rally or demonstration, you have a few options:

- "Do you need help handing out those flyers/pamphlets/pins?"
- "Want to help me hand these out?"
- "I love your 'Don't Blame Me—I Voted for Dole' T-shirt! Where did you get it?"
- "How much longer do you think we'll suffer the oppression of this cultural hegemony?"
- "We've got to get out of here! Those cops have tear gas!"

The important thing is to be sincere. Professing a love for the paintings of Jackson Pollock or an admiration for the '69 Jets is bound to backfire unless you know what you're talking about.

The Next Step: Do You Ask for a Date?

The evening's winding down and the conversation has been great, but it's time for one of you to go. Now comes the second hurdle: deciding if you want to see the person again and, if you want to, making sure it happens.

This is even more difficult than making an initial approach, because the stakes are higher. If you get shot down by someone you have been talking to for a while, it's even more humiliating because that person actually took the time to get to know you before rejecting you. It's so much more personal. Also, it's often unclear what the best move would be. Do you ask for a date?

Come on, It's the '90s Already

In general, who puts their pride on the line and asks for a date on campuses today? Some things don't seem to change very much, because 77 percent of the men still ask their potential mates out the first time, whereas only 16 percent of the women take that first step. Hey, you straight ladies out there, if you find yourself doing laundry on a Saturday night when you'd rather be out on the town, try following the example of your gay and bisexual sisters, 34 percent of whom do the asking when they want a date. Looks like it's still up to you guys out there to run the initial risk of rejection.

Or do you just ask for a telephone number? Do you just say, "See you around"? Again, the answer depends on the situation and what the environment at your school is like.

"Nondating" Schools

In recent decades, the students at small colleges seem to have moved away from the whole concept of dating. Maybe the intimacy of the situation makes formal dating unnecessary—you can be pretty sure of bumping into a person at a given social event, and you don't need to make special plans. Maybe people recognize that it's hard to keep your social life private at a small college, and they don't want to make the public commitment that a formal date would entail. Whatever the reason, the dearth of dating certainly doesn't mean that these students aren't pairing up regularly or that they aren't people who date. But the rules are different.

At a small college, asking for a date or telephone number can sound forced. The favored approach is just to play it cool and wait until you see the person again to develop your relationship further. Of course, you are free to turn up in places the person might frequent. You might also try inviting the person to an event you plan to attend, without making it sound like a one-on-one date. For example, "My friends are having a barbecue next weekend. Would you like to come?"

Big Universities and Dates

If you attend a larger university and meet someone interesting, the casual approach might not work. If you're a business major and he's a history major, your paths may never cross again, which puts you in the awkward position of

Getting Smooth		
Which of the following have students done to prepare for a date?		
Preparation	% Men	% Women
Had hair cut or styled	51	30
Bought clothing	40	59
Wore special underwear or lingerie	43	78
Bought condoms or other birth control	50	27
Rehearsed dialogue	18	16
Cleaned up residence	69	72
Changed bedsheets	30	20
Hid incriminating items from sight	43	40

having to ask for a minicommitment from a person you just met. The least invasive—and least effective—way to extract this commitment is to ask for a phone number, without mentioning any specific intention. It is unlikely that she will say, "No way, I wouldn't dream of giving you my phone number." On the down side, it is entirely possible that she will give you a fake phone number. Also, the spark of interest that springs up between two people has a way of dying out quickly if they're not reminded of it, and it can be most difficult to rekindle if you're stuck in the position of calling someone a week after you met and saying, "Um, hi, um, Mindy? This is Bruce. We met at The Bluebird last week? No, I have brown hair."

The move that requires the most commitment involves making a date right there and then—times and locations are set, and addresses may even be given. Some people have no problem with this, but others are uncomfortable giving near-strangers their addresses or agreeing to be alone with them somewhere. Such extreme caution is not unfounded. There are some dangerous

What Kind of Date Should You Go On?

As a college student you may not be old enough to go out to a bar, you may not be able to afford a nice dinner for you and your date, and you might not have wheels to get you somewhere other than the offerings within walking distance of campus. Don't despair. A little creative thinking—and a fun companion who's willing to go along—are all you need to have a great time.

> ### "Wanna See a Movie, Mary?" "My Name Is Amy." "Uh-oh."
>
> Overall, 76 percent of college students tend to date only one person at a time, but 24 percent like to date several people at once. Despite what you might think, there was no significant difference between men and women on this subject.

people out there (yes, even some dangerous college students as you'll see in Chapter 12), and women, in particular, are wise to be careful. If you want to go ahead and make a date, pick an event or location that is safe and comfortable. Daytime dates are safer than nighttime dates, so consider an afternoon meeting. Traditionally, it has been considered polite for men to pick up their dates at their homes and deliver them safely back to their front doors. Today, some women are leery of giving out their addresses, while others still feel safer with the traditional arrangement. It's best for men to present an alternative: offer to pick up your date or meet her somewhere, whichever she prefers. Of course, some women may want to pick up their dates. So be prepared for this guys, and throw out those old pizza boxes before she shows up.

Dating Etiquette

- In the immortal, ungrammatical words attributed to the late Paul "Bear" Bryant, who coached the Alabama Crimson Tide, "Dance with the girl what brung you." If you're out with a person and somehow another person catches your attention, the worst thing you can do is abandon your date or flirt outrageously with the other person. This will do terrible things to your reputation and your karma.

- Be prompt. Don't keep people waiting for you in front of a theater or alone in a restaurant. It's embarrassing. And it tends to piss people off.

- Call when you say you're going to call. If you make tentative plans for Friday night and say, "I'll call you Thursday to let you know when," don't expect a friendly reception if you call Friday at 6:30 and say, "So, can you be ready in twenty minutes?"

- Cancel in advance. If something comes up and you can't make it, let your date know as soon as you can so the person can make other plans. Never stand someone up if you can avoid it.

All this is pretty straightforward. What complicates things is people skipping over the whole dating thing and winding up lip-locked—or even naked—after their first encounter with each other.

Potential Outcomes of the Initial Encounter: Making Out and One-Night Stands

It is possible, of course, that the initial attraction between two people might be so strong that they wind up making out, seriously groping, or even tumbling into bed. These are certainly pleasant occurrences, but most of the time they immediately complicate the relationship. In order to deal with the levels of intimacy and commitment these actions bring on, we have come up with the **ball-and-chain rating** (on a scale of 1 to 5) to show you exactly what you're getting into. A ball-and-chain rating of five would mean that you had engaged in a very intimate act in which strong feelings and a certain level of emotional responsibility may be involved, and you should be prepared to deal with them. A ball-and-chain rating of 0 or 1 would mean that you should be able to go on about your business without much worry.

Hooking Up

You're at a party, you meet someone you like, and you wind up kissing or engaging in some clothed making out. You're more than mere acquaintances, but what you've done is essentially meaningless. You were almost certainly acting on physical attraction, not a well-formed emotional attachment, and there was no risk to either of you. You're under no obligation to date each other or call each other—nor should you expect to be called or dated—just because you made out. You should, however, behave respectfully if your paths should ever cross again. **Ball-and-chain rating: 1.**

What if you and/or your partner were very drunk? We'll say it now, and no doubt we'll say it again: you should never get so drunk that you do something you didn't want to. In reality, however, a great many college hookups occur when both parties are sloshed. Sometimes it's no problem at all and everyone can just have a good, sloppy time. But being wasted when you hook up renders the act meaningless.

Serial Hookups

Bumping into each other repeatedly and making out repeatedly is more serious. You obviously have a strong attraction to each other that could turn into

Hope he likes pistachio ice cream. Reuters/Corbis-Bettmann

something more serious. If your encounters are purely physical (that is, you find each other late at night and spend little time talking), the **ball-and-chain rating is 2.** That means you should be sensitive to the person's feelings and not do things like make out with other people when he or she is around. You should also acknowledge the other person's existence even when you're not fooling around.

If your encounters have more of a datelike feel, where you spend a lot of time talking by yourselves and getting to know each other, that's more serious. You are developing an emotional attachment—or at least you must assume that the other person might be developing an emotional attachment. This **ball-and-chain rating is 3.** You should treat this person with the respect and honesty you'd show a friend. This doesn't mean you can't see other people, but you should be friendly and considerate.

What if you're drunk every time you hook up with the same person? Sorry, that excuse works only once.

Oral Sex

When it comes to sexually transmitted diseases, oral sex is a risky activity—for both the recipient and the performer. AIDS can definitely be contracted through mouth-to-genital contact (see Chapter 4 on safer oral sex). So when two people decide to have oral sex, they must assume some responsibility for each other's health, even if they don't know each other well. Oral sex is also a highly intimate act. Some people find it more intimate than intercourse. If you have oral sex with someone, you must be prepared for some emotional involvement. Giving or getting a blow job or going down on someone may seem meaningless to you—and it might be meaningless to the person you're with, too. Unfortunately, there's no way to predict feelings ahead of time. If you know you have absolutely no desire ever to see someone again, maybe it's a good idea to stay away from her genitals, and keeps yours away, too. If you succumb to the temptation, don't say we didn't warn you. **Ball-and-chain rating: 4.**

Can You Remember Your Partner's Last Name? Did You Ever Know It?

College men who have had a one-night stand: 51 percent

College men who would do it again: 18 percent

College men who wouldn't: 13 percent

College women who have had a one-night stand: 42 percent

College women who would do it again: 9 percent

College women who wouldn't: 19 percent

The Infamous One-Night Stand

When you have sex, you risk an unplanned pregnancy—even birth control pills aren't foolproof (see Chapter 4 on birth control)—and any number of sexually transmitted diseases (see Chapters 4 and 11 for the details), some of which can stay with you for life and some of which can end your life. Aside from unprotected anal sex, vaginal intercourse without a condom is one of the riskiest sexual acts you can engage in.

Still, it is possible to indulge your spontaneity, as long as every appropriate precaution is used. Even if worries of pregnancy and disease are allayed, the fact remains that you have done *it*: the single human act that causes the strongest emotional reaction. Wars have been waged for sex, so be prepared. Maybe you go to bed thinking the sex will mean nothing to you, only to discover afterward that you can't stand to be separated from your partner for more than five minutes. Maybe the sex was pleasant but meaningless to you, but the guy you took to bed is talking marriage. Maybe you are both madly in love now. Maybe you never want to lay eyes on each other again and feel a strong need for a shower, but the fact remains that you have been intimate with this person. **Ball-and-chain rating: 5.**

The Etiquette of One-Night Stands   That's right, mind your manners and be honest. A little forethought and consideration go a long way.

If you realize almost immediately after you finish having sex that this will definitely be a one-time-only event and you really don't want to pursue any relationship—even a purely physical one—with this person, try not to sleep through the night with the person. It may seem awfully awkward and it may be late at night, but get up, get dressed, say, "Thank you for a wonderful evening," and go home. Waking up in the morning and trying to get away from someone you're not interested in is much more depressing and difficult than making a quick and graceful exit at night and sleeping in your own bed. (Plus, if you sleep through the night and wind up next to a willing, naked body in the morning, you may—whom are we kidding?—you *will* find yourself having sex again before you know what you're doing, and then you're in serious trouble.)

Leaving someone with whom you've just traded bodily fluids can seem strange, rude, and inconsiderate, but at least you'll have the knowledge that you were being honest, and it will make things less complicated down the

---

Paradise by the Dashboard Light

If you aren't saying it already, believe us, by the time you get out of college you could live the rest of your life without hearing that damn Meatloaf song and it wouldn't be long enough. But the song does pose a question that we also asked. How far do students go on the first date? Here's what our college respondents said:

Activity	% Men	% Women
Nowhere, save it for next time	24	22
Kissing	34	56
Copping a feel	9	13
Fondling genitals	4	4
Oral sex	2	1
Intercourse	1	1
As far as my date will let me	28	5

road. And if the person asks the dreaded question, "Will I ever see you again?," respond with a platitude of some sort, like "I really enjoyed spending time with you tonight, but I'm not into having a relationship." Sure, the person might be really pissed off or hurt, and, yes, it's your fault for trifling with people's feelings. Comfort yourself with the knowledge that, as long as you're not in Texas, gunplay is unlikely—and at least you were honest.

What if you brought the person home and now you want to be alone? You'll have to kick him or her out. Look, we told you this could get messy, so quit complaining. If you happen to be male, it is distinctly unchivalrous and possibly dangerous to kick a woman you just slept with out on the street in the middle of the night. Offer an excuse, like "I need to get up early and I don't sleep well with other people in the bed" or "I think I'm coming down with something—maybe you should go." Obviously, there is no smooth way to get out of this spot. If you have a couch, leave the other person in the bed and go sleep on the couch yourself. If you are faced with kicking a woman out, get up and walk her home, drive her home, or, if she's sober, call her a taxi (and pay for it, if possible). Women don't need to worry about men so much, but it would be polite to call a cab for a man and offer to pay for it, or, at the least, offer him the couch (if you do this, most likely he'll get the message and take off on his own).

You are under no obligation to call or date someone you had a one-night stand with, and you really shouldn't expect to be called or pursued either. Women and men who have romantic notions that a one-night stand is about being swept away or love at first sight are in for some disillusionment. If you had no emotional involvement before you had sex, you really shouldn't demand emotional involvement afterward. Again, though, feelings often override rationality. Here are two potentially unpleasant situations and how to deal with them:

- If it turns out you want more, but your partner isn't interested, you must respect his or her wishes. Of course, you might feel angry or hurt or used, but you are an adult and should know what you are doing.
- If the sex meant nothing to you, but your partner wants to pursue a relationship, you must be firm and honest. Clearly state that you are not interested in a relationship. Do not say that you will call or that "maybe" you'll see each other again. Be polite and apologize for any misunderstanding.

Can one-night stands turn into relationships? Of course! Quite often, after an initial sexual encounter, both parties will want to see each other again, if only for the simple fact that they enjoy having sex with each other. This type of relationship can fizzle out after a while if there is no emotional or intellectual attraction between the two people. Hopefully, this is mutually agreeable to both people involved. A purely physical relationship is fine and enjoyable, as long as both parties agree that that's what it is.

Often, however, one person develops an emotional attachment while the other one is interested only in the sexual part of the relationship. Welcome to the nasty quagmire of human relationships! Here's where things can get really ugly. It's always clear to at least one party when a relationship starts to go sour. Unfortunately, people will put up with a lot in order to be assured of a steady supply of sex. For this reason, it's almost always the task of the emotionally attached person to end a lopsided (hence, bad) relationship. But, again unfortunately, they are usually reluctant to do so because they have strong feelings for the person they are sleeping with. Dishonesty, rationalization, and self-deception run rampant in these types of relationships.

Love Conquers All . . . or at Least It Conquers Hormones

Is friendship or sex more important to college students? The majority of students value friendships more than a good lay: 87 percent of men and 96 percent of women value friendship more than sex.

Here are a few telltale signs that your partner wants you only for sex:

- The person displays a general lack of consideration: lateness, rudeness, indifference to your opinions or feelings or presence—maybe not all the time, but enough to bother you.
- The person doesn't invite you out anymore. You just meet at his place, have sex, then watch TV.
- You don't know many (or any) or your partner's friends. She doesn't invite you along to hang out with her friends.
- He is frequently drunk when you have sex.
- You catch her lying about plans, activities, whereabouts.
- She seems to avoid you at times, doesn't call, or avoids your calls.
- He tells you he wants you only for sex.

If these are familiar, you probably have a bad, unhealthy relationship going on, and you should kill it before it grows. Your partner may object to your ending the relationship and may even promise to be nicer, but remember, people lie, cheat, and steal for sex. Don't be a fool.

How to Dump Someone: The Good, the Bad, and the Ugly

For many people, the simple act of ending an unhappy dating or sexual relationship seems almost as traumatic as having all your teeth pulled without anesthesia. We hope to put a stop to all the rampant cowardice (or at least rein it in some).

The Good Way

Once you've decided that you don't want to see someone anymore, call that person up and say so, or wait until the next time the person calls you and explain the situation. You don't have to be creative. Simply say, "I've been thinking . . . this relationship isn't really working out for me. I like you, but I'm not interested in seeing you romantically anymore." Don't feel obliged to explain any further or justify yourself, but be honest about your feelings. (One big exception to this rule: don't try this in a relationship that has involved love and long-term commitment. Those important relationships are too complicated to be ended abruptly over the telephone, and you must explain your behavior and reasons to someone you had loved or been committed to, whether you want to or not. The only way to avoid it is to change your name and move out of state, which is both expensive and impractical.)

Breaking up isn't as bad as you think, especially if the relationship has not been a long one. Quite often, the person you're breaking up with already has the idea that something is wrong or maybe even feels like breaking up as well. The person you're breaking up with might be surprised or upset. That's not unusual—after all, it's not enjoyable getting dumped. Tears are not out of the question, either, but hysterics or tantrums are rare. This may sound unpleasant, but there really aren't any good ways of breaking up (for an inspiring exception, see the sidebar). The bonus with this method is that you get everything over and done with quickly and honestly. Like a clean wound, these kinds of breakups tend to heal rapidly. Believe it or not, the person you break up with in this way may even respect your honesty and courage, and you may wind up being friends. That's really the best of all possible worlds.

The *Casablanca* Farewell Speech

No one has ever had a breakup as phenomenal as that of Rick and Ilsa (Humphrey Bogart and Ingrid Bergman) in *Casablanca*. Most of the time, when you break up with someone, at least one of you feels lame for a while, or has some regrets, or feels like less of a person in some way. Not Rick. The situation is this: Rick and Ilsa had a liaison before she was married. After an interval of some years, they meet again in Casablanca. Rick has just slept with Ilsa the night before, making her an adulteress and causing her to fall in love with him all over again. She loves him so much, in fact, that she intends to stay in Casablanca with Rick, while her husband, Victor Laszlo, flies away to freedom. But at the last minute, Rick manages to break up with Ilsa and maintain his dignity, even as he gives her up to another man. But that's not all. He also does something so heroic (giving Ilsa his plane ticket to America, which he forced an official to authorize, so that she can go on to freedom with her husband) that he ensures that Ilsa will love him forever and probably regret spending the rest of her life with her husband! Is this guy cool or what? Check out this speech:

RICK: If you don't mind, you fill in the names, that will make it even more official.

LOUIS: You think of everything don't you?

RICK: And the names are Mr. and Mrs. Victor Laszlo.

ILSA: But, why my name, Richard?

RICK: 'Cause you're getting on that plane.

ILSA: I don't understand, what about you?

RICK: I'm staying here with him until the plane gets safely away.

ILSA: No, Richard, no! What has happened to you! Last night you said . . . !

RICK: Last night we said a great many things. You said I was to do the thinking for both of us. Well, I've done a lot of it since then and it all adds up to one thing: you're getting on that plane with Victor where you belong.

ILSA: No, Richard!

RICK: Now you've got to listen to me! You have any idea what you'd have to look forward to if you stayed here? Nine chances out of ten we'd both wind up in a concentration camp. Isn't that true, Louis?

LOUIS: I'm afraid Major Strasser would insist.

ILSA: You're saying this only to make me go.

RICK: I'm saying it because it's true. Inside of us we both know you belong with Victor. You're part of his work, the

thing that keeps him going. If that plane leaves the ground and you're not with him you'll regret it. Maybe not today, maybe not tomorrow, but soon and for the rest of your life.

ILSA: But what about us?

RICK: We'll always have Paris. We didn't have it, we'd lost it until . . . until you came to Casablanca. We got it back last night.

ILSA: And I said I would never leave you.

RICK: And you never will. I've got a job to do, too. Where I'm going you can't follow. What I've got to do you can't be any part of. Ilsa, I'm no good at being noble, but it doesn't take much to see that the problems of three little people don't amount to a hill of beans in this crazy world. Someday you'll understand that. *(Ilsa begins to cry.)* Now, now. Here's looking at you, kid.

The Bad Way

The most common ploy people use when they want to break up is the avoidance technique. They duck phone calls, sneak around, and make excuses, hoping the other person will get the hint and go away. This is not a very respectful way to deal with someone. The great appeal it holds, however, is that at least for a while you don't have to deal with the person you want to dump. The idea is that if you avoid them long enough, they'll disappear forever.

This never happens. You're bound to run into the person again, who will undoubtedly be pretty angry about your stupid behavior. Tantrums and hysterics are a far more likely result of the avoidance technique than they are if you go for the direct approach.

The Ugly Way

Some people try to get out of relationships by behaving horrendously toward their dates in an attempt to drive them away. Someone using this method might sleep with your best friend, abandon you in a strange place, tell nasty stories about you, degrade you in front of friends, steal your money, or perform any number of antisocial acts. Due to some bizarre twist in the human psyche, this method often serves to strengthen the victim's resolve to stay in the relationship. Have you ever wondered why some women date real assholes? Well, this is part of the reason. Maybe it seems like a challenge to some people when their boyfriends or girlfriends start acting like real shits—a challenge that they're meant to overcome. We don't know, but it happens with shocking regularity. The resulting relationship is monstrous: one person acts like a sadist, and the other tries pathetically to gain the sadist's approval. The ugly way eventually works, but only at enormous emotional cost to both parties.

Luckily, for most, once the sadism begins, it's good-bye.

Let the Relationship Begin

Finding a partner is up to you, but we thought a little advice couldn't hurt. This book is about sex, how to be happy with it, and how to do it well. We believe the best way to enjoy sex is within the context of a committed relationship, where both parties respect each other and can explore and grow their sexuality together. This chapter was meant to outline some ways to achieve that goal. We hope it's been helpful. But now it's time for the good stuff.

CHAPTER 3

Map of the Terrain

THE HUMAN REPRODUCTIVE SYSTEM: HOW IT WORKS

Don't go charging off into Sexual Adventureland without the necessary information and provisions. You're going to have to get familiar with the terrain, first of all. And before you roll your eyes and declare that you already know what's what, thankyouverymuch, consider these startling facts: according to a recent sex survey in *Glamour* magazine (November 1995), 50 percent of men don't know when a woman's most fertile time of the month is, and 41 percent of women don't know either. Do you know?

How about the answer to these questions? Is it possible for a woman to get pregnant if her partner doesn't ejaculate inside her? Where is the female urethra located? Is oral sex safe as long as the woman doesn't swallow? Can sexually transmitted diseases be transmitted nonsexually, that is, on towels or toilet seats? What are the visible symptoms of HIV infection?

If you can't answer all these questions confidently, you should read Chapters 3 and 4 very carefully. Even if you are pretty sure you know the answers, give yourself a brushup. We hope this won't sound too weird, but you literally have the power of life and death between your legs. Yep, what may seem like innocent organs are actually an awesome responsibility. For your sake, for your sex partner's sake, for the sake of anyone who cares about you, take control of your body and your reproductive system before you conceive, contract, or transmit anything you don't want to.

But before we talk about controlling and protecting the reproductive system, we have to know what it does when left to its own devices. There are some pretty explicit diagrams in the section, to prevent any possible misunderstanding, but it also might be a good idea for you to locate on your own body all the parts that are referred to here. So drop your pants, grab a mirror, and follow along.

THERE'S A VAS DEFERENS BETWEEN THE TESTES AND THE GLANS, OR THE MALE GENITALIA

You are going to see a lot of terms on these diagrams that you will probably never use, but we're including them anyway, just so you know. Since this is a book about sex, we're just going to cover the basics of erection and ejaculation. Of course, there is more to the male genitalia than these functions. The sperm-producing testicles, for example, are also necessary for the production of the male sex hormone *testosterone*, which gives men all their secondary sex traits (such as whiskers and deep voices) and makes normal sexual functioning possible.

Let's start on the outside and work our way in. The diagram below shows a circumcised penis on the left and an uncircumcised penis on the right. Circumcision is the removal of the foreskin—that hood of skin you see covering the head, or glans, of the penis. Many American men are circumcised by a doctor right after they are born, and it is traditional for Jewish males to be circumcised by a rabbi in a religious ceremony. Circumcision is not common throughout the rest of the world. So why do Americans like to

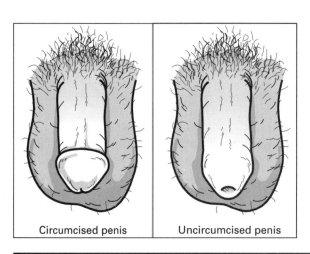

Circumcised penis   Uncircumcised penis

Frontal view of circumcised and uncircumcised penises.

have this part of their sons' penises cut off? Well, Americans have always liked to keep things sanitary. A circumcised penis is much easier to keep clean, especially for little boys. Of course, keeping an uncircumcised penis clean is not exactly rocket science. You just have to pull back the foreskin and rinse to make sure nothing gets caught underneath that flap of skin and causes irritation.

During arousal, as the penis swells, the foreskin on an uncircumcised penis is pushed back along the shaft as the glans emerges. The shaft is the outer area of the penis between the pubic bone and the glans. Once fully erect, circumcised and uncircumcised penises look pretty much the same.

At the tip of the glans, you'll notice the urinary opening, through which both urine and semen are discharged (but not at the same time, so relax). Semen is the clinical term for what is often called "cum," "jizz," or any number of even cruder things. It is the thick, milky liquid released during the male orgasm. It contains the sperm, or male sex cells, that fertilize the female egg (more on that in a minute).

Hanging behind the penis and looking like a wrinkly pouch is the scrotum. The scrotum is a sack of skin and muscle that is designed to keep the testicles comfortable. The testicles are oval-shaped glands (they're often called "balls"

Measuring Up

According to our study, college males are not plagued by insecurity about their penis sizes. A full 76 percent reported that they thought their penises were "about average" size, while 13 percent thought their members were larger than average. Only 11 percent thought they were undersized. And 12 percent reported that they would consider surgery to enlarge their penises.

So how big is average? When asked to estimate the size of their erect penises, our male respondents came up with an average of 6.5 inches, with 38 percent reporting 6 inches and 32 percent reporting 7 inches. About 16 percent of the men we surveyed are either heavily endowed or need a better ruler: they reported their penis sizes as over 8 inches. Conventional wisdom would have us believe that men are apt to exaggerate things like their height and their penis size. Given the fact that most sex researchers say the average erect penis is around 5 inches long, we might be tempted to believe that our male respondents were fibbing just a little and that our female respondents would be quick to set the record straight. What a surprise *we* got! The women reported that the average male penis is 6.9 inches long. A full 23 percent believed the average erect penis was 8 inches or longer. With these kinds of numbers, it should be no surprise that 55 percent of our straight female and bisexual male respondents said they would *not* want their partners' penises to be larger.

or "nuts") that produce sperm. There are two of them, and one usually hangs a little lower than the other in the scrotum. For some reason, testicles don't like to produce sperm when they are too hot or too cold. They prefer a temperature *below* normal body temperature. Usually, the scrotum is relaxed so the testicles can hang out and be mellow away from the piping-hot, 98.6-degree body. When it's cold outside or a man jumps into cold water, the scrotum obligingly contracts and pulls the testicles up very tightly, close to the body, so they can warm up. The scrotum also contracts like this during sexual arousal.

Now let's take a look from underneath. Look at the diagram below. You'll see that along the back of the penis, connecting the scrotum to the shaft, is a piece of skin, called a raphe, which looks like a ridge. The area of skin between the raphe and the glans is the frenulum. And that raised ridge all around the glans is called the coronal ridge. The frenulum and coronal ridge, as well as the glans, are all filled with nerve endings and are extremely sensitive to the touch—especially erotic touches. You'll also see the anus, from which feces are expelled. This opening is also filled with nerve endings, and stimulation of the anus can bring erotic pleasure (see Chapter 7)

On the inside, the penis and testicles are a mass of glands and tubes. Check out the diagram on page 65. One major tube we're concerned with here is called the vas deferens. It carries sperm from the testicles to the urethra, the tube that runs through the penis, and to the urinary opening. You'll also see the seminiferous tubules. Their job is to crank out new sperm, non-

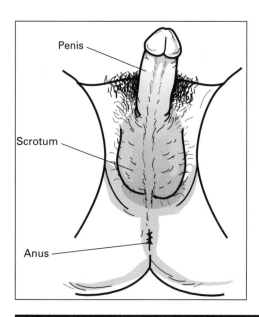

Spread-eagle view of male genitals.

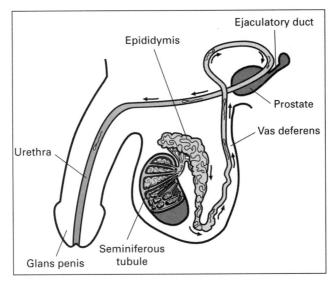

Cross section of penis and scrotum.

stop, from the time a man reaches puberty until he dies. They're the hardest-working tubules in show business.

Do you see the corpus spongiosum and the corpus cavernosa? These cylindrical parts of the penis are full of tiny blood vessels and spongy tissues that fill with blood during arousal. The blood makes the tissues in these cylinders lengthen and swell, causing an erection. A fully erect penis is firm and inflexible, and it usually points upward or straight out.

> Many men are even more concerned with the size of their penises than women are with the size of their thighs, as if penis size is the one thing that makes a man desirable or masculine. Just to set the record straight, the average size of an erect, adult male penis is five to seven inches. However, penises smaller or larger than this are not deficient. There is a lot more to being a good lover than having an enormous penis. After you finish the next two chapters, read Chapters 6 and 7 and find out.

THE BRAVE VOYAGE OF THE SPERM

The semen that you see after ejaculation is not all sperm—not by a long shot. Semen takes a lot of presex preparation. On their way out of the testicles, the young sperm enter a sort of maturation tube called the epididymis, which is a tight coil almost twenty feet long. In that tube, the sperm figure out how to swim straight. Once they pick up their little YMCA certificates, they head through the vas deferens to an ejaculatory duct just outside the urethra, where they hang out until they are given the signal to charge. While they're there, the seminal vesicles, right next door, produce a liquid that the sperm use for nutrition and protection against the acidity of vaginal fluids. The sperm are contained in this fluid upon ejaculation.

When ejaculation is occurring, the sperm, swimming in the alkaline broth, are pushed into the urethra. During arousal, the Cowper's gland secretes a fluid that gets the urethra ready and lubricated. This liquid is called pre-ejaculatory fluid, or, more commonly, "pre-cum," and is clear and odorless. Since the Cowper's gland goes to work close to the time of ejaculation, it is possible for some sperm to be present in the fluid (which means *it's possible to impregnate a woman even without ejaculating*).

The "sperm soup" slides along the lubricated urethra, pushed by tiny hairs called cilia, which move in a waving motion. Along the way, one other ingredient is added: another alkaline fluid that comes from the prostate gland. The prostate is also sensitive to sexual stimulation.

All this lubrication, fluid, and sperm mixed together is called semen. As mentioned before, it is thick, often gooey, and white immediately after ejaculation. It becomes runny and more liquid when exposed to air. Semen that is a different color—for example, clear, yellow, or gray—might be a sign of a health problem (see Chapter 10).

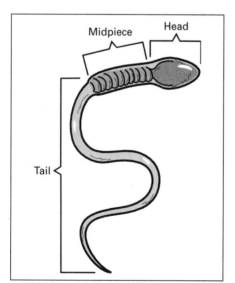

A sperm: Millions of these microscopic **gametes** (sex cells—an egg is a gamete, too) are released during most ejaculations, but it takes only one to fertilize an egg. Sperm can live in a woman's reproductive tract for *eight days,* and remain fully capable of fertilizing an egg even after waiting around for over a week. Persistent, aren't they?

Friction against the sensitive nerve endings in the glans and shaft brings on ejaculation, or expulsion of semen. The orgasm, a series of muscular spasms in the groin area, is what forces the semen out. Friction isn't the only thing that brings on ejaculation, however. Most males have encountered a "wet dream" at one point or another. These are ejaculations that occur during sleep. The technical term for this is nocturnal emission.

THE FEMALE PACKAGE

This may be unfamiliar territory, even for you females out there, simply because most of the female reproductive system is internal, and the stuff that's external is cleverly hidden by folds of skin. If you're female, we recommend that you grab a hand mirror, go someplace with good lighting, and figure out some way to follow along with this discussion.

Involving the Vulva

The vulva is the general term used to refer to all the parts of your genitals that are located on the outside. The vulva has several different parts, but the vaginal opening seems to be the one people are most concerned with, so we'll start there. Look at the diagram below. You'll see the vaginal opening is located under the much smaller urinary opening, which is where urine comes out. The vaginal opening is made up of soft tissue that is quite stretchy.

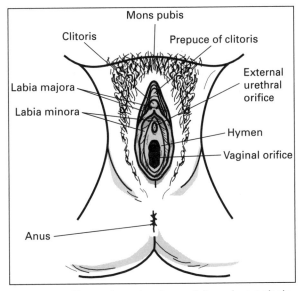

Spread-eagle view of female genitals.

In some young women, a very thin membrane called the hymen may partially cover the inside of the vaginal opening. This membrane, if intact, is the traditional symbol of virginity, although it is far from an accurate indicator. Women are born with this membrane, but it almost never stays completely intact and can easily be ruptured by nonsexual activity or injury. Even after sexual intercourse, small pieces of the membrane remain. The hymen can be torn during the first few times a woman has intercourse, and the tearing can cause some discomfort and bleeding. On the other hand, the membrane is flexible, and it is also possible for the hymen to stretch and accommodate a penis without tearing.

Some women are scared that, because the vaginal and urinary openings are so close together, it might be possible for a man to insert his penis in the wrong one. Don't worry—the urinary opening is far too small for this to be anywhere near possible. It can be difficult for a man's penis to enter the vaginal opening for a variety of reasons. If a woman is a virgin, the tissues are likely to be less flexible. Lack of arousal, nervousness, and a disorder known as vaginismus (see Chapter 11) can also cause problems. In general, however, if everything goes as it should, the vaginal opening can easily accommodate the penis.

If you are following along by looking in a mirror, you will have noticed that you had to move some folds of skin aside in order to look at the vaginal opening. In our diagram, these folds are already pulled aside and labeled. The larger, fleshier folds with pubic hair on them are called the labia majora, which means "greater lips." If you pull those folds aside gently, you'll notice another set of lips right around the vaginal opening. These are the labia minora, or "lesser lips." The labia minora are hairless, thin, and sensitive to the touch. When a woman is aroused, these lips can become swollen with blood, darker in color, and even more sensitive than usual.

What about the clitoris, you ask? Where is it? What does it do? These questions seem to have troubled more men and women than any other question involving female sex organs. It's no big mystery, as long as you're willing to do a little research and exploration. The clitoris, as you can see in the diagram, is located above the urinary opening where the labia minora meet. The meeting of the labia minora forms a hood that covers the glans of the clitoris. Yes, the clitoris, like the penis, has a glans. The glans is the supersensitive part of the clitoris, while the hood is much like the foreskin of the penis. The glans becomes swollen and erect during arousal. Because the clitoris is neatly tucked away under a hood and protected by the labia, it is hard to see unless you gently part the labia. Stimulation of the clitoris is a very important part of bringing about orgasm in women. See Chapter 5 for more details.

The part of the vulva with the coolest name is the mons veneris, which means "mountain of Venus." Venus, of course, is the ancient Roman goddess of love. The mons veneris is also called the mons pubis or just the mons. It is that fleshy area of skin covering the pubic bone. It doesn't really do anything, but there it is. Same with the perineum—that's the area between the anus and the labia minora. It doesn't do much either.

INTERNAL FEMALE SEX ORGANS

Inside a woman's body is where all the complicated stuff happens. In fact, so many different complicated things happen that we could devote several chapters to this topic—but we're not going to. We'll cover the basics that every sexually active man and woman ought to know.

Check out the diagram below. You'll see that after the vaginal opening comes—you guessed it—the vagina. The vagina is a muscular chamber about

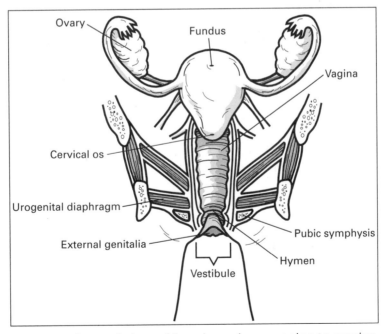

Internal view of female package, vagina to ovaries.

three or four inches long, when relaxed. Women following along can try gently inserting a clean finger into the vagina to feel it. Notice that the muscular walls of the vagina are not completely straight. There are soft folds of skin. It probably feels moist, but the vagina can be dry, especially right after your menstrual period. The vagina expands during arousal to accommodate the penis.

At the top of the vagina is the cervix, which is the opening to your uterus. You can feel your cervix with your finger, if you want. It's best if you trim your fingernail first; then, while standing in a slightly squatted position, gently insert your finger all the way into the vagina and bear down a little. You should feel a smooth, rounded bulge with a slight dimple in the middle. You'll probably also notice that while *you* can feel *it*, *it* can't really feel *you*. That's because the cervix has very few nerve endings. The slight dimple you feel is where the entry to the uterus is located, although it is plugged up with mucus. Semen can travel through this; tampons, penises, fingers, and contraceptive sponges cannot. During delivery, the cervix expands greatly to allow the baby to pass through, but otherwise it remains closed to keep the uterus well protected.

The uterus or womb is about the size of a man's fist. Above the uterus, connected by fallopian tubes, are the ovaries, two almond-sized glands that produce eggs and estrogen, the main female sex hormone. Actually, strictly speaking, the fallopian tubes and the ovaries are not directly connected. The fallopian tubes also produce progesterone, another sex hormone, along with a bunch of other hormones whose functions doctors have yet to determine. All of this is held in place by muscle and connective tissue.

The female menstrual cycle is roughly twenty-eight days long—give or take a couple of days. Menstruation—your "period"—lasts for anywhere from a couple of days to a week, and can vary widely in heaviness. Ovulation, the release of an egg (ovum) into the fallopian tube, happens once a cycle, approximately two weeks after the start of your period. This is the time of peak fertility for a woman. Technically, the few days after ovulation are the only days on which you can become pregnant. Unfortunately, it is hard to feel exactly when ovulation is occurring, and sperm can survive for more than a couple of days in a woman's body, so birth control remains a necessity.

WHAT ABOUT THE STUFF ABOVE THE WAIST?

The reason women have breasts is to provide milk to their babies. Their function as a food delivery system is usually obscured by all the hype and

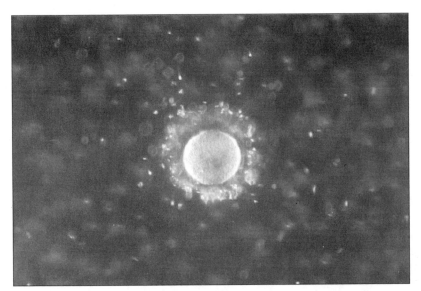

If one of these sperm penetrates this ovum—bang!—you may be looking at a future president. SCIENCE PICTURES LIMITED/CORBIS

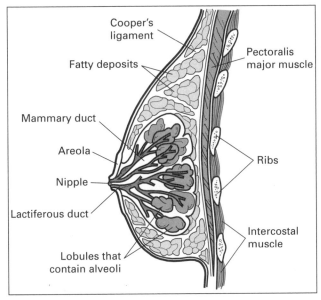

Cooper's ligament

Fatty deposits

Pectoralis major muscle

Mammary duct

Areola

Ribs

Nipple

Lactiferous duct

Intercostal muscle

Lobules that contain alveoli

Cross section of breast.

attention they receive during the time when a baby isn't attached to them. They are sexual organs in their own right. Most straight men are aroused by looking at, touching, or even just thinking about breasts, and most women are aroused by the skillful stroking or sucking of their breasts. Given the otherwise inexplicable popularity of the television show *Baywatch*, you might even say ours is a breast-obsessed culture.

D Cup or Bust?

If you could change them, would you want your partner's breasts to be larger? Forty-five percent of the men in our survey said they would, but that it was "no big deal," while 9 percent said they would "absolutely" like to have their partners' breasts enlarged. That means 54 percent of our respondents are out there hoping the titty fairy visits their girlfriends tonight.

Does this mean that college men have a skewed idea of what an average breast size is? Apparently not. Fifty-nine percent of our male respondents correctly identified B cup as the average bra size for women, and 28 percent listed C cup as average. Our female respondents report that 38 percent wear B-cup bras, and 34 percent wear C, while 11 percent wear A cups and 12 percent wear D. So the male perception is fairly accurate. We can only assume that, for most men, bigger is definitely better. It seems some of the women agree—11 percent say they would consider a breast enlargement operation.

Our lesbian respondents couldn't disagree more. One hundred percent answered no when asked if they would prefer their partner's breasts to be larger.

Luckily, nothing you can do to a non-milk-producing breast will result in a pregnancy or sexually transmitted disease (STD). Just so you know, the inside of a breast contains the mammary gland, which makes milk, and fat and connective tissue, which give the breasts their shape. The mammary glands do occasionally produce and release small amounts of fluid, even if a woman is not pregnant or nursing. The size of a woman's breasts cannot be increased with exercises (since they are mostly fat), but they can increase in size temporarily before each menstrual period and during pregnancy.

On the outside, you will find the areola, the darker area of skin that encircles the nipple. Arousal, cold air, or nervousness can cause the areola to contract and pucker, and the nipple to stand erect. Look for more information about breasts and how to keep them healthy in Chapter 10.

CHAPTER 4

Safer Sex

HOW TO CONTROL AND PROTECT IT (BEFORE IT KILLS OR CREATES SOMEONE)

As the previous chapter showed you, the human reproductive system is a complicated thing. As if the power to produce an entire, new human being weren't impressive enough, our sex organs also have the ability to give us unparalleled pleasure. Unfortunately, along with the power and the pleasure come a host of potential problems. Yep, we're talking about the two things no sexually active, unmarried college student wants to think about: unplanned pregnancy and sexually transmitted diseases. Just how common are these problems? Our survey reveals some disturbing answers to these questions.

? *Have you and a partner ever experienced an unplanned pregnancy?*

Unfortunately, 12 percent of the students we asked said that they had had to deal with an unplanned pregnancy. Of those students, 20 percent had been pregnant more than once. Most of these students—53 percent—chose to have an abortion, while 26 percent miscarried. The sad thing is that accidents don't have to happen with this kind of regularity. While no common method of birth control is completely foolproof, when used conscientiously, failure rates are very low.

It's Tough Being a Lady

More women report STDs than men for a simple reason: it's easier for a man to infect a woman than for a woman to infect a man. A man with any kind of STD, including HIV, may infect six out of ten women he has intercourse with, while a woman with the same disease would probably infect one or two of her ten partners. We're not saying it's fair, but that's just the way it is.

Have you ever been diagnosed with a sexually transmitted disease?

Our study shows that 9 percent of college women and 4 percent of college men say they have been diagnosed as having an STD. Why more women than men? Perhaps because women are more likely to have regular medical checkups, so their conditions can be caught and treated.

Luckily, through the miracle of modern medicine, you can avoid these hazards with relatively little effort. Notice, we said *relatively* little effort. Relative to what, you ask? Relative to the trauma of having to deal with an unplanned pregnancy. Relative to the medical and psychological costs of handling potentially incurable sexually transmitted diseases (there are more than one). There has been a lot of emphasis in the past several years on HIV

A gentleman and a scholar, ready for class and safer sex. JIM CORWIN/CORBIS

and AIDS and the fact that unprotected sex can be fatal. It certainly can. But AIDS is only one of the many hazards of careless sex. Even "minor" STDs can cause pain and embarrassment. Some can render you permanently sterile. Some develop into cancer if left untreated. And an unplanned pregnancy—no matter how you choose to deal with it—can change your life forever.

AIDS may be relatively rare on college campuses, but it's not likely to stay that way, considering that careless, unprotected sex is rampant. More than half of the students we surveyed—55 percent—admitted that they do not always have safe sex, and 37 percent don't always use birth control. It's true that dealing with condoms and birth control can be awkward, but there are ways to get around the uneasiness. Read on for ways to keep yourself confidently and comfortably protected.

Why Protection Fails

Before we get into a discussion of safe sex and all the different forms of birth control, we need to address the one factor that causes most methods of protection to fail: people who either forget or decide not to use protection *every* time they have sex. This won't do at all. It's kind of like remembering to put on your parachute nine out of ten times. A lot of good those nine careful times do you when you are splattered all over the ground. We asked our respondents why they had failed to use condoms during sex (just condoms, not other birth control methods) and here's what they had to say:

■ Drugs and alcohol strike again: 18 percent said that they forgot about the condom because they were too drunk or high. Clearly, six beers and half a joint do not tend to make people smart. Sex, alcohol, and/or drugs do not make a great combination, for many reasons. This is not the last time we will stress this important idea: if you or your partner seems too intoxicated to act responsibly, it's best to keep your pants zipped. Easier said than done, we know, but it's worth the effort.

■ Embarrassment is another derailer: 16 percent worried that they would spoil the mood by bringing up condoms, and 4 percent thought their partners might react badly. A woman might feel awkward demanding that her partner use a condom, because she does not want to seem too pushy or too knowledgeable about sex (the old double standard in action). She might think bringing up the subject of condoms will spoil the mood. Men might think that they would insult their partners by talking about condoms or, selfishly, might prefer not to use condoms because they believe unprotected sex feels better. There are many gullible, selfish people out there, and you might wind up in bed with one of them. That doesn't mean *you* have to be stupid. The best way to avoid a lot of awkwardness when it comes down to condom time is to be honest with yourself. Are you sexually active? If so, then keep your condoms handy. Keep one in your purse or wallet. Keep a box of them by the bed. Then, when clothes start coming off, whip one out. No need to ask first. If the condom is there and ready, it is much more likely to be used.

■ Some folks—5 percent—said their partners refused to wear the condoms, but they went ahead and had sex anyway. If your partner refuses to use the condom or objects to its use, offering such assurances as "I'll be careful" or "Don't worry, I don't have anything," you need to speak up right then and there. You might try a playful approach, such as saying, "Sorry, house rules" or "But it looks so cute on you/me. . . ." Or you might stress that you would feel much more relaxed using a condom. If neither approach works, your partner either has no respect for your health or your feelings, or he or she has some personal hang-ups you should work out together. Either way, stand your ground and *do not* have unprotected sex. See Chapter 4 for tips on satisfying each other safely until the condom issue can be resolved.

■ Ah, and then there's lust. The overwhelming attractiveness of a partner was responsible for 14 percent of the failures to use condoms, and it seemed to be slightly more of a problem for men, 17 percent of whom used this excuse. No doubt about it, wild, spontaneous sex can be fabulous. But that doesn't let you off the hook. If you have the serious hots for someone, you better make sure those condoms are nearby at all times. Stash them everywhere—glove compartments, kitchen drawers, book bags. If you do happen to find yourself revved up without a condom handy, remember: anticipation only increases desire. Get thee to a drugstore. If your lust is such that there will be no waiting, satisfy each other safely, without intercourse (again, see Chapter 4).

■ The unfounded belief that someone is disease free also leads to careless sex: 13 percent said they dispensed with condoms because they thought their partners probably had no STDs. How are you supposed to tell—the flashing green "all clear" light on the forehead? Clean-cut, well-mannered people can have STDs, too. They might not even know about it. Unless your partner has been examined by a physician and has shared the results with you, don't assume anything.

■ Finally, there's the truly inexplicable excuse: "I didn't care." Yes, 21 percent of the students who failed to use condoms just didn't care enough to protect themselves. What can we say about that? We are dumbfounded. At least the 13 percent who said they were too lazy have identified an area of potential improvement. We hope this is some sort of self-esteem issue that can be worked out in therapy.

You've Come a Long Way, Condom!

The condom concept dates back to 1350 B.C., when ancient Egyptians (fond as they are of wrapping bodies) figured covering up the penis might prevent pregnancy. Over the years, many strange casings have been used for prophylactic purposes: goat bladders, sheep and fish intestines, seed pods, linen, silk, and leather have all fallen in and out of favor. Vulcanized rubber made an appearance as a condom material in the mid-1800s.

Birth Control vs. Safer Sex

Safer sex means sex performed with the maximum precautions against contracting STDs—most importantly, AIDS. Conveniently, the precautions you must take to avoid STDs also serve well to prevent unwanted pregnancy. The reverse is not true. Many birth control methods, such as birth control pills and diaphragms, offer no protection against disease but plenty of protection against pregnancy. To clear up any confusion, we are going to use the following terms to distinguish between two kinds of protection:

Does Abstinence Make the Heart Grow Fonder?

Before we talk about safer sex, we have to come clean on one point: no method of protection or birth control is perfect. Even people who have had operations to sterilize themselves have been known to become pregnant or get someone pregnant. And mistakes do occur—condoms tear, that "less than 1 percent chance" happens to you, and so on. The only real way to make sure you don't get pregnant, get someone pregnant, or catch an STD is to stay away from sex. Period. With this in mind, many religious and educational groups across the country are urging young people to practice abstinence until marriage. It should be pointed out that marriage, in and of itself, is not some miracle guard against STDs (husbands and wives have been known to cheat); however, statistically, you are a lot better off the fewer partners you have, and zero partners offers you infallible protection.

Safer sex   Safer sex, as we just explained, is about preventing disease. It almost always involves a condom and preferably includes spermicidal jelly, which make it a very effective means of birth control, too. We'll further explain safer sex in a minute. Safer sex must be practiced by anyone who is not in a monogamous relationship with a disease-free person whom they trust.

Controlled sex   In this chapter, we are going to use the term "controlled sex" to mean sex with birth control (we're not talking about your wildness or lack of wildness in bed). Some kinds of controlled sex offer some protection against disease and some do not, but all offer protection against pregnancy. Controlled sex that is not combined with safer sex should be practiced only by two disease-free, monogamous people who trust each other.

There is overlap between safer sex and controlled sex, as we shall see.

SAFER SEX

Vaginal Intercourse the Safe Way

Most STDs are transmitted through direct, genital-to-genital contact. Often, STDs cause lesions (cuts or blisters) or bumps (see pages 92 to 95 for descriptions of symptoms). Simply putting your genitals into contact with these lesions or bumps can be enough to cause you to contract the disease. HIV is transmitted through body fluids, such as semen and blood. Any tiny cut or abrasion on your genitals could leave you open to infection. Because contact is so risky, the best way to protect yourself is with a barrier method of protection.

An AIDS Quick Reference

AIDS is an abbreviation that stands for "acquired immunodeficiency syndrome." People with AIDS have weakened immune systems, which means their bodies have trouble fighting off diseases. AIDS is incurable and deadly.

HIV is an abbreviation for "human immunodeficiency virus." Doctors believe HIV infection is what causes AIDS. It is this virus, not the disease known as AIDS, that can be transmitted through unsafe sex and other exchanges of bodily fluids.

HIV positive is the term used for people who have been infected with HIV, but may or may not have developed AIDS. Thanks to new, effective treatments, many people who are HIV positive can remain healthy for many years. However, most people with HIV eventually develop AIDS.

Condoms

The most common barrier method is latex condoms, or "rubbers." There are so-called natural or lambskin condoms out there that promise better sensations during sex. Make sure you use only latex condoms; materials other than latex do not offer much protection against disease, because they are porous enough to let viruses through, even while keeping semen in. Latex condoms

One size does not fit all.

are available in almost all drugstores, and they come with a stunning variety of options. Ribbed, studded, ticklered. Black, purple, glow-in-the-dark. It's probably best to stick with the basics. Pick one with a reservoir tip that can collect semen, or make sure you leave a little air space at the tip of the condom. This helps prevent uncomfortable tightness and tearing. Some condoms come prelubricated. These are a good choice. Lubricated condoms are easier to put on, more comfortable to wear, and reduce the friction during intercourse that could cause tears in the condom or, worse, tears in the skin that could transmit disease. Unlubricated condoms are OK, but you should have a water-soluble lubricant to use with them. K-Y Jelly, also available at drugstores, is an excellent choice. Vaseline or other brands of petroleum jelly are terrible choices. *You must not use petroleum jelly with your condoms.* It breaks down the latex and, since it does not wash off easily, can trap bacteria in some inconvenient places. Some condoms come with something called "dry lubrication." We have no idea what this is supposed to mean, but it sure isn't comfortable. Stay away from them or use them with the regular "wet" lubricating jelly.

The best choice is a condom lubricated with spermicidal jelly. Studies show the chemicals in spermicide offer additional protection against disease. As we will explain, spermicides really boost your protection against both disease and pregnancy. Unfortunately, some people with sensitive skin develop mild, but uncomfortable, reactions to the chemicals. If this happens to you, use condoms well lubricated with nonspermicidal jelly. Women who can't use spermicide might also want to use a backup method of birth control, such as birth control pills.

Looking for a good deal on condoms? Check with your college health center—it might offer free condoms or, at least, condoms at cheaper prices.

It's All in the Timing

Exactly *when* the condom gets put on is a tricky question for many people. As we pointed out in the last chapter, sperm are remarkably determined. Tiny drops of preseminal fluid released near the vagina can find a way of getting a woman pregnant. And any genital-to-genital contact, even if it does not involve penetration, is risky. The condom has to go on as soon as your genitals are exposed and have any possibility of coming into contact with those of another. But what if you want to roll around and make out some more? Our advice is to keep your underwear on or keep your genitals apart until you are absolutely ready to begin intercourse. Make sure the condom is within easy reach, preferably already opened, so when the time comes there won't be any awkward fumbling to mess up the mood.

How to Use a Condom

It gets very easy with practice. First, determine which side of the rolled-up condom is the "out" side, so that it will unroll correctly, then just place the ring of the condom over the top of the erect penis and gently roll it down over the entire shaft. Either partner can do this. Make sure to pull a little extra room at the tip of the condom between thumb and forefinger—just a half inch is fine. If you are using a condom with a reservoir tip, squeeze any air out of it. This helps prevent breaking and leaves room for semen. Apply lubricant or spermicide, and you're ready to go. After ejaculation, the penis must be withdrawn carefully. To prevent the condom from coming off inside the vagina, either partner should gently grasp the base of the condom as the man withdraws. It's important that the man withdraw soon after ejaculation, while the penis is still fairly firm. As the penis becomes smaller and softer, there is a danger that the condom could slip or leak.

Throw the condom away after use. Do not reuse condoms or use them after the expiration date printed on the package. Store your condoms at room temperature. You can carry them in your wallet or glove compartment for a day or two, but heat from your body or the sun can cause the rubber to break down.

Potential Problems and Troubleshooting

Condoms can take some getting used to. Some men complain that occasionally they lose a certain amount of sensation when using condoms, and this can cause them to have problems keeping erections. It's important not to lose your patience or your resolve. Some men say that by starting intercourse with fairly vigorous, rapid thrusts they can get their bearings and avoid problems. If the penis starts to become soft, either partner can massage it manually to help restore the erection.

Usually, all it takes to resolve these problems is a little experimentation. Try different brands of condoms. Make sure they fit comfortably. Regular condoms fit most men, but there are slightly larger and smaller sizes that might increase your or your partner's comfort.

"Female" Condoms

This is a relatively new form of barrier protection. It works pretty much like a regular condom, except it covers the inside of the vagina instead of the outside of the penis. It is shaped like a baggy tube, with rings at both ends. One end is covered. This goes over the cervix. The outer ring stays in place snugly against the outside of the vagina. Many women like this option because they believe it gives them more control. They can protect themselves, even if their partners are unwilling to wear condoms. Also, the female condom can be inserted ahead of time, so there is no interruption of sex.

Female condoms are not as widely available as regular condoms. Check with your campus health center to find out more about them.

Spermicides

Spermicides, as mentioned before, not only provide protection against pregnancy, but also give added protection against some STDs. If the condom should break or slip during sex, the spermicide provides an important fallback. There are a few ways to use spermicides. At the drugstore, you will find spermicidal jelly or cream, spermicidal foam, and spermicidal suppositories. Which you choose depends on your personal preference. Most come with applicators and are easy to use. Read the packaging information carefully, and ask your pharmacist or a doctor at your college health center if you have any questions.

We strongly recommend that you use spermicide with your condom for greatest safety.

Please! Don't Eat the Spermicide!

If oral sex is something you enjoy along with intercourse, using spermicides can cause a problem. They have a lingering taste and smell, and they numb your entire mouth. Not pleasant at all. Either work in the oral sex before spermicide gets applied anywhere, or keep a damp cloth on your nightstand full of goodies so you can clear the area before deploying. Since safer oral sex includes using a condom, keep the unlubricated variety around for this purpose.

Anal Intercourse the Safe Way

Check out Chapter 7 for some important information about engaging in anal sex. There are potential health problems involved with anal sex that are not covered in this chapter. Anal intercourse is considered the riskiest form of sex, in terms of the transmission of HIV. Despite this fact, only 17 percent of the students we surveyed said they used a condom every time they had anal sex. Since the anus is smaller and less flexible than the vagina, tears can occur in the tissue in and around it, even if you are very careful. These tears make it very easy to transmit or contract bloodborne disease such as HIV/AIDS. A condom must be worn during anal sex. In fact, even between committed, disease-free partners, it is a good idea to use a condom to prevent possible bacterial infection.

The same rules about condom use that apply for vaginal intercourse apply for anal intercourse. There should be no unprotected contact between the penis and anus. Plenty of lubrication should be used to minimize the risking of tearing the condom or the skin, and insertion of the penis should be slow and gentle.

Do not use the same condom to penetrate both the vagina and the anus—this can cause or spread infections. Switch to a fresh condom before switching from vaginal to anal or anal to vaginal penetration.

Oral Sex the Safe Way

The good news is that many STDs cannot be transmitted through oral sex. The bad news is that only the most unpleasant STDs can be transmitted through oral sex. A recent study showed that unprotected oral sex is riskier than was previously assumed. Any nick or abrasion on your gums or tongue could be an opening for AIDS. Cold sores on the lips can become herpes on the genitals. You can even develop gonorrhea in your throat. And it's important to remember that you run a risk even if you are just the recipient of someone's oral attention. The prospect of a getting a casual blow job might sound great, but you'd better take precautions.

To be safe when giving or receiving fellatio (a blow job), a nonlubricated condom should be used. To be safe when giving or receiving cunnilingus (oral sex on a woman), either plastic wrap or something called a dental dam

---

Oral Alert

Health officials have been warning us for years that AIDs and other STDs can be transmitted through oral sex, but college students have not gotten the picture: 77 percent said they never used a condom during oral sex, and 76 percent said they never used a dental dam. The problem seems to be worse among older students. Among freshmen, 73 percent reported never using a condom, while 81 percent of the seniors were having unprotected oral sex.

should be spread over the vulva and vaginal opening. Do you absolutely hate these ideas? Well, there is one way to get yourself out of this situation. You and your partner can get clean bills of health from the doctor, and that means getting AIDS tests. You can make arrangements at your campus health center to have this test done confidentially. Then you have to be sure that your partner isn't giving or receiving oral sex (or any other kind of sex) from anyone else. If you are both HIV and herpes free—and monogamous—you can toss the condoms during oral sex. Quite an incentive for developing a committed relationship, isn't it?

Making Safer Sex Sexy

Creams and jellies, condoms and dental dams, rules and regulations. Seems like being safer takes all the zip out of sex, huh? Trust us on this: it seems that way only at first. A little practice and ingenuity is all it takes. Here are some suggestions for getting over the initial rough spots.

In the heat of the moment, it can be difficult to open the condom package and get the thing on properly. The condoms that come in foil packaging are the hardest to open (although you get the hang of it with practice); however, they are the best ones for carrying around with you, since the tough packaging makes them more resistant to damage in your wallet or purse. (Remember, don't keep condoms in your wallet for more than a day or two.) Some condoms come in thinner plastic packaging with a convenient serrated tear line—not so damage resistant, but very easy to open. We suggest using the condoms in the foil packaging as your "road rubbers," but use the easy-to-open ones at home. As far as getting the condom onto the penis, only practice helps there. You men out there might want to invest in a box of condoms, shut yourself in the bathroom, and spend some quality time with yourself to build up your condom application speed.

Problem: Concentrating on getting the condom on causes the man to lose his sexual focus and erection. *Solution:* Having the condoms handy and getting familiar with putting them on will usually eliminate this problem. Some men just get plain embarrassed or frustrated by the whole procedure, though. Women can help with this by helping to roll the condom on or by taking over the condom job themselves. Make it something sexy, not some kind of chore. You can continue kissing and touching as you put on the condom. If the man's penis has gotten a little softer, try holding it firmly in your hand and massaging it as you kiss. Try to start intercourse as soon as possible, so you can both relax and forget about the condom.

Problem: You are out of condoms. *Solution:* You are not going to let this happen, right? Because the law of averages clearly shows that you need condoms most desperately when none are available to you. You may have gone months without requiring one, then—boom!—you come up shorthanded in your hour of need. Check your stash often—you never know if your roommate has been poaching your supply. However, if the unthinkable happens and you get caught without a condom, you have a couple of options. First, if you think the mood will last, go to the drugstore and get some. A sense of humor is key here. Take your partner with you and make it an adventure. If you leave him/her in your apartment, boredom will probably set in and the television will be on by the time you get back. If a trip to the drugstore seems unbearable, your other option is manual stimulation. This can actually be highly erotic and exciting—not like the sweaty groping you might have encountered in high school. Turn down the lights and take your time. Chapter 5 contains tips for satisfying your partner this way.

As we said before, safe sex is a requirement for anyone who is not in a monogamous, disease-free relationship. If you are settled down with someone you trust and you both have received a seal of sexual approval from a doctor (that is, you both had AIDS tests and physical exams), then you have some more options available to you.

Top Five Reasons to Have Safer Sex

1. It can save your life. You know the score. AIDS is not something you want in your body.

2. It can save your fertility. STDs can damage your reproductive organs and ruin your chances of having a family later. You may not want babies now, but you'll want that option down the road.

3. It can save you considerable pain and discomfort. STDs aren't always easy to treat. If liquid nitrogen and trichloroacetic acid sound like things you'd like to keep away from your genitals, practice safer sex.

4. It can keep you on the road to success. Unplanned pregnancies have a way of derailing people's lives or, at least, changing them dramatically. If you have hopes and plans for the future, in college and beyond, protect yourself.

5. It can enhance your sex life. No, we're not kidding. With so many things to worry about, sex can be a stressful thing. One of the main reasons many unmarried women have trouble experiencing orgasms regularly is that they are too worried about pregnancy to relax and enjoy themselves. Condoms can be effective aphrodisiacs.

BIRTH CONTROL OPTIONS

Here is another one of life's unfair jokes. Except for condoms and surgical sterilization, all the birth control methods currently available must be used by women. All the risk of side effects, all the responsibility of going to the doctor and acquiring some of these methods rests squarely on female shoulders. Luckily, there are several options. What you choose depends on your personal preference, your medical history, and your lifestyle. The doctors at your health center will be able to help you make the best decision. Following are the basic facts about the major forms of birth control, but many factors help determine what is right for you. We strongly recommend that you consult a professional for help with this important decision.

If it helps at all, the students we asked favored birth control pills and condoms: 68 percent usually use condoms for birth control and 40 percent rely on the pill. When asked to list their favorite methods—what they would use ideally—birth control pills won hands down with 42 percent, while condoms got 33 percent of the vote.

Of course, 19 percent of the students said they use the withdrawal method, which means the man simply withdraws before ejaculation. Don't take their advice on this one. The withdrawal method is notoriously ineffective. In the first place, it requires very good control on the part of the man, who must be aware enough of his sexual responses to pull out in time—not easy in the heat of the moment. Also, preseminal fluid does contain some sperm,

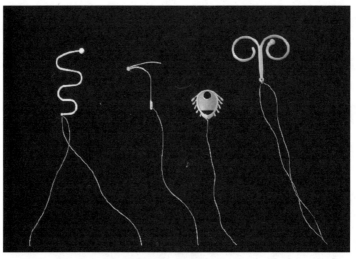

Yikes! IUDs are scary! ROBERT ESTALL/CORBIS

which can travel unmolested to the unprotected egg. Typically, almost 20 percent of women who use this method get pregnant within one year.

Over-the-Counter Methods

There are several birth control methods you can purchase at the drugstore, all of which involve spermicides. These can get expensive, especially if you have sex frequently. However, aside from minor skin irritations in some women with sensitive skin, these methods have no side effects. They are also completely reversible, meaning that if you want to get pregnant, all you have to do is just stop using them. On the down side, they are not the most reliable methods when used without condoms. Even under ideal conditions, your chances of getting pregnant within one year would be three to six in one hundred—and conditions are rarely ideal.

Jellies, Creams, Foams, Suppositories

These different forms of spermicide have different methods of insertion and slightly different levels of effectiveness. When used with a condom, research shows that the chance of accidental pregnancy is about 1 percent (in one year). Without a condom, the risk of pregnancy is anywhere from 3 to 20 percent. That's a big range, you might say. What's the deal? Well, human error seems to be at fault. Under clinical testing conditions, the risk of pregnancy is fairly low. But people don't always follow instructions correctly. If you choose to use these methods of birth control, make sure you read the instructions carefully and follow them exactly.

Contraceptive Sponges

The contraceptive sponge has become a popular nonprescription form of birth control for women, mainly because it allows for a little spontaneity. The sponge is round, and it is concave (indented) on one side. That side fits against your cervix. On the other side is a string you use to pull the sponge out. You can leave the sponge in place for up to twenty-four hours and have intercourse as many times as you want in that time—a big advantage over other spermicidal methods, which must be reapplied every time you have sex. You can put the sponge in hours in advance, if you think sex might be a possibility. You must leave it in for six hours after intercourse, though.

The sponge, even at its best, has a failure rate of 6 percent. It can also be a little hard to remove, especially after vigorous sex. The thrusting of the penis can turn the sponge around a bit. If this happens to you, don't panic. You *can* pull it out, even if you cannot reach the string. Try standing slightly squatted, bear down, and reach into your vagina with your fingers. Be patient and keep trying. If all else fails, go to the health center and let a doctor there remove it.

From Your Doctor

The most reliable methods of birth control must be acquired from your doctor.

The Pill (oral contraceptives)

One of the most reliable forms of birth control (aside from abstinence or sterilization) is the birth control pill. There are many different brands that employ varying levels of hormones, but basically they all work the same way: they fool your body into thinking it's pregnant, so no egg is released. If there is no egg for the sperm to hook up with, you can't get pregnant. If you take your pill every day, as instructed, there is a less-than-1-percent chance you will become pregnant within a year. That's the kind of reliability that makes the Pill so popular with young, single women who want to minimize any risk of pregnancy.

There are risks, however. Research over the past ten years has come to conflicting conclusions about whether there is any connection between higher breast cancer risks and the Pill. The biggest study to date, released in 1996, found no evidence that birth control pill use increases your risk of breast cancer. Smoking greatly increases your chances of developing potentially fatal blood clots while taking the Pill. Your doctor can discuss these

---

Missed a Period?

If your period is more than a week late, even if you have been very careful about using birth control, you should take a pregnancy test. You can pick up an easy-to-use home kit at a drugstore. These tests are extremely accurate if you use them according to the instructions. They are also pretty expensive ($15 to $20). If one of these tests says you are pregnant, make an appointment with a gynecologist and have your pregnancy confirmed. If you are short on cash, go to your campus health center and see if the doctor will give you a free or inexpensive pregnancy test. You can also go to a local women's clinic or family planning clinic (such as Planned Parenthood) for a urine or blood test. The blood test is more accurate.

rare, but serious, problems with you and help you decide if you are willing to take those risks. More common side effects of the Pill include weight gain, breast tenderness, and heightened emotionalism—much like the symptoms experienced early in pregnancy. Often, these side effects go away after a couple of months. Breakthrough bleeding, or spotting between periods, is also a common side effect. It is not serious, but it can be annoying. Let your doctor know about your side effects. There may be a different brand that might minimize them.

The Pill can be kind of expensive (sometimes up to $30 per month), but many college pharmacies offer much cheaper prices.

Norplant

Norplant is probably the most effective, lowest-maintenance form of birth control available right now (see photo) Six tiny sticks containing a synthetic hormone are implanted by a doctor into the fleshy underside of your upper arm. The hormone is gradually released into your system. The implant is effective for up to five years. There's no pill to forget, no trips to the pharmacy. Norplant is about as effective as the Pill, although its effectiveness drops slightly each year.

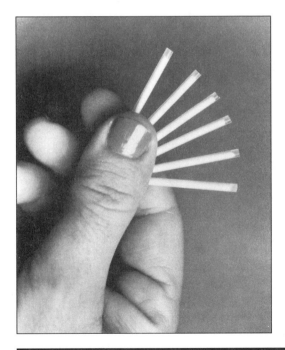

The Norplant birth control capsules. The capsules are placed under the skin in the upper arm and become effective within 24 hours when placed during the first 7 days of the menstrual cycle. The system has been called an alternative to sterilization and the most innovative contraceptive in 30 years.
REUTERS/CORBIS-BETTMANN

Getting Norplant does involve a high up-front cost if you go to a private doctor, but in the long run it works out to be cheaper than the Pill. It also costs to get the implants removed. Your campus health facility may offer less expensive insertion and removal services.

Since Norplant is a fairly new form of birth control, there is not as much long-term data about its safety—something you definitely want to bear in mind. Be sure to ask your doctor about the possible health risks.

The Diaphragm and the Cervical Cap

The diaphragm is a shallow rubber bowl that fits over your cervix. You put spermicide in the bowl and around the rim and insert it into your vagina. A doctor must fit you for a diaphragm. It has a failure rate of about six in one hundred per year if used correctly. Like the sponge, the diaphragm can be awkward to insert and remove, but it gets easier with time.

The cervical cap works much like a diaphragm, but it is much smaller and shaped sort of like a thimble. You fill it about one-third full of spermicidal jelly and place it over the cervix. It stays in place through the formation of a suction seal. It also has a failure rate of about 6 percent when used correctly.

Both the diaphragm and the cervical cap can be inserted hours in advance but, like the sponge, they must be left in place for six hours after intercourse. They are not as effective as the Pill or Norplant.

Other Methods

The intrauterine device (IUD) is an unlikely choice for college women. The IUD is a small metal or plastic device placed in the uterus. No one knows exactly how, but a foreign object in the uterus seems to prevent pregnancy. Unfortunately, there are all sorts of negative side effects that can occur, including pelvic inflammatory disease and impaired fertility. Since college-age women probably don't want to do anything that would hurt their chances of having children later, the IUD is not considered an ideal choice for them. But ask your doctor if you want more information.

Depo-Provera is a shot you get at your doctor's office once every few months. It is as effective as the Pill, but apparently has fewer side effects. However, there are few long-term studies on the safety of this method.

Abortion and Other Alternatives

No matter how many precautions you take, mistakes can happen. You will, we hope, never have to face it, but one of the hardest decisions any woman has to make is what to do about an unplanned pregnancy. If it does happen to you, you should know and weigh your options.

Abortion

Let's just set the record straight on one point: no one is *pro-abortion*. No one says, "Abortions are great! Everyone should have one." Abortions are not great, and no woman takes them lightly. However, they are—at present, anyway—very safe and legal, and, for some women, having an abortion is the best choice they can make when confronted with an unplanned pregnancy.

Abortions are safer and easier earlier in your pregnancy. It is important to determine whether you are pregnant as soon after you miss a period as possible. Many young women find it difficult to face the fact that they are pregnant and they go into a state of denial. This only hurts them in the long run. If your decision is to abort, you should decide as soon as you can—before you are eight weeks pregnant, if possible. If abortion is not your choice, you should begin seeking proper medical attention for yourself and your baby as soon as possible. Abortions performed after the first trimester (after your twelfth week) are legal, but are more expensive and difficult, pose more risks, are more emotionally upsetting, and can be harder to arrange.

Early abortions can be sought in several ways. You do not have to go to a hospital. Check your Yellow Pages under "abortion" for a list of clinics. Call one near you and ask about the procedure. You should make an appointment to speak with a nurse at the facility to find out exactly what the clinic offers. Some will administer short-acting general anesthesia, so you will be unconscious throughout the procedure. Others offer something called "twilight sleep," during which you are conscious, but tranquilized with medication. Make sure you are as comfortable as possible with the people and the environment at the clinic. Do not go someplace where you are left waiting for long periods of time, where you are treated rudely, where you are kept from speaking directly with the doctor who will be performing the procedure, or where you think that your feelings or questions are not given attention. Most important, if at all possible, do not go anywhere that is surrounded by anti-abortion protesters. Making the decision to have an abortion is hard enough—you don't need verbal abuse the day you go to the clinic; you need support and kindness.

If you aren't sure whom to call, try Planned Parenthood, a national, reputable organization that can give you assistance. Some smaller towns in some states might not have a choice of abortion facilities. Talk to the gynecologist at your health center. If he or she can't give you advice, you should visit a private doctor. You can also call the National Abortion Federation Hotline at 1-800-772-9100.

You will need someone to come with you the day of your abortion. That person will need to wait in the clinic the entire time and must get you home. You will not be allowed to drive. An early abortion should not be painful. Depending on what kind of drugs or anesthesia you are given, you will feel weak and perhaps a little nauseated afterward, and you will probably experience discomfort that feels like menstrual cramps. The doctor will probably prescribe some antibiotics and other medication, which you should pick up at a pharmacy immediately. You can take ibuprofen, Tylenol, or Aleve, but not aspirin, for the cramps. You will also experience some bleeding for a few days to a week and some spotting for a few days after that. The flow might be heavier than your normal period, and you will not be allowed to use tampons, so make sure to pick up some maxipads. You must also refrain from intercourse for a few weeks (follow your doctor's instructions). If you do have intercourse, use protection—you can get pregnant again right away.

Your doctor will probably give you a list of warning signs for complications. These include high fever, vomiting, very heavy bleeding, or bleeding that lasts longer than a week. Complications in an early abortion are not common.

Marriage

In times past, an unplanned pregnancy carried only one option for an honorable man: marriage. Unfortunately, these marriages of necessity do not always wind up joyously, and the child for the sake of whom the marriage was made winds up in an unhappy home. However, if you and your partner have been in a committed relationship for some time and think that getting married is something you wanted to do in the future . . . well, give it some more thought. If you can, see a marriage counselor together and talk about what you expect from a life together. Marriage and a family are a huge responsibility, especially while you are still trying to figure out what you want to do with your life. You have to consider that one or both of you might have to leave school and find work, and finding a good job without a college degree can be extremely difficult. Providing for a child limits your freedom, but it can be done, especially if you have a supportive family who can offer you assistance. Think very practically and carefully about your decision.

Single Motherhood

Unless you have plenty of support from the father of the child and your family, having a baby during your college years can mean the end of your education. If you have plenty of support—someone who can help you financially while you finish your education, someone who can watch and care for your baby while you go to class, study, and look for a job—then it is possible to continue at school.

Adoption

Adoption is another option you can choose if your religious or moral convictions keep you from seeking an abortion. Be very careful when seeking an agency, however. There are some shady characters out there who play fast and loose with the law regarding adoption. There are some desperate people who will go to desperate lengths to get babies illegally. Make sure the agency is reputable and legal.

If you go to church, talk with your minister about your options. You may find a family willing to help you with or pay your medical bills in exchange for an adoption agreement. Be aware that laws vary from state to state. If, some years after the adoption, you change your mind or decide you made a mistake, you will have an extremely difficult time getting your baby back.

THE ABCs OF STDs

OK, you are going to be careful, right? You are going to follow all the advice on pages 78 to 83. But, as we said before, mistakes do happen. STDs, in general, can be dealt with and contained. But in order to get proper treatment, you have to realize you have a problem and then take quick action—that is, hightail it to your doctor. We're not going to go into major detail here. Your campus health facility probably has a whole rack full of flyers and pamphlets that can give you more information. Following are some common and a couple of serious but not-so-common STDs and their major symptoms.

But first . . . some important information about STDs. In the first place, they are very common. If you have unprotected sex with more than one person, you run a pretty good risk of catching one. They can be transmitted in a number of ways (sometimes on towels and toilet seats), but intercourse is the easiest way. If you notice any of the following symptoms on your partner, don't have sex.

> **Who's Got What?**
>
> The students we surveyed who had been tripped up by an STD in the past reported that these were the culprits in question:
>
> | | |
> |---|---|
> | Genital warts | 31% |
> | Crabs (pubic lice) | 31% |
> | Chlamydia | 23% |
> | Gonorrhea | 17% |
> | Herpes | 15% |
> | Trichomoniasis | 7% |
> | Syphilis | 3% |

Gonorrhea

Women may have mild or confusing symptoms, or no symptoms at all. Pain in the lower abdomen, unusual discharge, or a urinary tract infection might be the only tip-offs. We must stress that any pain or unusual symptoms involving your reproductive organs should be checked by a doctor—don't wait until it becomes serious. Men might notice a thick discharge from their penises and feel burning during urination. Gonorrhea can infect the throat and be spread through oral-genital contact. It is treated with antibiotics.

Chlamydia

Chlamydia is transmitted mainly during vaginal or anal sex (unlikely, but possible, during oral sex). Chlamydia is especially dangerous because in women it very often has no symptoms, but if left untreated, it can leave a woman infertile. Burning during urination or an unusual discharge may be the only symptoms. Men with chlamydia usually do experience this burning. It is important that infected men inform all of their recent partners. Chlamydia is easily treated with antibiotics.

Syphilis

Syphilis causes rashes and sores on the genitals and elsewhere, and can be transmitted through contact with these rashes or through sexual contact. The symptoms of syphilis go through four stages as the bacteria that cause it spread and develop in the body. In the first stage, a chancre (pronounced "shanker") might appear on the genitals. This is a painless sore. It can also appear elsewhere in the body. During the second stage, which occurs weeks to months after infection, rashes on the body may develop then disappear; joints may ache; fever and headache might occur. This can go on for years. Late in the progress of the disease—say, ten years into it—there are no outward symptoms. The bacteria are too busy invading your internal organs. In the end, syphilis can cause blindness, madness, and death. Syphilis can be treated at any time with antibiotics.

Genital Warts (HPV)

The human papillomavirus (HPV) causes genital warts, which come in several shapes and sizes. Some look like common warts you might get on your hand or foot; some are as small as a pinhead; some are flat. Genital warts are very common and are spread through intercourse. Unfortunately for women, warts may be so small they can't be seen, or they may infect the cervix or vaginal walls, making them almost impossible for a woman to detect by herself. If left untreated, HPV can cause cervical cancer, so it is very, very important for women to have annual gynecological exams (see Chapter 10 for info). In men, warts usually appear as bumps on the penis head or shaft, or on the scrotum. They can itch. Women also may notice bumps on their labia. Genital warts are a viral infection, so they can come back after the initial treatment. They usually are treated with a prescription medication called podophyllin, but treatment may be more complicated for women and involve several trips to the doctor.

Herpes

Herpes is another viral infection. It is generally transmitted through sexual intercourse but can also be transmitted through oral-genital contact. Symptoms in men and women include an itching or burning in the genital area, followed within a day or so by the appearance of painful sores on the genitals. Urination may be painful. The sores, during an initial outbreak, can last for a couple weeks. Although nothing can cure herpes, there are effective medications that can reduce the frequency and severity of the outbreaks. With medication and proper diet and exercise, it is possible to go for years without an outbreak.

AIDS

AIDS is an incurable viral infection that doctors think is caused by the human immunodeficiency virus (HIV). It can be transmitted only through the exchange of body fluids such as blood, semen, and vaginal secretions. The disease is believed to be ultimately fatal, but more and more people are living for years with HIV and not becoming ill. They are, however, infectious. HIV infection has no symptoms. A person whose HIV infection has developed into AIDS might develop frequent infections, such as vaginitis. Weight loss and fatigue are other early symptoms of AIDS. Treatments do exist to make the disease more manageable.

Make AIDS testing a part of your yearly physical or gynecological exam.

Part Two

CHAPTER 5

Masturbation

THE HISTORY OF MASTURBATION: GUILT, INSANITY, BLINDNESS, DAMNATION, AND HAIRY PALMS

Since the beginning of time, the overwhelming majority of people have engaged in some form of autoerotic stimulation. Hey, monkeys at the zoo do it in front of visitors all the time, a good indicator that we humans knew how to masturbate before we knew how to walk upright. But since the beginning of time (or at least the beginning of recorded time) we've been told by lawgivers, church fathers, patriarchs, and moms that this particular form of pleasure is nasty, sinful, dangerous to our health, and just plain bad. But can eight billion masturbators really be that wrong? Let's see what the college students think.

▓ *Is masturbation wrong or sinful?*

Not according to the students we surveyed. Only 6 percent said they believe masturbation is wrong, while a whopping 79 percent said it is a perfectly "healthy and/or necessary" thing to do. Somewhere in between are the 15 percent who think it is "perverted." Positive feelings about masturbation increased with age and experience. It may seem surprising, but virgins really knocked self-stimulation: 15 percent said it is a sin. Freshmen gave masturbation the stamp of approval 69 percent of the time, while 80 percent of the sophomores, 86 percent of the juniors, and 87 percent of the seniors said it is a healthy thing to do. The highest approval rating from any one group came from gay and bisexual men, who gave masturbation a 98 percent approval rating.

Why do you masturbate?

When asked to describe their feelings about masturbation, about a third of those surveyed said that it isn't as good as sex, but 22 percent said they always enjoy it anyway. Collegiate masturbators don't seemed to be suffering any psychic damage as a result of their activities: only 6 percent reported feeling lonely or depressed because of masturbating. Many just look on it as a natural tension tamer: 29 percent reported that masturbating helped them reduce anxiety and frustration. Plus, it's reliable: 86 percent of the men and 55 percent of the women reported achieving orgasm through masturbation.

How often do you masturbate?

Folks were all across the board on this one. Almost one quarter—22 percent—said they masturbate two to three times a week. One in ten does so once or more a day. 14 percent said they give themselves a hand less than once a month. The real shocker? The most popular response to this question was *never:* 27 percent of our respondents claim they never masturbate.

The breakdown is even more interesting: 12 percent of the males said they never masturbate, and a full 40 percent of the women said they abstain, too. Even though 74 percent of women said they thought masturbation was a healthy/necessary thing to do, only 60 percent seem to be following through on their convictions.

Baby Self-Love

Thanks to ultrasonic snooping devices, doctors now know that male fetuses experience erections—and they stroke their penises.

THE ONUS ON ONAN

Thou shalt not spanketh thy monkey.

One of the earliest injunctions against masturbation comes from (where else?) the Old Testament in the Book of Genesis. It seems a guy named Onan wasn't too keen on the idea of impregnating the wife of his brother—even though God told him it was fine. "So," according to Genesis 46:12, "whenever he lay with his brother's wife, he spilled his semen on the ground to keep from producing offspring." This practice was deemed sin (apparently, even in Heaven, there's a substantial penalty for early withdrawal), and this sin was given the name "onanism," which referred both to coitus interruptus, or pulling out, and masturbation.

But why is spilling semen considered so bad, especially when compared to sleeping with your brother's wife? Most likely it has to do with the difficulty of procreation in biblical times. Childbearing may seem like a fairly straightforward proposition nowadays, but dying during childbirth was not rare for women of earlier times, and babies who were lucky enough to make it through childbirth often didn't survive infancy. Many Judeo-Christian teachings (including the Roman Catholic restrictions on birth control) focus on encouraging people to have as many children as possible, presumably to keep the faith going. A couple tablespoons of spilled semen, then, is like a wasted child. Of course, it's worth pointing out here that the Bible doesn't specifically forbid women from touching themselves—that idea was created, developed, and disseminated by religious patriarchs long after the death of Christ.

Thirteenth-century philosopher Thomas Aquinas, for example, listed masturbation as a grave sexual sin. Five hundred years later Onan's legacy was still going strong: in 1758 a Catholic medical doctor and Vatican advisor named Samuel Tissot published a study called *Onania* "proving" that masturbation caused insanity. Hundreds of pseudoscientific studies have been

A chronic masturbator gets the medieval cure. Reuters/Corbis-Bettmann

produced since then claiming that masturbation causes blindness, sterility, and a host of other physical and mental ills.

Incalculable psychic damage, immeasurable guilt, and countless sexual disorders have been produced by this morbid hysteria over masturbation. Thankfully, health researchers, doctors, and mental health therapists today agree that, short of masturbating so frequently that you rub your skin raw, there are no negative side effects to masturbation. In fact, the opposite seems to be true. Masturbation has been shown to enhance self-worth, release tension, and broaden people's knowledge of their own sexual responses. Sex therapists may even prescribe certain masturbation practices as a way of helping men increase their staying power with a partner and a way for women to learn how to be orgasmic during sex with a partner.

Before we go into some detail on various masturbation techniques, decorum requires that we list a few rules of the road. You do, of course, have the right to touch yourself, but, unless you have permission from your audience, touching your genitals in front of other people is not polite. Also, try not to masturbate so frequently that you miss class. Don't hog the bathroom all the time. And clean up after yourself!

SOLO SEX: A FEW POPULAR TECHNIQUES

Don't knock masturbation! It's sex with someone I love.
—WOODY ALLEN IN *ANNIE HALL*

People discover masturbation in a variety of ways. Some girls discover they have a pleasurable sensation when running, riding a bike, or riding a horse. Some boys discover the possibility on their own at the onset of puberty. Other kids hear about it from siblings or friends, read about it in books or magazines, or see it alluded to in a movie.

The early development of masturbation techniques often forms lifelong preferences. While no one masturbation style is necessarily better than another—the aim, after all, is to give yourself pleasure—some do more accurately simulate the sensations received during intercourse. For women especially, it may be worthwhile to include these techniques in your repertoire to enhance your orgasmic ability during intercourse. We'll deal with those methods first.

Clitoral Stimulation

For the majority of women, during intercourse or during masturbation, orgasm is brought about through direct or indirect stimulation of the clitoris. Naturally, then, most masturbation methods tend to focus on the clitoris.

Give Yourself a Hand (or a Finger)

Many women find it easiest to bring themselves to orgasm using their hands and fingers. This is one method that can closely resemble the clitoral stimulation during intercourse, so give it a try if it's not your usual way. And remember, a little lubrication goes a long way.

Position: Lying on your back allows you to relax and gives full freedom of motion for your hands. Try bending your knees slightly and spreading your legs apart. Some women prefer lying face down, which helps increase pressure on the clitoris. Choose whatever stance makes you comfortable, however: standing, sitting, squatting, whatever.

Touch: You might begin by using one or more fingers to rub the clitoris in an up-and-down or circular motion, starting slowly. Some women like direct pressure best, although some find that one side of the clitoris is more sensitive and prefer to concentrate on that side.

Gently petting or stroking the clitoris is also very stimulating and, like rubbing, simulates the clitoral stimulation of intercourse to some extent. "Pinching" the clitoris, or rubbing it between two fingers or finger and thumb, is another type of touch some women use.

Variations: Putting the fingers of one hand into the vagina or anus is a popular way to heighten the pleasure of clitoral stimulation. Many women enjoy a feeling of fullness when they climax, and using your fingers is one way to achieve this. There are many other ways, too, which we'll discuss in the sections on vaginal and anal stimulation that follow.

Some women also use an object other than their hands, like a pen or pencil (not the sharpened end of course) or paintbrush, to stimulate the clitoris.

Rubbing Yourself Against Something

Since rubbing up against an object such as a bicycle seat is one way girls discover masturbation, it remains a popular technique in adulthood. And since sexual intercourse, in the least romantic sense, is basically rubbing up against something, this method can also be considered good practice for orgasms with a partner. This is different from the preceding method, because this time you move yourself against something rather than moving it against you.

The object you choose for this must be fairly steady, because this technique can require a lot of hip motion from you, and you'll want something that stays still. You might try a twisted-up pillow or the edge of your bed. Lie down on the object or situate yourself so that it puts some pressure on or near your clitoris. Then grind or rotate your hips to increase the stimulation until you reach orgasm. This is one of the more energetic masturbation methods, so be prepared to break a sweat.

Flowing Water, Showers

Some women can reach orgasm just by letting flowing water from the bathtub spout hit the clitoris, but most prefer the control and range offered by a massaging showerhead with a hose (you can buy these at any home supply store). Shower massagers have various settings, ranging from heavy pressure to a fine spray. You also have the option of changing temperatures in the shower, which can heighten the pleasure.

Adjusting the water pressure to a medium setting first, hold the shower-head a few inches away from your clitoris. You may want to lie down to do this, but any comfortable stance is fine. Adjust the settings to find one you like, and experiment with warmer and cooler water. One word of caution: do not pump strong streams of water directly into your vagina. It can be damaging to delicate tissue.

If you don't have a massaging showerhead, there are always the jets in a hot tub. A little less private, sure, but effective.

Vibrators

Vibrators, whether the plug-in kind or battery driven, come in all shapes and sizes. Some are shaped, more or less, like a penis. Others are shaped and colored exactly like a penis. And some have a wide head and are sold in stores as "massagers." Actually, these massagers do feel pretty good on an aching back or tired feet, but they also do mighty nicely as a means of clitoral stimulation.

Vibrators are a great option for women who have trouble reaching orgasm through other techniques. For these women, vibrators can be a great way to become familiar with the feelings leading up to orgasm and the sensation of orgasm itself. Almost all women can enjoy the fast, effective orgasm on demand provided by a vibrator.

The penis-shaped vibrators are usually sold as novelty items in sex-toy stores, and they vary widely in quality. Even though they are shaped like a penis, they are not intended exclusively for insertion into the vagina, nor is that the most effective way to use them. If you are uncomfortable going into a sex-toy store or if there doesn't happen to be one in your community, you can order a massager through most electronics catalogs or pick one up at a major chain such as Service Merchandise or Wal-Mart.

Most vibrators have multiple settings. Start out with a low setting first. The stimulation from a vibrator can be intense, so some women prefer keeping their underwear on. Hold the vibrator against your clitoris, putting pressure on it or moving it if you like. Adjust the setting as necessary. This tends to bring on fast, intense orgasms.

Of all the techniques, masturbation with a vibrator does not adequately simulate the clitoral stimulation of intercourse. Who cares? some happy vibrator users might say. Well, it's up to you to determine what your goals are. Using a vibrator does temporarily numb your clitoris, but only for a few minutes after use. Even frequent use should not affect the sensitivity of the clitoris, so women who are satisfied with their level of orgasmic response during intercourse might not consider this a negative. But for women just developing their sexual responses, heavy vibrator use might not be a good idea if satisfying orgasms with a partner are a goal.

Vaginal and Anal Stimulation

As we mentioned before, lots of women enjoy stimulating not just the clitoris, but also the vagina and anus—sometimes all at once. Stimulating just the vagina or anus is a difficult way for most women to give themselves orgasms, but it is possible.

Once you locate a suitable object, it's up to you to explore. Many women find this easiest on their hands and knees, but some have success while on their backs with their knees pulled up toward their shoulders. Again, vaginal stimulation is not an easy way to achieve orgasm. Many women insert dildos (or other objects) in their vaginas just for added pleasure during clitoral stimulation.

Anal Toys and Stimulation

Yes, we know, this tends to be kind of a taboo subject, but the fact is that the anus, in both men and women, is full of nerve endings and can be a highly

These toys are not available at Toys 'R' Us. BARRY LEWIS/©CORBIS

Top Ten Favorites for When the Hands-on Approach Is Not Enough

Many students we surveyed like to enhance the masturbation experience by using extra props, but men were far more likely than women to go that extra mile. These are a few of their favorite things:

1.	Pornographic magazine	67 percent
2.	Pornographic video	60 percent
3.	Lubricants	45 percent
4.	Nonpornographic magazine	28 percent
5.	Advertisements	19 percent
6.	Clothing	10 percent
7.	Vibrator	6 percent
8.	Food	4 percent
9.	Household items	3 percent
10.	Dildo	3 percent

Topping the ladies' charts were vibrators, with 13 percent reporting having used them, and porno mags and video, at 13 percent and 12 percent, respectively. As a group, gay and bisexual men and women are the biggest fans of vibrators and dildos: 28 percent of the men and 39 percent of the women said they used vibrators, and 27 percent of the men and 28 percent of the women used dildos.

erotic area. By the way, for those of you worried about, well, shit being in there, you should know that as long as you've had a bowel movement fairly recently, there should be no feces within a foot of your anus. Of course, if you really feel like you have to go, that might be a different story.

Women often enjoy anal stimulation during oral sex (see Chapter 6) but also during masturbation. There are many devices designed specifically for this purpose. The (somewhat crude) name for these toys is "butt plugs," and they tend to be conical or have a wide base—mainly to prevent them from slipping into the rectum. Some even have straps to keep them on. They are usually three to five inches in length.

You can also use an ordinary dildo, a suitably shaped (i.e., long enough not to get lost) and cleansed household object, or your fingers for this purpose. No matter what you use, however, it's important to remember that a little lubricant will go a long way. Definitely apply petroleum jelly, K-Y Jelly, or lotion liberally to whatever you're using, and you'll find the experience much more pleasurable. Another word to the wise has to do with using a dildo for anal and vaginal stimulation. Do not use the same dildo to stimulate your anus and then use it in your vagina without cleaning it with soap and water. There is a danger of bacterial infection.

Again, few women stimulate themselves anally to orgasm.

Penile Stimulation

Whacking off. Jerking off. Beating your meat. Spanking the monkey. It seems like every slang term that has to do with masturbation refers to male masturbation specifically. That might be because men seem to be so much better at it. In fact, in some cases, they've raised it to an art form. But we'll start with the basics.

Stroking or Pumping

Here's the method most people think of in association with male masturbation. Using a little lubricant (like saliva, soap lather, or lotion), grab the penis with one or both hands and stroke up and down along the shaft. Some men like to use a loose grip, allowing the hand to slip up and down from the base of the penis to the head, while others prefer a firmer hold, actually moving the skin over their stiffened penises. Many also massage or cup their balls while stroking the penis.

The easiest places for men to masturbate are in the shower (the semen can go down the drain), near the toilet (plenty of toilet paper nearby), or in bed. Common sense, right? Well, some guys like to make it a little more complicated. If you're in a place where you feel comfortable and secure, you might, for example, experiment by prolonging your climax. Stimulate yourself right up to the point of orgasm several times, then stop. Take thirty minutes—or more—to do this. When you finally allow yourself to come, it's all the more satisfying.

The stroking method most accurately simulates intercourse. Luckily for men, however, their sexual responses are much easier to generate, so men don't have to worry too much about teaching themselves the "wrong" way to have an orgasm.

Paddling, Slapping, Beating

Instead of rubbing the penis, this technique involves paddling it between your hands, against your body, or against another object.

Rubbing up Against Something

Women aren't the only ones who can rub themselves against something for sexual pleasure. Men also use folded pillows, towels, or just the pressure of the couch, for sexual stimulation. Be aware that this type of stimulation is much more "forceful" than intercourse. You don't want to acclimate your sexual responses to this type of stimulation, for it might cause arousal problems later. Anything that can provide some sort of friction for the penis is suitable—including various melons and gourds. Yes, a ripe, room-temperature pumpkin (or watermelon, or cantaloupe) can be a satisfying masturbatory aid. But make sure it's at room temperature: cold melons are unfriendly places.

Water Works (for Men, Too!)

Those massaging showerheads are good for the goose *and* for the gander. Men also find the variable pressure and temperature afforded by this type of stimulation very pleasurable. Most enjoy moving the pulsing spray up and down the shaft of the penis, although some prefer direct stimulation of the head. Hot-tub jets are also pretty nice, but unless you have your own, ejaculating in a public tub is very uncool.

Vvvvibrators

Some men do enjoy running a vibrator up and down the shaft of the penis. The orgasms can be intense.

Penis Pumps, Plastic Dolls

Proceed with a little caution in the realm of electronic masturbation devices. They vary widely in quality. Order or purchase them only from a reputable (umm, at least responsible) company and always follow the guidelines for accepted use.

A penis pump uses a clear, plastic tube that fits over the penis and makes a seal. The tube is connected to a pump that creates a pleasurable suction. The pressure of the suction can be adjusted. There are vibrating sleeves that usually attempt to in some way resemble the female genitalia, they're usually electronic, and, like most vibrators, they have varying speeds of vibration to choose from. These sleeves don't form a seal around the penis, but, used in conjunction with some lubricant, they envelop the penis and vibrate it to stimulate and induce orgasm. Plastic dolls—well, you've probably seen

---

What Are "Friends" For?

It's nice to know that when most people masturbate, they fantasize about someone they know: 33 percent of the students we surveyed said they fantasize about their current sex partner, and 36 percent fantasize about an acquaintance. But 31 percent of our male respondents did admit to fantasizing about celebrities—and they got specific.

Their favorites? Drew Barrymore and Gong Li were tied at 27 percent, with Jennifer Aniston running a close second at 25 percent. Pamela Anderson rated 20 percent.

---

those in the movies. They usually have a couple of openings to choose from. You decide if you're the kind of guy who wants one in his closet. At least they're always there for you.

Anal Stimulation

As we mentioned before, men as well as women can enjoy anal stimulation during masturbation. Anal toys like the butt plugs previously described can give the desired stimulation, or you can use your fingers or a clean, smooth household object (like a candle or carrot) that is long enough not to slip into your rectum.

SWING YOUR PARTNER: LEND A HELPING HAND

One great by-product of masturbation is that you know exactly how you like your genitals to be touched. Unfortunately, it's not always easy to tell the person you're making out with "umm, no, up and down on the left side, not little circles" or "loose around the head, tight around the base." In a developing, serious, sexual relationship between two people, however, these kinds of preferences should be discussed at some point, and the earlier the better. Manual stimulation of your partner's genitals is often a part of foreplay or a good way to bring on orgasm if it hasn't happened during intercourse.

Are students making use of this erotic technique? Absolutely. Overall, 72 percent of the respondents to our survey said they had manually brought a partner to orgasm, and 67 percent had the favor returned. The difference between male and female figures here is not large: 64 percent of women versus 71 percent of men had received an orgasm thanks to their partner's ministrations, and 70 percent of women versus 74 percent of men had stimulated their partners to orgasm.

How do you know when it's time to make use of this "handy" skill? What if you haven't gotten around to having sex yet? What if this is your first or second date? What if you've been making out a lot, and maybe you don't know each other well, or you're just not ready, but things are getting a little hot and sweaty and tense? Manual stimulation is a good option in a situation like this. Lots of clothes don't have to come off, and it's a relatively low level of commitment.

If you are confused about what to do, the rest of this chapter will help. Men, start by reading the section on female masturbation above. Women, you read the section on men. That'll give you the basic training. But there are some important differences.

Women on Men

One thing a woman in the throes of passion might have a little trouble with is adopting the appropriate grip on a man's penis. Don't grab too hard, especially if you haven't lubricated your hand with saliva. In fact, to make sure your partner is comfortable, it is a good idea to lubricate your hand a little. Grasp firmly, but not squeezingly, and move your hand up and down in a slow, steady rhythm. The word "steady" is key: a consistent stimulation helps a man concentrate on orgasm. You might have to pick up the pace toward the end, though.

Also, pay attention to your partner's reaction to your touch. If his penis begins to stiffen or swell at your touch, you can be sure you're doing something right. If he tries to suggest something to you or adjust your grip, adapt to his style (as long as you're comfortable with it). Many men like to keep kissing during this, but some like to just concentrate on the sensation, so don't worry if the kisses stop for a little while. Enjoy his reactions!

Like to Watch?

As the students in our survey confirmed, manual stimulation with a partner is not necessarily something you have to do *to* each other. Sometimes, it's fun to watch your partner pleasure him or herself—or be watched yourself. Thirty-five percent of our respondents said they had masturbated while another person watched.

You'll know when his orgasm is about to occur, usually because the penis will swell and stiffen even more, his muscles will become tense, and his breathing will likely become heavy. Keep doing whatever you're doing at that point, no matter what, and do it throughout his orgasm until he seems to level out.

Men on Women

You do not necessarily have to get your hands in a woman's pants to bring her to orgasm, though it probably is easier that way. If, after prolonged necking, you are both highly aroused, you might be able to bring her off simply by pressing firmly on her clitoral region through her clothes and moving your hand in a circular or back-and-forth motion. Take your cue from your partner to see if this is working. If she starts moving with you or pressing her hips toward your hand, she probably likes what you're doing. Since this is indirect stimulation, it may take a while (like several minutes) for her to achieve orgasm this way, if it is possible for her at all. Keep it up as long as you can or as long as she wants.

If your partner is comfortable with it, get some of those clothes out of the way. Through her underwear, you'll probably be able to feel the swollen clitoris. That's your goal. With a couple of fingers, rub it firmly and steadily. If your partner is comfortable with you touching her genitals directly, you have a lot more freedom. First, gently stroke her vaginal area, inserting a finger or two gently into her vagina. Then, using the moisture from her vagina as a lubricant (if that's not enough, lubricate your fingers with saliva or Astroglide or the like), slide your fingers up to her clitoris and rub it or stroke it. Steady, consistent rhythm is important. If what you are doing seems effective, don't change it. Also remember, when a woman becomes more excited and aroused, the clitoris actually retracts and it can be hard to find. Don't stop what you're doing and go looking for it! Stay in the area and continue the stimulation or let her guide you to the sweet spot.

Women often need to concentrate more than men in order to reach orgasm, so take it as a good sign if your partner closes her eyes and seems to withdraw for a while. If she clenches her fists, tightens her muscles, or holds her breath, that's a sign that she is close to orgasm. Don't speed up or change pressure. Just keep doing what you're doing. A sudden release in her body—a deep sigh or relaxation—may be the only signs of an actual orgasm in some women. Others might cry out, shudder, or jerk their hips. Even if your partner is moving around a bit, try to keep your motion going on her clitoris through her orgasm. If you're ambitious, you might keep going and try for two.

CHAPTER 6

Oral Sex

Changing mores and social attitudes have brought oral sex into the mainstream. Forty years ago, the average age of people who had experienced oral sex, either as giver or receiver, was significantly lower than it is today. One of the reasons for this, as indicated by the Kinsey report of 1953, was that oral sex was pretty much the province of married couples. Even then, Kinsey found that only 50 percent of married women had participated in oral sex, suggesting that it was not a widely accepted form of sexual expression.[1] More recent research has found that at least 90 percent of wives have experienced oral sex.[2] Further, surveys have revealed that many women—married or not— derive greater satisfaction from oral sex than from intercourse, finding it easier to achieve orgasm through cunnilingus.[3]

Of course, oral sex is no longer something that is postponed until the wedding night, so let's see how many people on campus are down with going down.

What percentage of female students have performed oral sex?

The percentage of female college students engaging in oral sex is about the same as the percentage of those who have intercourse. Our survey revealed that 80 percent of today's female coeds have performed oral sex, but the important distinction to be made here is that oral sex is not an activity restricted to sexually active nonvirgins. While 91 percent of nonvirgin college students have performed oral sex, 33 percent of their virgin classmates also have.

The finding that one third of college-enrolled virgins has experienced oral sex has been supported in research over the past ten years. A 1994 study showed that 37 percent of female college virgins had performed fellatio and slightly over 48 percent had experienced cunnilingus.[4]

Getting back to the present, it is also worth noting that, while 79 percent of heterosexual women have performed oral sex, an overwhelming 91 percent of gay and bisexual college females have performed it. This high number is beaten only by the gay and bisexual men on campus, 94 percent of whom report having performed oral sex. Is the loud sucking sound that Ross Perot said he could hear really American jobs swirling into Mexico because of NAFTA, or is it something completely different?

Lip Service

While there have been numerous studies devoted to the occurrence and frequency of premarital intercourse, there has been relatively little research done on the topic of premarital oral sex. One of the best studies was done by Herold and Way in 1984, and their findings indicate that 61 percent of college women had performed oral sex on their partners and 68 percent had received oral sex from their partners.[5] Other studies reveal numbers that coincide with Herold and Way's findings: the reported range of female students experiencing cunnilingus is from 68 to 72 percent, while the number of females performing fellatio ranges from 73 to 86 percent.[6] In other words, there is no paucity of oral sex happening on campuses today (our survey found even higher numbers than these). For the women who reported having performed fellatio, 97 percent had also experienced cunnilingus. Oral sex is a healthy and reciprocal sexual experience for college students.

What percentage of female students have received oral sex?

A slightly higher percentage of college women—85 percent—have received oral sex than have performed it. Separating the virgins from the nonvirgins again, we also see a slight increase in the number of virgins who have received oral sex: 38 percent. Once again, the 84 percent of hetero females who have received oral sex are eclipsed by their gay/bi sisters, of whom 95 percent have received oral pleasure. The gay and bi women finally occupy the number-one spot over the gay and bi men, of whom 90 percent report having received oral sex.

❓ *What percentage of male students have performed oral sex?*
What percentage of male students have received oral sex?

Keeping right in step with the women, 82 percent of college men have performed oral sex and nearly the same amount of men, 83 percent, have received oral sex. As we have already discussed, they are outranked by the gay and bisexual community on campus, regardless of gender, who quite actively pursue oral sex. In fact, according to our stats, the gay and bisexual college community participates in and has experienced oral sex more than any other sexual activity.

A steady increase in oral sexual activity can be seen as students progress through college as well, with an average of approximately 76 percent of freshmen going oral, 83.5 percent of sophomores, 85 percent of juniors, and 88.5 percent of seniors. Only 13 percent of the college population report that they have never experienced oral sex. As we can plainly see, college really sucks, and with all this oral love going around, the question that begs to be asked is . . .

❓ *Do you spit or swallow?*

Chances are there have been times when you've really wanted to ask this question before it was too late or when you've tried awkwardly to warn your partner before you jizzed somewhere she wasn't exactly anticipating. It's a deceptively simple question, yet it's one people don't often ask each other, preferring to find out through trial and error (we'll talk more about that later). So, to help assuage your potential embarrassment, we asked the question for you. As it turns out, 41 percent of college women do, in fact, swallow, as do 40 percent of the men who perform fellatio. Virgins who perform fellatio fall short of their nonvirgin classmates in this area, with only 32 percent of this demographic group swallowing. Interestingly, 50 percent of the bisexual women responding said that they swallow semen when performing fellatio.

The most popular method that 50 percent of heterosexual women use during fellatio, however, is pulling their mouths away and using their hands to climax their partners. This method is also the most popular among 52 percent of gay and bisexual men and the 64 percent of virgins who don't swallow. It is least popular among the 35 percent of bisexual females who don't swallow. And 18 percent of the entire college population spit out their partners' semen after climax.

? Under what conditions will you engage in oral sex?

The numbers here are interesting in the way they vary from an identical question we asked about intercourse. Whereas 10 percent of students responded that they would have sex "whenever possible," a slightly higher response rate of 13 percent said they would have oral sex whenever possible, with 23 percent of the men agreeing with this statement but only 5 percent of the women do. The percentages for both women and men who responded that they would have oral sex whenever possible were higher than for those saying they would have intercourse whenever possible.

At the opposite end of the spectrum, 34 percent of the guys said they would have oral sex only if they were "in a steady relationship" (a full 10 percent higher than those who said the same of intercourse), as opposed to 57 percent of the women (5 percent higher than those who said the same of intercourse). Again, as was the situation with intercourse, having oral sex in a steady relationship was the most popular response, with 46 percent of the college population in agreement (and again, this was 7 percent higher than the overall percentage who said the same about intercourse).

Gay and bisexual males varied from their college peers, with 34 percent saying they would have oral sex whenever possible and only 5 percent saying they would do it only in a steady relationship, as opposed to 36 percent of their straight male classmates who would engage in oral sex only in a steady relationship.

? Is oral sex considered more or less intimate than sexual intercourse?

Since the level of intimacy ascribed to any sexual act will be different for every person, it is hard to say what college students' overall opinion is on this subject. Given the ratio of nonvirgins to virgins who engage in oral sex (ranging from 33 percent for virgins to the high-80 and low-90 percentiles for nonvirgins), it is evident that oral sex for nonvirgins is viewed as a natural and pleasurable extension of lovemaking, occurring in tandem with intercourse and enhancing the experience, as opposed to being a substitute for intercourse.[8]

Preference for oral sex as opposed to intercourse then becomes less of an issue, because the activities go hand in hand. But when asking the deceptively simple question "Why do students have oral sex?," more than one answer is possible. Oral sex may be a foreplay activity to enhance the level of stimulation prior to intercourse, or it may be another method of helping

> ### Tough Luck for the Singles, Again
>
> The factors that most significantly contribute to oral sexual behavior are a high degree of dating commitment, high frequency of dating, minimal guilt factors over oral sex, high self-esteem, high frequency of intercourse, and high frequency of masturbation. Religiousness has not been found to be related to frequency of oral sex among students.[7] Studies indicate that there is a clear correlation between the intimacy of a relationship and the frequency of oral sex. That is not to say that oral sex does not occur outside of the parameters of a steady relationship, but oral sex between nondating students is much less likely than it is between coupled students.

one's partner achieve orgasm (as already mentioned, many women find it easier to achieve orgasm through oral stimulation). Really, then, the reason people have oral sex is to achieve sexual satisfaction.

Do students enjoy performing oral sex?

This came as a happy surprise to us: 47 percent of the college population responded that they "loved" performing oral sex. Of those responding that they loved giving head and going down, the gay and bisexual men loved it most, with a 79 percent approval rating, followed by hetero men, coming in at 60 percent. The hetero men were closely followed by the bi/gay women, of whom 58 percent said they loved performing oral sex. Bringing up the rear were hetero females, with only 32 percent of them claiming to love giving head.

Heterosexual women giving a low rating to fellatio is not a new phenomenon. Nearly a fifth of college women—19 percent—said that they can't stand performing oral sex, while only 4 percent of their gay/bi counterparts said the same. Only 6 percent of the men said they couldn't stand performing oral sex, while none of the gay/bi men reached that conclusion.

Responses in between made up the difference, with 25 percent of the college population (29 percent of the women, 20 percent of the men) feeling a general ambivalence toward oral sex and 16 percent of college students (19 percent of women, 13 percent of men) describing their fatalistic attitudes toward oral sex as "you have to give some to get some."

Why do they hate it?

We asked the 19 percent of respondents who said they hated performing oral sex to tell us why they hated it. The most common complaint was that it made

---

Spit? Swallow? Yuck!

In a fascinating, albeit dated, 1982 study of college students by Waterman and Chiauzzi,[9] pleasure ratings for sexual enjoyment were generally higher for both males and females when oral sex occurred without orgasm. This might seem illogical, but when rating the pleasure achieved through oral sex for both men and women, women rated fellatio the least pleasurable of all sexual activities when it occurred with orgasm. The question "Do you spit or swallow?" might be misguided, since it appears that women seem to want to avoid male orgasm during oral sex altogether.

Examining the pleasure factor across genders for oral sexual behavior reveals more reasons why students engage in oral sex. Women indicate receiving a great degree of pleasure from cunnilingus, while the men performing cunnilingus rate it significantly lower than the women who are receiving it. For fellatio, the same is true. Men give fellatio a significantly higher pleasure rating than women do, regardless of whether it results in an orgasm. Out of all the sexual activities studied by Waterman and Chiauzzi, fellatio received the lowest marks from women. Not only did females rank it the least pleasurable of any activity, it rated lower than any activity ranked by men. Apparently, according to our results, this attitude toward oral sex might have changed in the past sixteen years, but our results also show that heterosexual women are still the group least likely to enjoy performing fellatio.

---

45 percent of the students "uncomfortable." Of the students made uncomfortable by oral sex, 50 percent were women and 26 percent were men. The second most common complaint, which 43 percent of respondents agreed with, was that they didn't like the smell or taste of their partners' genitals. Of these respondents, 62 percent were heterosexual men and 38 percent were heterosexual women. A third of the students said they thought oral sex demeaned them—but, interestingly, only 9 percent of the heterosexual men felt that way, while 39 percent of the heterosexual women felt that way, and a very high 57 percent of the gay and bisexual women felt it was demeaning.

Rounding out the numbers, 19 percent said they didn't like oral sex because "it doesn't feel good," 4 percent because it "demeans my partner," and 12 percent because they feel incompetent performing the act. Of this last group, 2 percent were men and 15 percent were women. To these people we say, read on, because we know we can help you become competent.

Are you satisfied with the amount of oral sex you're getting?

Overall, students are more pleased than displeased with the amount of oral sex they're having, as the 39 percent of our respondents who said they were "very" satisfied can attest to. Perhaps not surprisingly so, only 28 percent of the men were "very" pleased with their frequency of oral sex, as opposed to 49 percent of the women. Men and gay/bi women were also the hardest to please, with 33 percent of heterosexual males, 25 percent of gay and bi males, and 27 percent of gay and bi women stating that they were not at all satisfied with the amount of oral sex they have, while only 19 percent of hetero women agreed with them. Students who were somewhat satisfied with their oral sex experiences accounted for 35 percent.

HOW TO ENJOY ORAL SEX

Getting Un-Hung up

The problem many people have with oral sex is the simple, understandable aversion to the thought of having their mouths come into contact with their partners' genitals. People also tend to shy away from the prospect of having someone's nose buried in their nether regions, mainly because they are worried about the way they smell down there. Both of these hindrances to good oral sex can be overcome with a little enlightenment and a pioneering spirit.

First, become more familiar with your partner's genitals by simply looking at them when you are both naked. Try exploring them with your hands and kissing them through clothes. As you progress, begin lightly kissing on and around them during foreplay or sexual intercourse. Most likely, you and your partner will find this exploration exciting, and that will be incentive enough to continue.

If you still have a nagging sensation that for some reason oral sex is really gross, think about this: you like kissing your partner, and when you French kiss you are exchanging fluids through your mouths. The human mouth is actually likely to have more bacteria than the genital area.

If you're worried more about the acceptability of your own genitals than the acceptability of your partner's, you can just stop your hand-wringing right now. If you bathe daily (and you give the various folds and crevices of your genitals a good sudsing), it's unlikely that any overwhelming odor will be emanating from your body. If you don't bathe daily, you or your partner may notice a certain smell around the genitals. This is not necessarily a bad smell. In fact, men and women often find their partner's particular aroma very, very sexy. There is evidence to suggest that these odors contain a high concentration of pheromones—the hormones that cause a sexual response in others. Too much of a good thing can be harmful, though, and for modern American tastes, the smell of a body unwashed for more than three days might be unusually pungent.

Some temporary disorders can cause unpleasant odors around the genitals. For a description of these disorders, turn to page 204.

How to Perform Fellatio

Talk About It

You should have open communication with your partner about any sexual act you wish to experiment with, and oral sex is no exception. Discuss your feelings about oral sex with your partner. If you are intimidated by the prospect of fellatio, tell your partner what you don't like and what you are afraid of and ask for his help in getting beyond these feelings. You might be surprised how sensitive men can be when the prospect of a blow job is on the horizon. You need not feel pressured to continue through to climax. Your partner can always stop whenever you feel you have gone as far as you can go or if you are tired. The man can find relief through other means (intercourse, manual stimulation). If your partner does get out of line and pressures you to do things you aren't ready for, you have two options: dump the inconsiderate clod or remind him that you have his penis between your teeth.

Of course, you might find that you want to continue through to orgasm, and he will most likely not object. Even if you are confident and comfortable performing fellatio, it is still a good idea to talk about it, because you can learn about each other sexually, discovering what you do that makes him feel good, and what you could do differently.

Get to Know the Penis

A man's penis is often responsible for some of his more questionable—or at least illogical—decisions. For better or worse, the penis is hardwired into his brain, and the better you know it, the better for both of you. Find out where he likes to be touched and where he is most sensitive. The head of the penis contains the most sensitive nerve cluster, but there are many areas on and around the penis that are sensitive. Have him guide you or tell you what feels good to him, and feel free to experiment.

Gettin' Comfortable Goin' Down

Fellatio can be performed in any position that is comfortable for both partners. The man can lie on his back while the woman kneels beside him or saddles herself between his legs, or the woman can lie on her back while the man kneels beside her or straddles her face. Both the man and the woman can be lying down; the man can be sitting or standing. Are we beginning to see the possibilities here? Each partner can take a separate turn for oral sex or both partners can give and receive it at the same time in the so-called 69 position, with both parties side-to-side or one partner on top. Why is it called "69," you ask? Look at those frisky little numbers and the way their shapes complement each other. Get it?

While the 69 position is a lot of fun, you might want to alternate turns for oral sex if either partner is having difficulty becoming aroused. Most people are unable to fully experience their own sensations while trying to give pleasure to a partner, and a lot of the time you'll end up with one person just breathing heavily on the other (which is fine, too). In any case, it's tough to keep your attention on the matter at hand when your partner is performing oral sex on you simultaneously. This can lead to a fun game of sexual one-upmanship, a contest to see who can concentrate long enough during 69 and who will be the one who gives up and decides just to enjoy what's going on. This gives the word "loser" a whole new meaning.

And guys, do keep in mind that arousal also can affect a woman's receptivity to oral sex. Oral sex may seem very unappealing if it is attempted too early, before she's had a chance to become sexually excited.

Giving Good Head

Teasing can be quite a turn-on. Kiss all around the penis—on the thighs, the stomach. The anticipation of the mouth meeting the penis can be incredibly exciting. Once oral-genital contact has been made, the woman can circle the tip of the penis and/or flick the head of the penis lightly with her tongue. Try licking the shaft as if it were an ice cream cone, taking your time.

When your partner is fully aroused (or you feel you've teased him enough), try inserting the penis into your mouth and then circling or flicking the head with your tongue. Then lower your mouth over the shaft and gently move up and down. You may want to steady his penis with your hand or move your hand up and down the shaft of his penis along with your mouth. Only take as much of his penis in your mouth as you can—no need to gag yourself. As you become more relaxed, you'll find you can allow deeper penetration into your mouth.

You can blow on the penis with hot breath or cold breath or become a human vibrator by humming with the penis in your mouth (popularly known as a "hummer" on college campuses, and a perennial favorite among men). This is also good for a healthy laugh. Play name that tune or spontaneously break into "The Star Spangled Banner." Be creative, because by this point, you've got a captive audience. One piece of advice: watch those teeth.

From *Clerks*

What really makes men jealous? Well, if you've seen the movie *Clerks* you might have one opinion. When disclosing the number of men she has slept with, the character Veronica admits to three, to which her boyfriend Dante has little reaction. When he admits to her that he has slept with twelve women, she gets angry. They patch it up quickly until Dante discovers how many oral sex partners Veronica has had. Read on:

DANTE: Oh my god, why did you tell me you only had sex with three different guys?

VERONICA: Because I did only have sex with three different guys. It doesn't mean I didn't just go down on people.

DANTE: Oh my god, I feel so nauseous.

VERONICA: I'm sorry, Dante, I thought you understood.

DANTE: I did understand. I understood you had sex with three different guys and that's all you said.

VERONICA: Please calm down.

DANTE: How many?

VERONICA: Dante.

DANTE: How many dicks have you sucked? How many!?

VERONICA: Let it go!

DANTE: How many!!?

VERONICA: All right, all right! I'll tell you! Jesus, I didn't freak out like this when you told me how many girls you've fucked.

DANTE: This is different. This is important. How many! Well . . .

VERONICA *(under her breath in a whisper)*: Something like thirty-six.

DANTE: What!!? Something like thirty-six!?

VERONICA: Lower your voice.

DANTE: What is that anyway? Something like thirty-six? Does that include me?

VERONICA: Thirty-seven.

DANTE: I'm thirty-seven!!

(A customer walks into the store and approaches the counter.)

VERONICA: I'm going to class.

DANTE *(to the customer and in disbelief)*: Thirty-seven! My girlfriend sucked thirty-seven dicks!

CUSTOMER: In a row?

Most men like firm pressure when a woman moves her mouth up and down on the shaft, but many women complain that their mouths get too tired. So stop making your mouth do all the work. Instead of just using tight lips, grasp the base of the penis firmly with a hand and move it up and down the shaft in tandem with the mouth.

Some men may like to have their scrotums touched by both the mouth and the hands while experiencing oral sex, so don't be afraid to experiment with this, but keep in mind that the testicles are probably the most sensitive part of the man's genitals, so be more gentle with them than with his penis.

Icing on the Cake

There are things you can do and use to make fellatio even more stimulating. A variety of sensations can be created for the man by placing different substances in the mouth prior to and during oral sex, such as very warm or very cold water, crushed ice, carbonated water, or champagne. Another interesting effect can be created by sipping crème de menthe or using a few drops of Binaca, mentholated cough drops, or any other mentholated mouth freshener prior to and/or during oral sex and then blowing on the moist penis.

"Enough ice for a marathon session . . ." CORBIS-BETTMANN

This is known in some college circles as the "Binaca blast!" and can be very pleasurable, both in fellatio and cunnilingus.

Your partner may also want other areas of his body touched during oral sex. The best way to find out about such preferences is to ask or to experiment. Some men enjoy having their breasts, nipples, and thighs stroked, having their testicles stroked or sucked, having a finger placed between the testicles, or having the whole scrotum pushed up. For many men, the area between the scrotum and the anus is very sensitive, especially to deep pressure or massage. This is because the prostate gland lies directly underneath. The male prostate is somewhat like the area of the Grafenberg spot in women (see page 152) and both are highly sensitive to pressure. The prostate also can be reached through the rectal wall.

For this reason, and also because of the presence of many sensitive nerve endings around the rectum, many men enjoy anal stimulation during oral sex—either by circling the anus or gently inserting a finger. You might want to approach this delicately, as having a finger suddenly intrude into your butt during oral sex can be quite surprising, and not always pleasantly so. Also, straight men sometimes have mixed feelings about anal stimulation or penetration, perhaps feeling that it's not macho to enjoy this kind of stimulation. It is also possible, of course, that your partner might simply dislike the sensation. Always respect his wishes, but feel free to discuss the matter later.

All Choked Up?

There are a few obstacles to overcome even for those who greatly enjoy oral sex, the most common of which is the gag reflex. Sometimes when engulfing an erect penis, the woman will find herself choking or gagging. There are ways to avoid this unpleasant sensation, the easiest being to use your hand to hold the penis steady. That way, you can control the depth of the thrust.

Most gagging takes place when the woman is on her back with the man thrusting. If you find that this is a problem, avoid this position or use your hands to control the depth of thrusting. Obviously, no one wants anyone choking or puking during oral sex. Some women have found that they are able to "throat" or "deep throat" their partners' penises by relaxing their throat muscles and allowing deep penetration of the penis into the oral cavity. Don't feel bad if you can't do this—it is not a necessary component of a blow job. If you want to, however, you can try to teach yourself how to do it. The best way to experiment is for you to be on top during oral sex. That way you can control how deeply you take the penis into your throat and you can abandon ship quickly if you have to.

Taking a penis too deeply into your mouth is not the only problem. A woman also may respond by gagging just from the fear that her partner will ejaculate in her mouth. Luckily, there are ways around this.

The Protein Shake

Although fellatio is often used only to heighten arousal, many men enjoy continuing the act through orgasm (just as women like to have cunnilingus performed through to climax). Some women feel fine about letting their partners ejaculate in their mouths, and they either swallow the semen, swallow some of it and let the rest run where it may, or just spit it out into a tissue or the handy spittoon thoughtfully placed in the corner by their cowboys. If you are uncomfortable about letting your partner come in your mouth, you can set up a signal of some kind with your partner (he can just announce "I'm coming!" if he's not feeling creative, or you can institute some sort of secret hand gesture), so you can switch to manual stimulation when ejaculation is about to occur.

A Note to Men: What Women Hate

Women enjoy performing fellatio much more when it is their idea. Men should make it clear to their partners that they like oral sex, and they should feel free to say how frequently they like it and whether it's important to them to have oral sex performed through to orgasm. After your preferences are clear, try to leave the decisions about when to perform it to your partner.

You can, of course, make a request for oral sex if you're in the mood, but never, never grab a woman's head and push it toward your crotch. At the very least, that maneuver is irritating and impolite. Women hate that.

A Very Important Warning

Sexually transmitted diseases can be transmitted via oral-genital contact. Oral herpes can be transmitted to the genitals. Genital warts can be transmitted to the mouth. It's not likely, but it does happen.

AIDS is another disease that can be contracted through oral sex. Remember, any sexual activity that involves the presence of bodily fluids such as blood or semen can spread HIV. Unless you are in a monogamous relationship and both you and your partner have been given a clean bill of sexual health by a doctor, you must use a condom. Yes, a condom. Don't mope, it's not so bad. Just make sure to get a nonlubricated condom, and especially avoid condoms with lubricants containing a spermicide (you don't want to be swallowing that). See Chapter 4 for a more detailed description of safe sex and how to keep it *fun!*

How to Perform Cunnilingus

Talk About It

Some men may be apprehensive about having oral contact with the female genitalia. They may also have a certain degree of performance anxiety. Other men like nothing better than to perform cunnilingus. No matter what your feelings, you should talk them out with your partner. It will only serve to open up the lines of sexual communication between you. Lots of guys out there just don't know what they're doing when it comes to going down on a woman. Don't be afraid to admit your ignorance, and get your partner to tell you specifically what she likes and doesn't like. If she's not sure, you can at least have fun experimenting together.

For those of you out there who think a vulva is a safe, Swedish automobile, here's a word of advice: the most important step you can take to make yourself proficient with oral sex is to get to know your partner's parts.

Get to Know the Vulva

Sometimes formal introductions are appropriate, and if you are interested in giving your partner as much pleasure as possible through cunnilingus, then you must be familiar with your subject. Before we begin our discussion, please refer to the diagram on page 67 to review the names and locations of all the relevant components. Familiarize yourself with your partner's genitals, because, although the wiring is the same, each woman has different needs and wants. Find out where she does and doesn't want to be touched and licked (the clitoris is the most sensitive cluster of nerves, but the entire vagina is an erogenous zone and should be treated as such). Find out how much pressure is too much and how much is not enough. Be sensitive to the fact that at different times of the month her vagina will be more sensitive than normal and you might have to adjust to her sensitivity.

Goin' Down

Like fellatio, cunnilingus can be performed in virtually any position that won't give your partner a charley horse. The woman can lie on her back while the man positions himself between her legs or the woman can straddle the man's face by sitting above him (in a chair, on a table top, or whatever is available) or sitting on him (just make sure your partner is able to breathe comfortably). The woman can be lying on her side, stomach, or back during cunnilingus; she can be standing; she may also enjoy the 69 position; she can, essentially, be in any position she finds intriguing. In this way alone, cunnilingus opens up many doors for sexual experimentation.

Cunnilingus can also be a great part of foreplay, because oral stimulation brings on the flow of vaginal juices. In addition, a woman can experience an orgasm from oral sex and be prepared to have intercourse almost immediately afterward. This can be very satisfying for both of you because just after and just before orgasm, the vaginal walls become swollen and stiff, which enhances the sensations of intercourse for both partners. Some women, however, find that their vaginal area is sensitive after orgasm and may want to wait a few minutes before engaging in more sexual activity.

Monty Python's Recipe for a Happy Life

Sit on my face and tell me that you love me
And I'll sit on your face and tell you I love you.
Life would be fine if we'd all do sixty-nine,
So sit on my face and tell me that you love me!

Giving Good Head

Just as a woman must be physically ready for intercourse, she must also be ready for oral sex. Take your time. As in fellatio, teasing can greatly increase the pleasure of the act. Kiss all around your partner's genitals, kiss the abdomen, the thighs, and the soft area immediately surrounding the vagina, before you ever even make direct contact with the vagina. This will heighten her arousal and sensitivity. Don't neglect your partner's breasts during oral sex. Remember, a woman's breasts are a very sensitive erogenous zone and oral stimulation of her nipples will also increase her overall sexual arousal.

If you are wondering how to gauge how much teasing is enough, you will notice that the vagina swells and changes color slightly (due to increased circulation of blood in the region during arousal). This is a sure sign that she is sexually aroused. You may also notice the moisture of her vaginal juices. If this is the case, you can assume that you've stimulated the area long enough. Of course, she may be squirming with anticipation, thereby letting you know that she's quite ready for you to touch her clitoris. Again, any of these signals will let you know that you're headed in the right direction.

Once the woman is ready to receive oral stimulation, there are several ways to please her. Remember that it is best to start out gently and gradually increase the pressure exerted on the vaginal or clitoral area. One piece of advice: never be rough. The area is very sensitive and doesn't require you to exert a lot of pressure. Think of rolling an olive around your mouth by manipulating it with your tongue and pressing the olive with your tongue hard enough for it to push in the olive's skin but not hard enough to crack it. That's the amount of pressure we're talking about. As always, feel free to ask your partner whether you are applying enough pressure.

The vulva has several areas that can be stimulated orally. Try moving your tongue around the outer lips of the vagina, gently parting them with your tongue to expose the more sensitive inner lips. Absolutely use your hands to assist your mouth in cunnilingus (if your mouth had a second, opposable tongue, this might not be necessary). You can use your hands to part the outer lips of the vagina so that you may readily access the vagina with your mouth. Let your tongue explore the inner lips and her vaginal opening, making your tongue stiff to gently probe the inner walls of the vagina. Let your tongue and lips explore your partner's vagina.

Stimulation of the clitoris is what will normally bring your partner to orgasm. The tongue can be stiff while stimulating the clitoris, or it can be soft and flat, laid out across the clitoris. You can use a stiff tongue to circle on and around the clitoris, to move back and forth from the vaginal opening and up to the clitoris. You can use a flat tongue to lick and stimulate the entire vagina or the clitoris alone. Don't forget to use your lips, too, as simple kissing of the vagina can be very pleasurable to your partner. The lips can also be used to form an air pocket and suck on the vagina or clitoris, gently pulling on the vagina in the same way you would suck liquid through a straw.

While oral stimulation is occurring, some women may like you to touch or caress them with your hands. You can run your hands over the rest of her body while you perform oral sex and/or you can use your hands to further stimulate the vagina. Many women enjoy having fingers inserted into the vaginal opening while experiencing cunnilingus. It is possible to stimulate the Grafenberg spot while performing oral sex to add to your partner's excitement and arousal (for the scoop on the G-spot, please see Chapter 7).

Others enjoy having manual stimulation of the clitoris while the oral stimulation focuses on the areas surrounding the clitoris. Some women also like having their vaginas laid open by the hands (spreading the lips of the vagina and parting the thighs wide apart) while receiving oral sex. You might also try stroking the vaginal lips softly with your fingers while licking the clitoris—the vaginal lips themselves become swollen and sensitive during arousal, so this can be very pleasurable. Again, you should experiment with all of these. It's our hunch you won't get many objections from your partner.

It is best to use all of these approaches, stimulating your partner in many different ways during oral sex, moving among the different areas of the vagina, varying the speed and pressure with which you stimulate the clitoris and vagina. However, no matter how aroused she is, a woman will need a consistent touch to bring on orgasm. When you decide you're ready for that "wow" finish, start doing something she really likes and keep doing it, without changing speed or pressure, until she climaxes. If she's very aroused, this will probably take a matter of seconds.

Some women, however, need to concentrate much harder to experience orgasm. For them, it may take a little while to climax. Keep going as long as you possibly can, switching to manual stimulation if necessary (see page 103 for some how-to advice). Bringing a woman to orgasm is very rewarding—especially so if it's not something she experiences easily.

Icing on the Cake

If all of that doesn't sound like enough variety, there are more things you can do to enhance and increase the pleasure of cunnilingus for you and your partner. Mentholated mouth fresheners and cough drops can become welcome partners during cunnilingus. Using any of these mentholated products prior to and/or during oral sex creates a cool sensation on the genitals. However, avoid getting the mentholated saliva up into the vaginal opening—it can burn if it is too concentrated, but for topical applications it is safe and can be fun. By blowing onto the vagina when the mentholated effect is occurring, you can increase your partner's arousal and awareness of her vaginal area.

Women often want other areas of their bodies touched during oral sex. Some women enjoy having the area in and around the anus stimulated during oral sex, and others enjoy having manual stimulation of both the vagina and the anus during oral sex. The anus is a very sensitive area that can heighten sexual arousal, so feel free to experiment with it. But, as we said in the discussion on fellatio, this can be an unwelcome surprise to some women, so either talk about it first or try it gently and let her tell you if she wants you to continue, because for every woman who enjoys this type of stimulation, there is one who doesn't.

One important health tip: do not use the same finger or fingers to stimulate the anus and vagina. More specifically, do not insert fingers into the anus and then into the vagina (the other way around is OK). Bacteria from the rectum can cause very painful infections in the vagina and urinary tract (see page 157 for other tips on avoiding these infections).

What Is the Oral Sex Equivalent of Tennis Elbow?

A female's partner usually need not worry about having to swallow ejaculate (although it is possible, through stimulation of the G-spot, for a woman to ejaculate, and if this occurs during oral sex, a guy might get an unexpected splash in the face—for more information, see Chapter 7). One problem that men and women both face during oral sex is fatigue. Men complain that sometimes their jawbones or their tongues tire out before their partners are able to achieve orgasm. Of course, cunnilingus does not always have to involve an orgasm, but there are times when both partners would like it that way.

If cramping of the jaw or tongue fatigue occurs, take a break for a minute and continue stimulating your partner with your hand, or try doing something different with your mouth. Often the cramping that occurs is simply due to repetitive motion and, if you change your game plan and stimulate your partner orally in a different manner, you can relieve some of this stress. And if it comes down to it, you can just stop, but try tensing and relaxing your jaw a few times before you give it up.

References

1. Kinsey, Pomeroy, Martin, and Gebhard, *The Kinsey Institute Report on Sex*, 1953.
2. Hunt, 1974; Tarvis and Sadd, 1977.

3. Hite, Shere, *The Hite Report: A Nationwide Study of Female Sexuality*, 1976.

4. Kenneth J. Davidson and Nelwyn B. Moore, "Masturbation and Premarital Sexual Intercourse Among College Women: Making Choices for Sexual Fulfillment," *Journal of Sex & Marital Therapy*, Vol. 20, No. 3 (Fall 1994).

5. Edward S. Herold and Leslie Way, "Oral-Genital Sexual Behavior in a Sample of University Females," *Journal of Sex Research*, Vol. 19, No. 4 (November 1983), pp. 327–338.

6. Davidson and Moore, loc. cit.

7. Herold and Way, loc. cit.

8. Ibid.

9. Caroline K. Waterman and Emil J. Chiauzzi, "The Role of Orgasm in Male and Female Sexual Enjoyment," *The Journal of Sex Research*, Vol. 18, No. 2, (May 1982) pp. 146–159.

CHAPTER 7   # All the Way

When questions about the sexual behavior of Americans were first explored in depth, the facts uncovered about college students (or eighteen- to twenty-two-year-olds) were shocking to most people. Back in 1953 when the Kinsey report was first published, college students had their cover effectively blown: the world discovered that books weren't the only things their noses were buried in and that, for many, a wedding ring was not a prerequisite for a toss in the hay.

By the time the 1960s arrived, parents and grandparents were fainting left and right in the face of hordes of sexual revolutionaries rallying to the cause of free love (we have since discovered that there is no such thing as free love—please see Chapter 1). The impact of the radical social changes of the '60s reverberated through the following decades. When the dust settled, premarital sex had gained widespread acceptance in the national mainstream, and from the looks of things, there is no turning back. All surveys of sexual attitudes and practices of college students since the '70s have confirmed that the amount of sexual activity on college campuses has continually been on the rise.

This doesn't exactly mean that students are more promiscuous today than they were in the '60s. While the number of sexually active students has increased, the number of partners per person has tended to decrease.[1] Of course, there may be many reasons for this, not the least of which is increasing awareness of sexually transmitted diseases like AIDS. But whatever the reason, it remains clear that under-graduates are more likely now to explore their sexuality than they once were.

？ *When did you lose your virginity?*

The majority of our respondents lost their virginity in high school, with the percentages of men and women coming in dead even at 63 percent for both genders. Only 2 percent say they lost their virginity before junior high school, 9 percent while in junior high school, with the remaining 26 percent of students losing their virginity during their college careers. Women were more likely to have lost their virginity in college than men, as evidenced by the 29 percent of women who remained virgins until college and the 22 percent of men who did so.

I Want to See You Naked

Of the college students we polled, we found that 72 percent of the men felt confident the first time they got naked with a new sex partner and would be happy to keep the light on while they went about their business. Only 36 percent of the women felt as confident about being naked for the first time in front of a new partner, 64 percent of them preferring to turn those lights out for the big moment.

？ *What percentage of college students are having sexual intercourse?*

The reported percentages of sexually active college women today range from 72[2] percent to 85 percent.[3] There must have been some pioneering women during the '80s, because one 1982 study showed that only 58 percent of female undergrads had engaged in sex, while at the end of that decade another study reported the percentage of sexually active women at 86 percent, and throughout the '90s the 86 percent standard has remained fairly constant.[4]

The numbers for men are a little lower: 66 percent[5] to 74 percent.[6] This is one of the rare cases in which women exceed men in some sort of sexual behavior.

? *How many sexual partners do college students have?*

An eighteen-year-old guy going to college might fantasize about having sex with a new girl every week of his freshmen fall, and that's OK, because fantasizing is healthy. Unfortunately, the odds are that this guy won't be able to live up to his lofty goals: sixteen women in one semester is apparently a lot, even for a senior. A 1992 study showed that 18.9 percent of undergraduate males reported having three or more partners, while only 5.1 percent of the women reported as many.[7] Other studies have shown higher numbers, with 40 percent of the men and 25.2 percent of the women reporting at least five partners, and 21.3 percent of the men and 8.6 percent of the women reporting at least ten sex partners.[8] The most common number of sex partners for both sexes seems to be in the range of two to six and our study confirms this: of our respondents, the average number of sex partners students have had was 6.4.

One for You, One for Me

How do college students feel about having multiple sex partners? Heterosexual students felt this way:

- Is it OK for men to have multiple sex partners: 26 percent of the men said yes; 12 percent of the women said yes.
- Is it OK for women to have multiple sex partners: 21 percent of the men said yes; 12 percent of the women said yes.

Apparently, there is still a small double standard here among men.

There was not much disparity between the numbers for men and women, so there's not one really lucky guy or gal out there getting all the action. The most popular answer to our question "How many sex partners have you had in your life?" was one (23 percent of students responding). As you might imagine, the second most popular answer had 19 percent of our respondents saying that they have had two sex partners, but coming in third with a 14 percent response were students saying that they have had between six and nine partners. A respectable 7 percent owned up to having between ten and fourteen sex partners and from here the numbers started getting lower and lower, with 4 percent having had fifteen to nineteen partners and 3 percent saying they have had twenty-five or more sex partners.

When you get into the higher number of sex partners, what we assumed would be true *was* true: juniors and seniors are more likely to have had a higher number of sex partners than their younger peers. The percentages climbed just like a ladder for freshmen, sophomore, juniors, and seniors who had twenty-five or more sex partners, with the class breakdown reading 2, 3, 4, and 5 percent, respective to their year in college. There was one interesting anomaly that we noticed. Gay and bisexual men beat out their straight and female counterparts at least two to one, with 13 percent having had twenty-five or more sex partners as opposed to 4 percent of straight men, 2 percent of straight women, and 6 percent of gay and bisexual women. In fact, in every category for number of sex partners, ranging from ten to fourteen up to twenty-five and over (we stopped asking respondents to count after 25), gay and bisexual men always came out on top, so to speak.

Every Tom, Dick, and Harry . . .

One study asked if undergraduates had more than twenty-five sex partners: 13 percent of the men answered yes, while none of the women in the survey reported having that many sex partners and only 2 percent of the women reported having sixteen to twenty-five partners.[9] Hmmm.

How often do students "do it"?

In the film *Dazed and Confused,* a college hopeful looks down over his suburban town and says, "Look at all those people fuckin' " as if he believed that, like him, everyone would want to be having sex at any given moment. Is this true of the college population in general? Not really. When asked how often they have sex, only 7 percent of our respondents answered "Every day." An identical percentage answered that they have sex less than once a year, and 13 percent answered that they have sex less than once a month.

A third of the respondents, 31 percent, said that they have sex two or three times a week, and of this percentage, women again beat out the men, with 25 percent of the men claiming to have sex two to three times a week as opposed to 36 percent of the women. Go girl!

Sorry, singles, but students who are in steady relationships are far more likely to be getting regular action: 35 percent of men in relationships and 48 percent of women in relationships report having intercourse more than once per week. Contrast this figure with unattached women, of whom 15 percent are having sex more than once a week, and unattached men, of whom 10 percent can say the same. Virtually no one, male or female, who is not in a relationship is having sex every day. In fact, between 20 and 26 percent of unattached students have sex less than once a month—considerably less than their romantically involved peers. There are some valiant loners out there trying to make up for this (10 percent of unattached men and 15 percent of unattached women have sex more than once a week), but the outlook for steady sex is bleak for the uncommitted.

What sexual positions do students favor?

What was it about those missionaries that made their sexual position so popular? After 400 years on the charts, man-on-top, woman-on-bottom, face-to-

What's your favorite position? UPI/Corbis-Bettmann

face is still among the most popular—38 percent of students say that the missionary position is their favorite sexual position. But don't go thinking college students aren't interested in variety: Thirty-nine percent of our respondents said their favorite position was woman on top, edging the missionary position out by one percentage point. Doggie style was also popular, with 19 percent citing this as their favorite position, although more men liked this than women. The spoon position was left in the dust, with only 4 percent favoring it. Finally, there are some contortionists out there whose favorite sexual positions fall under the alluring category of "other."

However, there is an interesting disparity between men and women when it comes to their favorite positions. The majority of women, 48 percent, favor the missionary position, while only 25 percent of men say it is their favorite (as many men said doggie style was their favorite position). When it comes to the women being on top, 45 percent of men say this is their favorite position, while only 33 percent of women agree with the guys. Looks like the majority of folks, men and women alike, enjoy being on their backs while they're getting laid.

? What percentage of students have had anal sex?

How do students feel about anal sex? Is anal sex generally thought of by students as an activity that is practiced by close couples in longstanding or steady relationships, not as a typical activity for a one-night stand or casual sex? Or is it an option for intercourse without the risk of pregnancy?[10] Exactly what accounts for the relative rarity of anal sex as a sexual practice (when compared with vaginal intercourse or oral sex) is subject to individual opinion.

According to our survey, fully 20 percent of our college students have engaged in anal sex at least once. Break this response down by gender and we found that 6 percent of college men had experienced anal sex as the "catcher" (or the passive partner), as opposed to 31 percent of college women. Because 20 percent of the undergraduate population reports participating in anal sex, it certainly can't be called rare or unusual, but it is less common than vaginal intercourse and oral sex. As one might suspect, if you further analyze the responses, 61 percent of gay and bisexual men in the college community engage in anal sex as a catcher, far higher than the 1 percent of straight men who responded in the affirmative (we guess their girlfriends are using strap-ons). Also interesting is the fact that straight women, of whom 30 percent have had anal sex, are eclipsed by their gay and bisexual female peers, of whom 45 percent have had anal sex.

The numbers from other studies are fairly consistent and support our findings, although we found the rate among current college women engaging in anal sex to be higher. Two studies done in 1990 and 1994 found that a range of 18.6 percent[11] to 20.1 percent[12] of female undergrads have engaged in anal sex, while the range for men (as the "pitcher," or the active partner) is from 9 percent[13] to 14.3 percent.[14] According to a study comparing sexual practices among college students across ethnic boundaries, it was found that 15 percent of sexually active undergraduates had experienced anal sex. The same study showed that when these students were engaging in anal sex, a high-risk sexual act (see Chapter 4 *now* if you're even considering it), they used condoms an average of only 18.5 percent of the time.[15]

What else have you had up your butt?

We wanted to know more, so we asked our respondents to tell us which of the following has been up their butts: a finger, a tongue, a dildo. Our results showed that 37 percent had had a finger in the butt (30 percent of men, 42 percent of women), 17 percent had had a tongue up the butt (15 percent of men, 18 percent of women), and 4 percent had had a dildo up the butt (4 percent of men, 3 percent of women).

Again, when you single out the gay and bisexual community among the respondents who answered in the affirmative, you get much higher numbers. While 25 percent of straight college men had experienced a finger in the rear, 87 percent of their gay and bisexual peers had. Of straight women, 40 percent had had a finger you-know-where, while 69 percent (no kidding) of gay and bisexual women had experienced the same. Of those who had experienced tongues in the nether regions, 12 percent of the men were straight, while 49 percent of the men were gay or bisexual, and 18 percent of the women were heterosexual, while 28 percent of the women were omnisexual. And when you get to dildos, only 2 percent of the heterosexual population across the board had had dildos up their butts, while 45 percent of the gay and bisexual females had. The majority of gay and bisexual men—61 percent—had experienced dildo in the butt.

Do students have sex for nonamorous reasons? Is love important?

It is hard to say how many or what percentage of college students have had sex to obtain a good grade, to exact revenge on a lover or friend, or to win some sort of bet, but what is clear is that students will have sex for nonamorous reasons in the sense that there is no emotional investment involved. When asked "Under what circumstances will you have sex?," 19 percent of the guys responded "whenever possible," as opposed to only 3 percent of the women. On the opposite end of the scale, 24 percent of the guys responded that they would have sex only if they were "in a steady relationship," as opposed to 52 percent of the ladies, and, overall, this was the most popular response, with 39 percent of the college population in agreement. Once again, however, our gay and bisexual male sampling varied widely from their college peers, 33 percent saying they would have sex whenever possible and only 3 percent saying they would restrict sexual experience to a steady relationship (heterosexual females differed only slightly from their gay and bisexual sisters).

I'm Bored—Let's Have Sex

In a study from 1985, students were presented with the statement, "If I am feeling the need for a release of sexual tension, I would rather masturbate, have sex, indulge in some vigorous activity, or watch television." The overwhelming response by male undergraduates was "have sex" (80 percent), while the most popular female response was "vigorous activity" (50 percent). This should give you some insight into just who is willing to have sex for nonamorous reasons and who'd rather watch a rerun of *Melrose Place* while using their Thigh-Master.

The same study revealed that 46 percent of male undergraduates would "never neglect an opportunity" to have sex, regardless of how well they knew the other person. None of the women in the study mirrored their sentiments. When asked if emotional involvement was a prerequisite for sexual intercourse, 6 percent of the men said it was never an issue, while only 1 percent of the women said it wasn't an issue. Conversely, 45 percent of the women said the emotional involvement was always necessary for them, and 8 percent of the males said it was necessary.

When asked if they had ever had sex without an emotional involvement, 84 percent of the males responded with a resounding yes, while half that number of women—42 percent—responded yes to the question.[16] Clearly, the nonamorous side of sex is largely still a male province.

? *Have you ever had sex with someone you didn't like?*

While the overall majority (64 percent) said no, 36 percent said yes. Only nine percentage points separate the men (41 percent having slept with someone they didn't like) from the women (32 percent), but the gay and bisexual males again top the charts in this category, 60 percent of them having been intimately physical with someone they didn't like. Fifty percent of the gay and bisexual women overshadowed their hetero peers as well.

We asked these cross-gender campus lotharios why they had sex with someone they didn't like and, after the cop-out response of "It just happened" (47 percent), the number-one answer was "I was drunk or high," to which 40 percent admitted. What does this tell you? Well, sex and drugs aren't always the best combination, because you might wake up and feel the coyote response, meaning that you want to chew off your arm in order to get out of bed with the person next to you. Things can also get much more complicated than just a simple regret, as we'll discuss in Chapter 10. However, our gay/bisexual male population defied the averages again, with only 7 percent saying they had had sex with someone they didn't like because they were drunk or high, as opposed to 44 percent of the hetero males and approximate 40 percent of all women regardless of their sexual preferences, showing that in terms of alcohol and drugs, the gay male college population is straighter than their classmates.

Rounding out the responses, 5 percent of the guys had sex with someone they were less than inspired by "to be nice," as did 11 percent of the women (women are just more *giving* than guys, we guess) and, in a nearly perfect flip, 11 percent of the men and 6 percent of the women had sex with an

You're So Ugly, Fat, Dumb . . .

When asked what reasons are least likely to cause students to jump in bed with someone, they responded as follows:

Reason you won't sleep with someone	% Men	% Women
Because the person is ugly	40	28
Because the person is fat	37	23
Because the person is dumb	26	14
Because the person is of a different race	10	7
Because the person is poor	3	3

A surprising percentage of both male and female students don't seem to be aware that we're all pink on the inside, regardless of what color we are on the outside. Women are apparently not quite as shallow as men are about physical traits, but women also seem to like their bimbos a little more than men do. A man's cranial capacity stops only a small percentage of women from taking advantage of him. Talk about dumb luck.

undesirable because "they were desperate" (men are just weaker than the gals, we guess, too). So perhaps the statistical evidence here indicates that people are being nice to those who are desperate. Oh, the humanity.

⍰ *Have you ever had intercourse while intoxicated?*

Gee, what do you think? One might think college students more often have sex when they are intoxicated then when they aren't and, judging from our responses, that might not be too far off base. A full 68 percent of our respondents have had sex under the influence of alcohol (the drug of choice, it seems), 53 percent of those saying it enhanced the experience, only 26 percent saying it made the experience worse, and 19 percent maintaining that it had no effect. The use of marijuana was not as prevalent, only 28 percent having been under its influence while getting naked. But 63 percent of those said it enhanced the experience, only 16 percent said pot made sex worse, and 19 percent claimed it had no effect on the sex.

College students definitely seem to take inventory of the pharmacy when it comes to having sex under the influence of drugs. Here's a quick breakdown of the drugs they've used while having sex: LSD (6 percent), Ecstasy (5 percent), cocaine (3 percent), heroin (1 percent), crystal meth (2 percent), and barbiturates (2 percent). Only in the case of barbiturates did the majority of college students say that the drugs made sex worse (31 percent said barbiturates enhanced sex, while 43 percent said they made it worse). Also, Ecstasy was a big hit, with 83 percent saying the drug enhanced the sex and the detractors accounting for only 8 percent.

And we thought sex was a physical act, not a chemical one! All of these drugs, however, can negatively affect your sexual performance and desire, not to mention creating the arena for awkward, and quite possibly criminal, sexually related behavior. We're not even going to go into what some of these drugs do to your brain and your health, but in Chapter 12, we will talk about how these drugs can contribute to the more unfortunate and serious aspects of sexuality on campus.

⍰ *For women: have you ever had sex when you didn't feel like it?*

A 1993 study of college women found that 69.8 percent of the women surveyed said they had been verbally coerced into having unwanted sex.[17] These numbers become even more disturbing when the coercion became truly threatening, and physical force, violence, or drugs were involved. A 1994 study revealed that 47 percent of college women had experienced unwanted sex, of which 45 percent said it happened only once, 39 percent reported that it occurred two or three times, and 16 percent reported unwanted sex having occurred four or more times in their undergraduate experience.[18]

These are staggering and alarming numbers. It is difficult to say how many men engage in coercive sexual behavior, because no one wants to admit to such behavior in a survey. One study indicated that 6 percent of the men who were surveyed admitted to forcing a date to engage in some form of sexual activity.[19] You don't need to be a statistician to see that something is quite amiss here. The figures quoted above are instances of verbal coercion (the use of verbal pressure through insinuation, emotional blackmail, or actual verbal threats) and do not necessarily indicate the presence of alcohol or drugs, although the statistics for women experiencing unwanted sex under these circumstances are also disturbing. All of the issues raised by these contradictory statistics and the subject itself will be addressed in Chapter 12. One thing is clear and that is that there is a lot of sexual foul play happening at universities and those who plan to be sexually active on campus should assume that no does indeed mean no.

It is important to remember that good sex is good fun for both people involved, and that takes a lot of communication, understanding, and technical expertise.

Going Greek (As in Fraternities and Sororities)

Fraternities—and sororities, too—encourage some of the more nonamorous reasons for engaging in sexual intercourse. The presence of alcohol at Greek parties has caused many people to pair off together for reasons neither of them can quite remember. Sometimes bets are placed on which member can sleep with certain women, sometimes cash rewards are offered for the member who can sleep with the heaviest woman, and so forth. These issues are related less to sex than to larger problems, which we will discuss in Chapter 12.

▸ *Where have students had sex?*

Enough doom and gloom—let's get back to the fun that sex is supposed to be. Did you ever have sex in your college's library? Well, 3 percent of today's college students have. The most popular places college students have had sex these days, aside from your average bed, are a car (70 percent), in the great outdoors (65 percent), on a waterbed (48 percent), in their parents' bed (41 percent, and we hope they washed the sheets), and in public buildings (28 percent). Only 2 percent of college students have joined the mile high club and had sex in a plane; the same percentage have had sex on a train, and 4 percent have had sex on a bus (we guess it can be tough at those commuter schools).

Interestingly, 10 percent of students have had sex online. While 8 percent of both hetero men and women have had cybersex, 17 percent of gay/bi women and 41 percent of gay/bi men have had sex online, perhaps illustrating that it easier to come out anonymously online. But what we can conclude is that the Internet is a safe and viable sexual outlet for today's college community. Also worth noting is that 4 percent of the general college population have had sex in a nightclub, while between 12 (females) and 16 (males) percent of the gay community have. None of our hetero respondents even admitted to having been in a sex club, much less having had sex at one, but 10 percent of the gay/bi men had and 1 percent of the gay/bi women had as well.

What's on Your Mind?

How often do you think about sex? Well, the largest segment of college students—30 percent—think about it every few hours, and that stretches across gender lines. Those hormonally overactive college guys are more preoccupied than the women, with 17 percent of them thinking about sex every ten minutes, as opposed to only 5 percent of the women who think about it as often. However, 28 percent of women more than double the 13 percent of men who think about sex once a day, so never let it be said that certain women aren't as obsessed as men.

? What's the longest students have gone without having sex?

Apparently there is a small (1 percent) but very lucky percentage of students who have never gone more than a few days without having sex. This, however, is not the norm. So, if you are in a dry spell, don't feel terrible, because 34 percent of our respondents (the highest percentage answering to any of our options) have gone a year or more without getting laid. The second highest response rate showed that 23 percent of students tend to go three to six months without getting happily hot and sweaty.

? *Are students satisfied with the amount of sex they're having?*

Overall, 56 percent of the college population are satisfied and, of those, 46 percent of males and 64 percent of women are satisfied. The least satisfied are the seniors: 50 percent of them are dissatisfied with the amount of sex they're getting, whereas freshmen have the fewest complaints: only 39 percent of them are dissatisfied. The hetero and gay/bi women are in agreement, but of the gay/bi men, only 36 percent are satisfied with the amount of sex they're having. And, among college men who have had fewer than six sex partners, the satisfaction rate is at 45 percent.

? *What's preventing students from having more sex?*

Is it shyness? Not exactly—only 11 percent say that's why they're not having more sex. Is it laziness? Nope, only 2 percent say they can't get motivated to try and get laid. How about an unwilling partner? Getting warmer, since 12 percent say their partner won't play (15 percent of men, 8 percent of women, if that tells you something). The survey says the number-one reason people aren't having more sex (47 percent of respondents) is that they simply don't have partners. Perhaps naïvely, only 9 percent of the college population cite fear of disease as a reason preventing them from having more sex, but of that subset, hetero women seem the most aware, with 14 percent of them giving fear of disease as a reason, more than doubling the rate of the gay community and twice that of their prospective male mates.

In a very telling statistic, 27 percent of gay and bisexual male students gave "no one wants me" as the reason they are not having more sex, three times the percentage of their straight male classmates. Gay and bi women also beat out their straight counterparts on this sad option, with 11 percent saying no one wants them, as opposed to 7 percent of female heteros.

? *Do college students often feel unsure about how to satisfy their sexual partners?*

Apparently there are a lot of confident people out there, because 65 percent of students said they don't feel unsure about how to satisfy their partners. We believe this is a great thing! It follows that 35 percent said they did often feel unsure. The percentages for these answers stayed pretty close across all gender and sexual preferences. Well, the next part of this chapter is for all of you, regardless of how you answered this question, because there's always room to learn.

THE INS AND OUTS OF INTERCOURSE

Are You Any Good?

Seems like, as soon as you start having sex, you start worrying about whether you're doing it right—or, more accurately, whether your partner thinks you're doing it right. Of course, mutual orgasm (not necessarily concurrent!) is a sign that things are going fairly smoothly (see Chapter 5 for the inside scoop on female orgasm). If someone's not climaxing, it's time to roll up your sleeves and start talking.

You are not a mind reader. Neither is your partner. You can learn a lot by being very observant about what turns your partner on, but at some point you're going to be stumped. It may be awkward, but you're going to have to talk to the person you're sleeping with. Ironic, isn't it? You get naked with this person, but saying something like "You know, it really hurts when you scratch my back that hard" or "Sometimes it feels like you're chewing my nipples off" is somehow too personal.

A good way to open the lines of sexual communication is to ask your partner what he or she likes and doesn't like. Then tell your partner what you like. Be specific (saying something like "Sex with you just doesn't feel good" is not likely to bring about good results). Show your partner, if necessary. If you're nervous, don't do this while you're in bed. Pick a time when you're relaxed and fully clothed to bring up the subject. As long as you're hon-

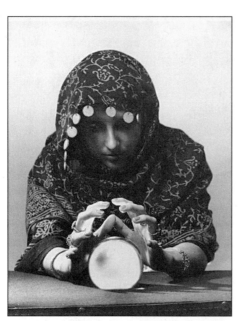

Your place or mind? HULTON DEUTSCH COLLECTION/CORBIS

est, specific, and tactful, you should have nothing to be afraid of. Your partner, if he or she cares about pleasing you, will be open to hearing your preferences.

And once you get comfortable talking about sex, once you're sure you know what your partner likes and how to do it, you can consider it official: you are a good lover. Of course, a little technical know-how never hurt anyone trying to be a good lover either, so get your notepad out.

Doin' It

Sex, so we're told, is the most natural act in the world. Fish know how to do it, cats know how to do it, hippos know how do it. Humans have complex and somewhat quirky wiring systems when it comes to sex, and gut instinct might not cover all the situations you'll encounter in your college years. Plus, being the highly evolved creatures that we are, we have centuries of ingrained paranoia, repression, misinformation, guilt, and neuroses about sex to further complicate our responses.

Get Your (Partner's) Motor Running

Would you take your new sports car out for a spin if it was low on oil? Would you try to fry some pancakes without putting butter in the pan?

Bees gettin' it on. F. Stuart Westmorland/Corbis

The point is to show that proper preparation (read: lubrication) is necessary for good driving, good frying, and good sex. Arousal is the issue here, and without it, sex is painful, uncomfortable, or even impossible.

Tips for Gals

As you probably already know, it is generally not that hard to arouse a young man. A passionate kiss, a glimpse of flesh, even a sexy suggestion is often enough bring on an erection. If you are putting the moves on a guy, just letting him know you're interested in having sex might be enough. Some good old-fashioned making out always helps, too.

The University of O, Part I: Happy Students

College guys who have had an orgasm: 94 percent.

College gals who have had an orgasm: 87 percent.

College virgins who have had an orgasm: 68 percent.

But not all men are turned on by the same things. For some, passions are more difficult to arouse. If, after ample kissing, embracing, and caressing, your partner does not have an erection—but seems willing and interested in having sex—do not assume he isn't attracted to you, and, whatever you do, do not say, "Aren't you attracted to me?" or "What's wrong?" The male erection isn't always automatic, and you might have to do more than just be there in order to turn a man on.

Try whispering sexy things in your partner's ear. Tell him you want him. Tell him what you want him to do with you, and what you want to do with him. A willing, involved female is highly arousing to men. Many men enjoy having their nipples stroked or licked, as well, so you may want to give it a try. If that doesn't work, try a direct approach: gently stroke or squeeze his penis, either through his clothes or directly. If you feel like it, perform oral sex (Chapter 6) on him until he has an erection.

If all these tactics fail, you may have to reevaluate the situation. This may be his first time. He may be too tired (or drunk) to have sex, or there may be a deeper problem. (See Chapter 11 on sexual difficulties). Be caring and tactful: this can be an embarrassing situation.

Tips for Guys

First, we should get some troubling myths about female sexual responses out of the way: women have sexual urges, they feel horny, and they become highly sexually aroused when stimulated properly. Even nice girls! Unfortunately, family, religious, and social pressures on women make some believe that they shouldn't have sexual feelings at all, much less show them. As you can imagine, it makes matters worse if you, as a man, share these misconceptions. Do yourself, and your partner, a favor and embrace female sexuality freely.

One of the most important prerequisites for female arousal is comfort. Women find it hard to let down their guard when they feel nervous or threatened, so make sure you're some place private and secure, if possible. It may sound like a cliché, but dim the lights and maybe put on some music (it wouldn't be a cliché if it didn't work, right?).

The University of O, Part II: Good Liars

College guys who have faked an orgasm: 18 percent.

College gals who have faked an orgasm: 61 percent.

College virgins who have faked an orgasm: 13 percent.

It usually takes women longer to become fully aroused than men, but that should not be seen as a negative. The escalation of excitement during foreplay should be relished. Kiss and caress your partner slowly and passionately. Take your time, enjoy your sensations, and enjoy your partner's responses. Don't pressure or rush her.

Most woman become extremely aroused when their nipples are rubbed, licked, or sucked. Different women have different preferences about touch and pressure, so experiment, but be sensitive to your partner's responses. Naturally, women also become aroused by clitoral stimulation. If your partner is clothed, try pressing firmly with your hand and moving it in steady circular motions near where you presume her clitoris to be. If you have more ready access to this hot spot, gently part the outer vaginal lips and slide a couple of fingers to the clitoral area (see the diagram of the external female genitalia on page 67). Very likely it will be swollen and easy to detect. Using one or two fingers, stimulate the clitoris using a small circular motion, taking your cue from your partner for what speed or pressure feels best. Try stimulating your partner vaginally as well by gently inserting one or two fingers.

At this point you may be asking, "OK, but how do I know when she's fully aroused?" Unfortunately, women don't have an indicator quite as obvious as an erection. Generally speaking, heavier breathing and a flushed complexion are indicators of at least initial arousal. As a woman gets more turned on, she might start arching her back or moving her hips against yours. There are a couple of surefire signals, as well: if her clitoris and vaginal lips are swollen and if the entrance to the vagina is wet and slippery to the touch, she's physically ready. Of course, she might also say, "Stop teasing me, I can't wait any longer!" and that's always a good sign.

One other method that ranks very high on the arousal scale is oral sex. Some women feel awkward about being stimulated in this way, but once their inhibitions are overcome, they find they enjoy receiving oral sex just as much as men do. See Chapter 6 for more details.

Positions of Interest

Once both parties are revved up, intercourse is just a matter of inserting tab A into slot B, right? Well, yes and no. As the ancient Indian framers of the Kama Sutra, a sacred text on the art of love, would tell you, there's more than one way, and some of them are more fun.

In all configurations for vaginal intercourse, it follows that the man inserts his erect penis into the woman's vagina and makes and returns thrusting motions. The male orgasm is brought on by the friction of his penis against the vaginal walls, while the woman's orgasm depends on the stimulation of her clitoris (and sometimes the G-spot) by the base of the penis or by manual stimulation by her partner or herself. (Please note that not all women achieve orgasm easily through intercourse. See Chapter 11.)

Most couples naturally find themselves in the missionary position (man on top). This position allows for face-to-face intimacy and pretty good contact between the clitoris and the base of the penis. The man usually keeps his legs between the woman's, but it is also pleasurable for the man to move his thighs outside the woman's. This increases pressure on the penis. One thing for men to avoid in this position: crushing your partner. A woman can't have much fun or freedom of movement if she's gasping for breath under 170 sweaty pounds.

Women often find they enjoy the control and freedom of motion they get from being on top—and men are happy to oblige (they can see and touch their partners more easily that way). In this position, the man reclines and the woman straddles him, usually resting her weight on her knees. She may either move herself up and down over the shaft of the penis or move her upper body forward and rotate her hips to stimulate her clitoris against her partner's pubic bone.

Another variation of this position is the seated position, which gives women good control over the depth of thrust and clitoral stimulation. In this position, the man sits himself down in a chair. Important: this should be an armless chair, because your partner will proceed to straddle you. The chair should be low enough so that she can rest both feet comfortably on the floor.

Nude Twister?

The variation of sexual positions is a great way to explore and enhance your sex life. From making love on a swing to swinging in a hammock, there are many ways to alternate your positions from the customary missionary position. Some companies even sell products to encourage alternative positions. If you're adventurous or curious, or maybe just want a good laugh, you should check some of these out in adult catalogs.

The most interesting (and humorously named one we've found) is something known as the Vietnamese Spin-Fuck Chair. Yup, we're not joking. This chair, if you want to call it that, is really more like a short table on ball bearings. In the center of the table is a hole wide enough for an erect penis to pass through and on the edges are handles for the woman to secure herself to. The man lies under the chair and the women sits on top of it as he penetrates her through the opening in the middle. The chair can then be spun 360 degrees. Sound like fun? Maybe. But it might be hard to pass off this piece of furniture as a card table since it's only about a foot high. And please don't ask us why it's considered Vietnamese, as opposed to any other nationality. It's probably made in Taiwan anyway.

The rear-entry (doggie-style) position doesn't allow for any clitoral stimulation, but it does allow for deep penetration by the penis and it's pretty easy for manual stimulation to be worked in. The woman gets on her hands and knees or lies on her stomach, and the man, either kneeling or standing by the edge of the bed, enters her. He can then reach around her to rub her clitoris, or she can do this herself. If your passion doesn't quite allow you to make it to a bed, this is a great position to use when standing up with the women bracing herself with her hands against a wall, desk, her partner's legs, or whatever else is available.

These four positions barely scratch the surface of infinite possibilities (oh, the things you can do with legs!), but they should give you some basic

---

The University of O, Part III: Consistently Happy Students

College men who always achieve orgasm during sex: 56 percent.

College women who always achieve orgasm during sex: 13 percent.

College men who achieve orgasm during sex most of the time: 35 percent.

College women who achieve orgasm during sex most of the time: 40 percent.

---

ideas. The main point to remember is that sex should always be good for both parties involved. Don't do something that one of you finds painful or uncomfortable. Experiment!

ENHANCING INTERCOURSE

What's that? Sex can get better? Of course it can, if you are communicative, open, and willing to experiment with your partner.

What's This I Hear About the G-Spot?

Stimulation of the G-spot can enhance sexual arousal and the intensity of orgasms. Some women have reported multiple orgasms as a result of G-spot stimulation and others have reported an orgasmic expulsion of fluid—a female "ejaculation." In any case, stimulation of the G-spot is a great way to get primed for intercourse and can also add to the intensity of intercourse itself.

The G-spot can be felt through the anterior vaginal wall about halfway between the back of the pubic bone and the cervix. It is hard for women to locate the G-spot by themselves, because the angle is not right from most

---

G-Spot Trivia or T-Spot?

Although it was first widely discussed by Dr. Grafenberg, sex researchers Dr. John Perry and Dr. Beverly Whipple named this area after Grafenberg when they claimed to have proven its existence. We say "claimed to have proven" because the existence of the G-spot is still debated. However, Dr. G. is getting more credit than he deserves. The G-spot has been known for thousands of years by Tantra practitioners, who called it "the sacred spot." A-men!

---

positions. If you want to try for it yourself, the best way to do this is to empty your bladder (for reasons we will soon discuss) and crouch in a knee bend.

Take your fingers and explore the anterior (or upper-front) wall of your vagina, pushing up toward your belly with firm pressure. You may find it useful to apply complementary pressure on your abdomen or pelvis, just above the pubic hair line, pushing back down at the fingers inside your vagina, as if they were trying to meet each other.[20] You'll know it when you find it, and it will begin to swell when stimulated. Once you've discovered the spot and find it pleasurable, you may want to teach your partner how to get at it.

The G-spot can be stimulated by a dildo or a finger, or with a penis, so you have many options as you explore your sexuality during intercourse and foreplay. But before any of that can happen, your partner has to know where the G-spot is. The easiest way for your partner to locate it is with his (or her) fingers in much the same way you would find it yourself. Once the vagina is aroused and lubricated, insert either your index or middle finger inside (the longer the finger, the better) as far as it will go comfortably and make a motion similar to the one you would use to signal someone to come here. Using that motion, apply pressure to the vaginal wall as if you were trying to (gently!) touch her belly button through the wall.

Aha! That's What Those Are: (Partial) G-Men

Ever seen one of those vibrators that looks more like a trailer hitch than a penis? Well, those are G-spot vibrators and that's why they are shaped that way, to put pressure up against the vaginal wall.

It is perfectly normal for the woman to feel as if she has to urinate when the G-spot is first touched, because some pressure is exerted on the nearby bladder and that's why it is a good idea to empty your bladder before stimulating this area. Have no fear, though, and persevere through the amount of time (ten or so seconds) that this feeling lasts, after which the initial reaction changes to a distinctive feeling of sexual pleasure. It may not happen the first time you try, and several exploratory ventures might be required to find the G-spot. (*Note:* like all things sexual, this is not true for *all* women, so don't feel strange if you do not experience this sensation.) When stimulated, the G-spot swells noticeably and can usually be felt through the vaginal wall.

A heavier pressure is needed to stimulate the G-spot than the clitoris, so don't be afraid to be a little more aggressive when massaging it.

The penis can also stimulate the G-spot. The best position for G-spot stimulation is with the woman on top. Since the erect penis tends to bend up toward the man's torso, this exerts a natural, steady pressure on the anterior wall of the vagina while the woman is on top during intercourse. The woman can also control the angle at which the penis enters and thrusts inside her when on top, giving her better control of G-spot stimulation. To enhance the female-superior position, place a couple of pillows under the small of his back so that his pelvis is arched upward at an angle while she is on top. This position, a variation on the old-favorite missionary position (see below) allows the angle of penetration to exert pressure on the upper wall of the vagina, thus stimulating the G-spot during intercourse. Women report that the stimulation of the G-spot during intercourse feels "deeper" than clitoral stimulation and, because of this, it is intensely arousing.

The University of O, Part IV: Lucky Students

College guys who have had multiple orgasms: 47 percent.

College gals who have had multiple orgasms: 63 percent.

College virgins who have had multiple orgasms: 37 percent.

We wonder if the guys really meant multiple orgasms or just a lot of sequential orgasms in one night. We tend to think it's the latter. . . .

G-spot stimulation has been known to produce multiple orgasms (just think of what simultaneous stimulation of the G-spot and the clitoris can do!) and, as we mentioned, female ejaculation. The fluid that is ejaculated in this kind of orgasm is not urine, nor does it smell or stain, so don't be afraid to unleash if you feel like it. It comes from the urethra and it's released due to the intense muscular contractions that occur under this form of stimulation.

Most men probably envy the fact that some women can experience multiple orgasms (and some women envy the ones who can, too). Well, there's hope for us all in the form of something known as Kegel exercises. These exercises were created and named after Dr. Arnold Kegel and were originally intended to help women overcome urinary incontinence. They worked, but an interesting and fortuitous discovery was also made in conjunction with

---

The Male G-Spot?

You may have heard that there is a male equivalent of the G-spot. When referring to a male G-spot, people are actually talking about the prostate gland, which is located opposite the interior wall of the anus. The prostate gland, like the G-spot, is sensitive to pressure and can add to and intensify male arousal. It's not as hard to find as the female G-spot. The prostate gland can be stimulated by applying firm pressure to the area between the scrotum and the anus, using two fingers to press the area in. The prostate also can be reached through the rectal wall by inserting fingers into the anus and using the same type of motion one would use to stimulate the G-spot, again putting firm pressure on the area. This can be pretty hard to do during intercourse, so it might best be left as an activity to perform during foreplay or oral sex, unless you are a contortionist. Regardless, stimulation of the prostate gland can produce intense orgasms in men.

---

these exercises. The "Kegels," as the exercises are known, strengthen the pubococcygeal muscle, and, as this muscle is strengthened through voluntary contractions (the exercise), there is a heightening of vaginal sensitivity. The improved muscle tone affords women greater ease in reaching orgasm. In fact, Drs. Perry and Whipple, whom we mentioned in connection with the G-spot, found that women who ejaculate on orgasm have stronger pubococcygeal muscles than those who do not ejaculate.[21] And also, guys, a 1984 study showed that men can experience multiple orgasms when they practice contracting their pubococcygeal muscles.[22]

During intercourse, you can use the pubococcygeal muscle to contract your vagina tightly around your partner's penis, creating a sensation he's not likely to forget. It also might make it easier for you to achieve orgasm during intercourse. For men, try contracting the muscle during intercourse. You'll notice that the rigidity of your penis increases during this contraction, as well as its angle. This can be very pleasing to your partner and it may also increase the intensity of your orgasm. Not a bad trade for an exercise you don't even have to go to the gym for. If you're interested in learning more about these techniques, pick up *For Yourself: The Fulfillment of Female Sexuality*, by Dr. Lonnie Garfield Barbach.

"I Say, She Say in the Butt, Bob"

If you decide with your partner that anal intercourse is an area of sexual expression you would like to explore, there are some things you should

The Love Muscle

The pubococcygeal muscle can be located by flexing the muscle you use to stop the flow of urine. It's the same for both men and women. Familiarize yourself with the feeling of contracting and releasing the muscle while you urinate. Once you're familiar with it, you can exercise it. It's a muscle, and like any muscle in your body, you can develop it and tone it. The first exercise goes like this: squeeze the muscle for three seconds, and then relax it for three seconds. Repeat this in groups of 10, three-second squeezes and do this exercise three times a day. If it is difficult for you to do this at first, shorten the length of time you contract the muscle and work your way up to three-second intervals. (Better than Jane Fonda videos, isn't it?) No one will be able to tell you are doing this, so you can do it whenever you want, even in that boring lecture class of yours. Keep in mind that if you are moving your stomach, thighs, or buttocks, you are exercising the wrong muscle.

The second exercise is a variation on the first, except this time you contract and relax the muscle in intervals as quickly as possible. Perform this exercise with the same number of repetitions as the first. Again, it may be hard at first, but you'll figure it out with practice.

The third and fourth exercises are for women only. In the third exercise, imagine that you are sucking something like a tampon up into your vagina. In the fourth exercise, bear down on your muscle the same way you would during a bowel movement, with the emphasis on the vagina as opposed to the anus. The sucking-in and bearing-down exercises should both be held for three-second intervals. If any cramping or discomfort is felt due to the exercises, reduce the frequency with which you do them and gradually work up to the level suggested, although three times a day is considered a minimum. When you are comfortable with all of the exercises, all four should be practiced ten times each, three different times a day.

This all might sound a little absurd, but the benefits can be worth it. To see how you're progressing, women can insert a finger in the vagina and contract the pubococcygeal muscle. See if you can feel the contraction around your finger. After you've worked out for a few weeks, try the same thing and you'll notice a difference in the strength of your vagina's grip on your finger.

know. The anus is a very sensitive spot and is considered an erogenous zone, so there is nothing wrong with wanting to experiment in this way. But people have their own preferences, so if your partner has an aversion to anal sex, don't belabor the point. No one likes being pushed into sex of any kind and doing so is really the quickest way to alienate your mate.

Even though the anus is an erogenous zone, it has different rules of engagement than any other orifice. The anus is not self-lubricating (at least not to the extent necessary to allow for anal penetration, although it does lubricate itself enough to allow the passage of waste). It is also primarily an exit and not an entrance. Still, among some frequent anal-sex participants, such as homosexual men, the preferred method of prepping for anal sex is to perform an enema beforehand. Because of its purpose, the anus is home to many bacteria, and anal sex is a high-risk activity. Infections more easily spread through anal intercourse than vaginal intercourse, because of the presence of bacteria and the likelihood of tiny tears in the rectum. A condom is an absolute must, even between committed partners.[23]

Lubrication is all-important in anal sex. Attempting anal sex without lubrication can be painful and even impossible. Petroleum jelly is not recommended, especially in the presence of condoms, because its petroleum base can break down the rubber in rubbers and cause them to fail. Saliva is one option, but, again, it is not the best, as it tends to rapidly evaporate. The best lubricants are those designed specifically for use as a sexual lubricant, such as K-Y Jelly or EZ Glide. These products are safe to use with condoms and have the viscosity necessary for maximum comfort. The best way to lubricate for anal sex is to put some directly on the anus and work a little inside with a finger, then lubricate the penis or finger itself. After this is done, you are ready.

It is not recommended that you thrust into the anus the same way as you would into the vagina at first. It is best to enter the anus slowly, giving the tight sphincter muscle a chance to relax and more readily let something inside its walls. It is also important to listen to your partner to find out what

The University of O, Part V: Consistently Frustrated Students

College men who rarely achieve orgasm during sex: 3 percent.

College women who rarely achieve orgasm during sex: 14 percent.

College men who never achieve orgasm during sex: 1 percent.

College women who never achieve orgasm during sex: 15 percent.

depth of penetration is comfortable. You may not be able to insert your entire penis into your partner's anus, and forcing it in can be damaging to the rectal walls. Open communication is extremely important, as anal sex can be quite painful if the sphincter is not relaxed or ready, so be prepared to alter your thrusts or back off altogether. Together, you can work up to something that is comfortable for both of you. If at any time your partner wants you to stop, do so immediately (not in "just a sec" or after a couple more thrusts). Anal sex is something that takes a lot of trust, and you can destroy that trust in a matter of seconds by hurting or ignoring your partner.

Your partner may enjoy other areas of his or her body being touched during anal sex. A "reach-around" stimulation of the genitals can add to the pleasure the passive partner experiences during anal sex.

After it's over, don't do anything else with your penis until it's been washed thoroughly (especially if a condom was not used—which isn't going to happen, right?). The risk of spreading infection is great. Do not have vaginal intercourse before cleaning off your genitals *including* the scrotum, and do not have oral sex either. You must put on a fresh condom.

Actually, in some states, anal sex is illegal. Just ask your senator. . . . MARK THIESSEN/©CORBIS

The anus may bleed a little after anal sex. If no pain was felt during intercourse, then this is probably nothing to worry about, but be aware of it. If the bleeding is significant (more than anything that causes a tiny stain) or persists for any amount of time, you might have caused some damage. It is imperative that you have this checked out by a doctor immediately, because the presence of an open scrape or tear in the rectal wall can lead to serious infection due to the passing of feces over it. Don't panic, but check yourself. If there is no blood at all, then you are most likely safe and sound, but if a pain lingers up inside your anus for an extended amount of time (say a few hours after), you should consider having that examined as well.

There are a lot of downers to consider in association with anal sex, but safe sex practices and mutual respect and communication can cut down on these risks. For many people, anal sex is a very enjoyable practice that adds to their sexual satisfaction with one another. Despite the fact that anal sex is hardly rare, it is still a touchy subject for many people. Approach this level of intimacy with your partner openly, but gently.

The University of O, Part VI: Students Who Care

College men who think it's essential that both they and their partners have orgasms during sex: 33 percent.

College women who think it's essential: 16 percent.

College men who think it's very important that both they and their partners have orgasms during sex: 48 percent.

College women who think it's very important: 44 percent.

College men who think it's not important that both they and their partners have orgasms during sex: 14 percent.

College women who think it's not important: 31 percent.

College men who think it doesn't matter if both they and their partners have orgasms during sex: 5 percent.

College women who think it doesn't matter: 10 percent.

We urge and implore all of you—men, women, gay, and straight alike—to reread Chapter 4 and Chapter 10 on safer sex and sexual health, respectively, before you go crazy with all of this information. Being careless about intercourse can lead to ruined friendships, unwanted pregnancies, numerous infections and diseases, situations that can change your life for the worse, and even death. It is important not to forget that—especially when it is estimated that one in every five hundred college students is infected with HIV—a number that is most likely on the rise because, although you college students are among the most informed people on the planet when it comes to safe sex practices, you tend to ignore all warnings. Don't.

References

1. Marilyn D. Story, "A Comparison of University Student Experience with Various Sexual Outlets in 1974 and 1984," *Journal of Sex Education and Therapy*, Vol. 2, No. 2 (1985).

2. L. Downey, "Intergenerational change in sex behavior: A belated look at Kinsey's males," *Archives of Sexual Behavior*, Vol. 9, No. 4 (1980), pp. 267–317.
3. R. W. Hale, D. F. B. Char, K. Nagy, and N. Stockert, "Seventeen-year review of sexual and contraceptive behavior on a college campus," *American Journal of Obstetrics and Gynecology*, Vol. 169 (1993), pp. 1833–1838.
4. K. Davidson and N. Moore, "Masturbation and Premarital Sexual Intercourse Among College Women: Making Choices for Sexual Fulfillment," *Journal of Sex & Marital Therapy*, Vol. 20, No. 3 (Fall 1994).
5. J. D. Baldwin, S. Whiteley, and J. I. Baldwin, "The Effect of Ethnic Group on Sexual Activities Related to Contraception and STDs," *Journal of Sex Research*, Vol. 29, No. 2 (1992), pp. 189–205.
6. N. MacDonald, G. Wells, et al., "High-Risk STD/HIV Behavior Among College Students," *JAMA*, Vol. 263, No. 23 (1990).
7. Baldwin, Whiteley, and Baldwin, loc. cit.
8. MacDonald, Wells, et al., loc. cit.
9. J. I. Carroll, K. D. Volk, and J. S. Hyde, "Differences between males and females in motives for engaging in sexual intercourse," *Archives of Sexual Behavior*, Vol. 14, No. 2 (1985).
10. Davidson and Moore, loc. cit.
11. MacDonald, Wells, et al., loc. cit.
12. Davidson and Moore, loc. cit.
13. Story, loc. cit.
14. MacDonald, Wells, et al., loc. cit.
15. Baldwin, Whiteley, and Baldwin, loc. cit.
16. Carroll, Volk, and Hyde, loc. cit.
17. R. J. Ogletree, "Sexual coercion experience and help-seeking behavior of college women," *American Journal of College Health*, Vol. 41 (January 1993).
18. S. Sprecher, E. Hatfield, A. Cortese, et al., "Token resistance to sexual intercourse and consent to unwanted sexual intercourse: college students' dating experiences in three countries," *Journal of Sex Research*, Vol. 31, No. 2 (1994).
19. B. L. Yegidis, "Date rape and other forced sexual encounters among college students," *Journal of Sex Education Therapy*, Vol. 20, No. 2 (1990).
20. B. Whipple, "The G Spot and Female Sexual Response," presented at the *YPO Annual Meeting*, May 1994.
21. J. D. Perry and B. Whipple, "Pelvic muscle strength of female ejaculators: Evidence in support of a new theory of orgasm," *Journal of Sex Research*, Vol. 17, No. 1 (1981), pp. 22–39.
22. W. Hartman and M. Fithian, *Any Man Can* (New York: St. Martin Press, 1984).
23. Kathleen J. Sikkema, Richard A. Winett, and David N. Lombard, "Development and evaluation of a high risk reduction program for female college students," *AIDS Education and Prevention*, Vol. 7, No. 2 (1995), pp. 145–159.

CHAPTER 8

Coming Out on Campus
Gays, Lesbians, and Bisexuals

Gay and lesbian organizations are now commonplace on college campuses, but, as you might imagine, it has not always been this way. Even today, gay and lesbian organizations exist on campuses for different reasons than the Spanish Club or a community like Princeton's eating clubs. The organization for gay and lesbian communities at colleges exists because these groups are a minority on campus and still experience prejudice from their classmates as well as from the world off campus. Our survey revealed that 92 percent of college students consider themselves to be heterosexuals, 5 percent consider themselves to be bisexual, and only 2 percent declare themselves homosexual, which makes homosexuals among the smallest minority group on college campuses today.

Who's Out, Who's In and Out

Among the small homosexual population on today's campuses, 3 percent of the men are homosexual and 1 percent of the women are homosexual, making lesbians the smallest minority in the college population. More students consider themselves bisexual than homosexual, with 4 percent of the men and 6 percent of the women going both ways to class. In such an environment, it is easy to see why it can be hard to be homosexual in college.

In short, these groups and organizations exist because they need support from each other in the face of adversity and in a largely closed and heterosexual community. A lot of young adults first feel comfortable enough to come out while in college, where a gay community is a recognized entity. This is one possible way to read the statistics that reveal the 1 percent of freshmen who consider themselves homosexual, as opposed to the sophomores, juniors, and seniors, of whom between 2 and 3 percent consider themselves homosexual. A similar rise is seen in the bisexual community, with 4 percent of freshmen considering themselves bisexual, as opposed to 7 percent of seniors.

Most gay and lesbian organizations are far from being dens of liberal whining and political finger-pointing. These organizations frequently host fund-raising events for local institutions like Planned Parenthood and any number of charitable businesses and causes. They host awareness days that promote acceptance of diversity, both sexual and racial, on college campuses and beyond. They also speak out against injustices, both political and sexual, in the policies of the government and even in a university's administration. And you can bet they throw parties as wild as any fraternity or sorority party you're likely to attend.

What Gay Community?

When we asked if there was a strong gay community at their schools, 42 percent of students answered yes, 28 percent answered no, and 30 percent didn't know. Of the students who didn't know, approximately 31 percent were heterosexual, while approximately 15 percent were gay and bisexual, which kind of tells you right there who's paying more attention to whether there is a gay presence on campus.

If you are unfortunate enough during your tenure at college to experience the shock wave that goes through a campus when a sex crime is reported, the gay and lesbian community will likely be crying foul the loudest, because they are used to fighting for the right to a safe, normal sex life. If you are not yet convinced, consider the following results. (Unless otherwise noted, the following questions were asked only of the gay and bisexual students in our survey.)

Have you ever been teased, harassed, or attacked because of your sexual orientation?

The majority of homosexual students—52 percent—answered yes to this question. It appears that homosexual and bisexual men are more often the targets of prejudice, because 62 percent answered in the affirmative, while 43 percent—still a very high number—of the women answered yes. It also seems that the older the students get, the more prejudice they are exposed to. We saw a steady increase in the positive response rate to this negative question throughout the course of gay and bi students' college careers: 33 percent of freshmen, 52 percent of sophomores, 58 percent of juniors, and 64 percent of seniors have been teased, harassed, or attacked because of their sexual preferences.

⚇ Do you consider yourself openly gay or bisexual?

Of the homosexual students surveyed, 65 percent considered themselves to be out (60 percent of the men and 69 percent of the women), while 35 percent remain in the closet. With 34 percent of homosexual freshmen openly gay, they were the least likely among their classmates to be out. The number of openly gay sophomores jumped to 74 percent, juniors to 76 percent, and seniors to 66 percent, supporting the idea that a large number of gay students either come out or discover their sexual orientation during college. Gay and bisexual females (69 percent) were also more likely to be open about their sexuality than the men (60 percent).

⚇ Do your parents know you are gay or bi?

Being openly gay or bisexual on campus doesn't mean that these students have confronted their parents with their sexual orientation. While 39 percent of the students had told their parents, 69 percent had not. Again, women were more likely to have come out to their parents, as evidenced by the 35 percent of females whose parents knew. Twenty-six percent of the men's parents knew their son might one day bring home his husband—that is, if the courts lose their prejudices and recognize same-sex marriages.

⚇ When did you become aware of your sexual orientation?

The largest segment of homosexual and bisexual students—48 percent—became aware of their sexual preference in high school, but 26 percent found their true sexuality in college. Interestingly, 13 percent of the men realized they weren't heterosexual in college, while 37 percent of the women did. Still, that is a quarter of the homosexual population who first

---

I Now Pronounce You Husband and ?

If college students were in control of the U.S. court system, homosexuals would have the right to marry each other. The majority of our respondents—64 percent—believe that gay people should have the legal right to marry. Even the majority of heterosexual under-graduate men, who tend to have the most conservative attitudes toward homosexual behavior, thought that gay marriage was acceptable, with 52 percent of them offering their support. Over 90 percent of the gay population agreed, as well as 70 percent of the hetero females. If it's not legalized soon, it will be when these students go on to become judges.

---

really found their sexual orientation in college. The men appear to have discovered their sexuality at an earlier age than the women all through their academic careers, with 20 percent knowing they were gay or bi in junior high and 17 percent realizing back in grade school. Only 6 percent of the women can say they knew in junior high, while 11 percent said they already knew in grade school.

When did you have your first homosexual encounter?

Although much of the gay/bi population knew of their sexual orientation prior to entering college, the largest segment of our respondents—44 percent—didn't have their first homosexual experience until they got to college. But of that 44 percent, 30 percent were men, while 55 percent were women. The majority of homosexual and bisexual men—53 percent—had their first homosexual encounter in high school, while 29 percent of the women did. A small number—5 percent—had their first experience in junior high, while 11 percent had their first experience in grade school (9 percent of the men and 12 percent of the women). However, it should be noted that it is not uncommon for grade-schoolers to have explored their fledgling sexuality, be it eventually gay or straight, with a member of the same sex.

Now let's get some idea of what it is like to be gay or bisexual on campuses that are predominantly the domain of heterosexuals, so you can see how a conflict of ideologies can lead to prejudice. We asked all students, regardless of their sexual orientation, to answer the following questions.

> **High-Risk Behavior**
>
> We know we go over this in Chapters 4 and 7, but it is important enough to reiterate here. Anal sex, a high-risk sexual activity, is more popular among gay and bisexual students regardless of their gender than it is among heterosexual students. However, 20 percent of the gay/bi men and 37 percent of the gay/bi women say they *never* use a condom during anal sex. To their credit, they put their heterosexual classmates to shame: 68 percent of straight men and 72 percent of straight women say they never use a condom during anal sex. While 30 percent of the gay/bi men and 48 percent of gay/bi women say they always use a condom for anal sex, that just don't cut it, boys and girls. You want to know why? Go to Chapter 4.

Do you find the idea of sex between women alluring or sexy?

Overall response to this question was split down the middle, with 51 percent of students saying they did find the idea to be a nice one, while 49 percent disagreed. Are you ready for this, ladies? We're sure it won't surprise you much, but 80 percent of heterosexual men really like the girl-on-girl thing and they were surpassed, naturally, only by gay and bisexual women, 95 percent of whom found the idea enticing. The gay male population's opinion on the matter mirrored the overall numbers, while 23 percent of hetero women found the idea alluring. So, do you think the numbers will be similar for our next question?

Do you find the idea of sex between men alluring or sexy?

The resounding answer from college students: hell no. From these results you can see why gay men have experienced much more ridicule than gay women. An overwhelming majority of 88 percent of the college population polled said that they did not find this idea alluring or sexy, and 90 percent of hetero men agreed with the general college populace. While 23 percent of hetero women found sex between women alluring, only 10 percent found the idea of men getting it on arousing. The majority of gay and bisexual females—57 percent—didn't warm up to the idea of men having sex together either. As you may have assumed, the only overwhelmingly positive response to this question was from the gay and bisexual men, 94 percent of whom liked the idea. But as you can see, they don't share that opinion with very many of their classmates.

❓ Which of the following have you experienced with a person of your own gender?

Activity	% hetero men	% gay/bi men	% hetero women	% gay/bi women
Kissing	12	96	14	84
Caressing	8	94	11	79
Manual genital stimulation	7	86	5	67
Manual anal stimulation	2	61	1	15
Oral sex	7	85	4	60
Penetration	4	60	2	33
Nothing	84	2	83	12

❓ How did you feel about it?

We gave students four options to choose from to describe to us how they felt about the above activities: (1) Great, can't wait for the next time; (2) Nothing special, could take it or leave it; (3) Definitely not for me; and (4) Ashamed. Not surprisingly, 84 percent of the gay/bi men answered "great," along with 93 percent of the gay/bi women. What was surprising was the 22 percent and 25 percent of heterosexual men and women, respectively, who also chose "great" as their answer, but we must bear in mind the small percentages of heterosexuals who have had sexual experiences with a person of the same gender, as shown on the table above, so the heteros answering this question are more experimental than the majority of the hetero population at large.

On the flip side, 11 percent of the hetero men said they felt ashamed (choice 4, along with 17 percent of the hetero females, while 4 percent of the gay/bi men felt ashamed, and none of the gay/bi women did. Overall, 30 percent chose response 2 and 17 percent chose response 3. No gay or bi respondents chose the third response, which only makes sense. Thirty-three percent and 19 percent of straight men and women, respectively, found, through experimentation, that sex with a member of their own gender was not for them.

? If you haven't done so already would you ever consider having sex with a person of your own gender?

We're looking only at the responses of heterosexuals, and the resounding answer from straight college men, 96 percent of them, was "never." The women weren't quite as adamant, with 77 percent of them also responding that they would never consider it. The "maybes" in response to this question came in at 4 percent of the guys and 21 percent of the women, while the percent of men who answered "absolutely" was too small to calculate, and a mere 2 percent of the straight women answered that they would absolutely consider sex with another women. So, in light of these responses, you could postulate that heterosexual college males are the least accepting of homosexual activity, and that's exactly what we found in the answer to our next question.

? How do you feel about homosexuality?

The largest group of college students—44 percent overall—are ambivalent toward homosexuality, expressing that they feel "it's a little weird, but whatever." However, of the students who feel that homosexuality is wrong or sinful, 36 percent of them were heterosexual men, while 20 percent were straight women. Hetero college males clearly have the biggest problem with homosexuals. Hetero females are much more accepting of homosexuality: 31 percent of them had no problem with homosexuality, feeling that whatever turns you on is fine, no matter if it is homosexuality. Only 18 percent of the straight men were so open-minded in their opinions of homosexuality.

? In your opinion, making a distinction between "gay" and "straight" is . . .
A) an accurate description of the way things are
B) an outmoded distinction in an increasingly omnisexual world

This is another attitudinal question we used to gauge college students' feelings toward homosexual activity. The majority of students—62 percent—agreed with statement A; 38 percent with statement B. Breaking down the responses to A, we see that 71 percent of hetero men agree with this, as opposed to 61 percent of hetero women, 28 percent of gay/bi men, and 16 percent of gay/bi women. Judging from this, it would seem that the status quo between gays and heterosexuals still strongly exists.

Despite a fair amount of support from the nongay community, we can see from our results that there is still a lot of bias toward homosexuals on today's college campuses. The results of a 1988 study printed in the research journal, *Sex Roles,* sounds like our results: college students tended to have negative attitudes toward homosexuals and, consistent with previous studies, males had stronger negative attitudes than females. But things have gotten better than they used to be. The same study asked a couple of questions nearly identical to ours. When students in the late '80s were asked if they agreed with the statement, "The idea of homosexual marriages is ridiculous," a full 64 percent agreed. Our survey shows that the exact same percentage of students now agrees with the statement, "Gay people should have the right to marry"—quite a change of opinion. Where our study revealed that 26 percent of students thought that homosexuality is wrong or sinful, nearly double that number of students in 1988—57 percent of them—agreed with the statement, "Homosexual behavior is just plain wrong."* There has been improvement in the attitude toward gays on college campuses.

Don't lose faith out there, people, things have changed for the better and, hopefully, they will keep getting better. Though college may be tough, it's just as tough, if not tougher, to be gay in the world that awaits you after college. Keep fighting until the rest of the world catches up with you.

* Lawrence A. Kurdek, "Correlates of Negative Attitudes Toward Homosexuals in Heterosexual College Students," *Sex Roles,* Vol. 18, Nos. 11/12 (1988).

CHAPTER 9

Alternative Nations

R ecently, while doing some research for this book at New York's famous alternative sex club, the Hellfire Club, your humble authors were labeled as people who like "vanilla sex," meaning that we don't stray too far into the realm of the unusual or kinky. Feeling a little defensive, as if the term were some sort of accusation, we tried to explain that we were into experimentation, that we'd pretty much try anything once just to check it out and that we have no problem with taking pictures or videos or the occasional foray into role-playing (we were at the Hellfire Club on Schoolgirl Nite) and, hey, maybe even some light bondage—as long as there wasn't any *real* pain involved. "Yup, vanilla sex," was the response. OK, so we didn't try spanking any of the "school girls" there, who were all convinced they had to stay after class because of their misbehavior, but then again, there weren't many college students to be seen in the Hellfire Club, even if it was Schoolgirl Nite.

For some of us, the traditional methods of sexual intercourse just don't seem to float our boats. Even more advanced sexual practices such as oral gymnastics, anal sex, restraints, and role-playing aren't enough. Some of us like shoes, stockings, or, in the case of Rosanna Arquette's boyfriend in the Martin Scorsese film *After Hours*, Dorothy from *The Wizard of Oz*, and it is only these things in which we find true pleasure and sexual gratification. Others still are curious about what it might be like to dress up like men and dominate their partners. Or they're interested to see if the mix of a little pleasant pain might enhance their awareness of pleasure in the sexual act. And some of us are so far out there that no else can understand what the attraction is to, say, defecating on your loved one. In any case, if you ever wonder about these things, or if you wonder if anyone shares your certain, secret or not-so-secret proclivity, then read on as we explore the acquired tastes that some college students find themselves reveling in.

ACQUIRED TASTES, ODDITIES, AND JUST PLAIN OFF-THE-WALL SEX ACTS

❓ *What has held you back from acting on the things you've only fantasized about?*

The overwhelming majority of students, 57 percent of them, said that they were too embarrassed to bring up their fantasies with their partners. Heterosexual women were the most embarrassed, 67 percent of them admitting that disclosing their sexual fantasies was too embarrassing for them. Heterosexual men were the second most embarrassed; just under half of them—49 percent—couldn't tell their partners what was on their minds, while a similar number of gay and bisexual women (47 percent) and men (45 percent) were also too shy to admit what naughty bit of business they wanted to try.

Only 16 percent of the college population as a whole said that they haven't acted on their fantasies because they were just too scary to try. Again, female undergrads were more intimidated by their fantasies then men, with 25 percent of gay and bi women and 21 percent of hetero women having fantasies that were too much for them to handle. The gay/bi guys came in a close third, with 19 percent of them paralyzed to inaction by their secret sexual desires. The straight men were the most intrepid (or perhaps the least creative) and only 8 percent of them said that their fantasies were too scary to act on.

Having a partner unwilling to help you fulfill your fantasy, whatever it may be, was more problematic for those trying to explore their fantasies than those who were simply too scared to try. Overall, 43 percent of the men said their partners were unwilling to help, while only 14 percent of the men were unwilling to help their partners. If we break out the responses by sexual preference, it is the hetero men who are having the most problems with unwilling and/or unadventurous partners on campus: 44 percent have had their fantasies left unfulfilled by their partners, while just 13 percent of the hetero women have the same problem with their fellas. See, men can be more understanding than women sometimes, at least about sex it seems. About a third of the gay and bisexual community (39 percent of the men, 34 percent of the women) had partners who offered them no help in realizing their wildest dreams.

❓ *What do college students fantasize about?*

After seeing the results above, we just had to know, so here are the top eighteen things students are fantasizing about and the corresponding percentage of all students who are having these fantasies. *Note:* with one exception, the respondent's year in college and whether or not the person was in a relationship made little difference to where these fantasies ranked in the popular college sexual id.

1. **A threesome (40 percent).** More men (55 percent) are thinking about this than women (27 percent), if that comes as a surprise to anybody, but more gay and bisexual women (44 percent) are thinking about it than their hetero female classmates and more gay and bisexual men (56 percent) are thinking about it than anybody else.

2. **Using a video camera (28 percent).** Again, a more popular flight of fancy among men (35 percent) than among women (22 percent), but no real differences across the lines of sexual preferences. However, women who were in a steady relationship were much more likely to have this fantasy than those who were not.

3. **Bondage (24 percent).** This fantasy is most common among gay male (40 percent) and gay/bi female undergraduates (32 percent), but 24 percent of the hetero women share this fantasy, more than the 21 percent of the hetero men who do, so we have our first fantasy that is more popular among female coeds overall (25 percent of the college population) than it is with the guys (23 percent overall).

4. **An orgy (22 percent).** The idea of an orgy is much more enticing to the men on campus, with 32 percent of them having this fantasy, more than

---

The '70s Preservation Society

We found a study of one hundred students done in the mid-1980s showing that only 5 percent of college students have participated in a group sex orgy, with the breakdown of males and females being 4 percent and 1 percent, respectively. That's one very daring woman, wouldn't you say? If you are going to college looking to participate in a lot of group sex, you're living in the wrong decade. In the 1970s, the percentage of undergraduates participating in group sex was nearly triple the number reported in the '80s.[1]

doubling the 15 percent of women who have the same fantasy. While the heterosexual respondents deviate only slightly from the percentages for the college population overall, 51 percent of gay/bi males share this fantasy, along with 33 percent of their gay/bi sisters.

5. **Taking photographs (22 percent).** Those who aren't thinking of taking motion pictures with a video camera are thinking of taking some nice shots for the family photo album. Everyone was pretty much in agreement here, with 25 percent of all the men sharing this fantasy, but only 18 percent of the hetero women imagining this, as opposed to 28 percent of the gay/bisexual female students.

6. **Sex with a much older partner (22 percent).** Twenty-nine percent of the men are pining for that sexy older lover of their dreams. But, again, there is dissension among the women, with only 15 percent of the hetero women sharing this fantasy, as opposed to 24 percent of the gay/bisexual femmes.

7. **Talking dirty (13 percent).** Can we say "vanilla sex"? Still, not everyone does it. Men and women come a little closer together on this one, with 14 percent of the men on campus thinking of dirty things to say, along with 13 percent of the women, but this time the nonheterosexual women overtake everyone else, as 20 percent of them yearn to whisper sweet and sour nothings into their partners' ears.

8. **Role-playing (13 percent).** The overall percentages are exactly the same as the overall percentages of students who fantasize about talking dirty to each other, but this fantasy was more popular among the gay and bisexual community, as evidenced by the 16 percent of women and 19 percent of the men who found this idea alluring.

9. **S&M (11 percent).** Again, this fantasy was most popular in the gay and bi community, with 15 percent of the men and 21 percent of the women longing for some sadomasochistic sex. It was least popular among hetero females, of whom 9 percent said they fantasized about it.

10. **Sex with violence (11 percent).** For the first time, male heterosexuals encounter a fantasy that they have less frequently than any other group. While 9 percent of the straight men fantasize about this, 11 percent of the hetero women do, and 16 percent of all members of the gay and bisexual community do as well.

11. **Spanking (10 percent).** Men, regardless of their sexual preference, came in about even on this topic, with between 12 and 13 percent of all college men sharing a spanking fantasy, while 16 percent the female gay and bisexual campus disciplinarians doubled the 8 percent of their hetero counterparts who felt like a good spanking.

12. **Sex with a person of the same gender (10 percent).** We asked heterosexual students if they've ever had this fantasy and 4 percent of men said they had, while 14 percent of the women had.

13. **Golden showers (5 percent).** Overall, 7 percent of the men had this fantasy (see Glossary for definition) and 4 percent of the women did. This was also one of the rare instances where the heterosexuals outfantasized the gay and bisexual students. A full 8 percent of straight men thought fondly upon a golden shower, as did 4 percent of the straight women, while only 2 percent of the gay community, both men and women, yearned for this particular brand of shower.

14. **Phone-sex lines (5 percent).** Heterosexual male undergrads outflank everyone else with this fantasy, because 6 percent of them ponder the idea, while only 4 percent of all women and gay/bisexual men consider the seductive possibilities of 1-900-SCREW-ME.

15. **Online sex (3 percent).** Hetero men again fantasize about this the most, with 4 percent of these would-be World Wide Web Casanovas beating out the rest of the population. But as we saw in Chapter 7, in practice it is the gay male community which most frequently hooks up on the Internet.

16. **Cross-dressing (3 percent).** Only 1 percent of the straight women fantasize about this, along with 3 percent of the straight men; however, 6 percent of the gay/bi women do, along with 8 percent of the gay and bisexual men.

17. **Sex with an animal (2 percent).** That's right. Of the heterosexual college population we polled, 2 percent had erotically charged zoomorphic fantasies, while 12 percent of the gay/bisexual men thought about scenarios with animals and 8 percent of the gay/bisexual women also had barnyard fantasies.

18. **Sex with the opposite gender (1 percent).** We asked homosexual students if they have fantasized about having sex with a member of the opposite sex and 13 percent of gay men responded in the affirmative, while 9 percent of the gay women did. But because the overall gay population is so low, fantasies about same-sex liaisons are more popular on campus, which is why that fantasy came in at number 12.

Finally, 3 percent of our respondents specified their fantasy as "other"—or perhaps they were just too embarrassed to share it with us.

Fantasy is one thing and, as we have seen, just because you have a fantasy doesn't mean you get to live it out, but we wanted to know how many college students had actually done these things that they fantasized about. So we asked, and here's what we found.

? *What sexual activities have college students done?*

1. **Talking dirty (64 percent).** While it came in seventh in terms of what college students are fantasizing about, 65 percent of men and 63 percent of women say nasty things to get each other off. Results from the gay community were slightly higher, with 70 percent of the men and 76 percent of the women arousing each other with dirty talk.

2. **Spanking (27 percent).** Ranked eleventh by fantasizers, spanking is popular enough on college campuses to come in at number two on this list. Hetero men and gay/bi women do it the most, with 30 percent and 33 percent, respectively, while gay/bi men and hetero women both come in at 24 percent on the spank-o-meter. Spanking is most popular with upperclassmen, freshmen falling behind them by 6 percentage points.

3. **Bondage (26 percent).** Bondage comes in at number three on both lists! Bondage is most popular among gay female (48 percent) and gay/bi male undergraduates (34 percent), while 24 percent of the hetero ladies enjoy restraints, as do 26 percent of the straight men. Of the students who participate in bondage, freshmen appear to have their appendages free of restraints most of the time, with only 20 percent of the first-years engaging in this activity, as opposed to 29 percent of all the upper classmen.

4. **Sex with a much older partner (16 percent).** The gay and bisexual females top the charts in this activity, as evidenced by the 36 percent of them that have had sex with an older partner. The bisexual and gay men are next in line, 26 percent of them having bridged the generation gap, leaving the average of 15 percent of heteros who have enjoyed someone older and wiser.

5. **Taking photographs (13 percent).** It was ranked number five on the previous list and it's number five again here, with 13 percent of the student population having taken some illicit photos of themselves, 9 percent below the number of those who have fantasized about it. The gay and bisexual population has apparently used more rolls of film, because 22 percent of them have raised eyebrows at the FotoMat.

6. **Role-playing (12 percent).** Just about as many people fantasize about this activity as actually do it. As was implied by the split across sexual preference lines in the people who fantasized about it, it is the bisexual, gay, and lesbian community who role-plays the most, with an average of 27 percent engaging in this activity. Only 9 percent of hetero males participate in this activity (strange when you think that a lot these guys probably loved the role-playing game Dungeons and Dragons when they were younger), while 13 percent of hetero women do. About one fifth of seniors engage in role-playing, the most of any class, while 8 percent of freshmen do.

7. **A threesome (11 percent).** It was the most popular fantasy, with 40 percent of college students having sex with two partners in their imaginations, but it comes in at number 7 on the "I've done it" list. While hetero men fantasized about a threesome more than gay and bisexual women, the gay and bisexual women are beating the straight guys out in practice: 40 percent of the gay and bisexual women have had a threesome while 11 percent of the hetero men have. Only 7 percent of hetero women have tried a threesome, while 42 percent of the gay/bisexual men have.

8. **Online sex (10 percent).** The overwhelming majority of participants in online sex are gay and bisexual undergraduate men, 47 percent of whom have sex online.

9. **Phone-sex lines (10 percent).** More men do this than women: 12 percent of hetero men and 26 percent of gay/bi men. Women don't accrue as many charges to their credit cards, as an average of only 7 percent of the women call phone sex-lines, considerably less than the percentage of congressmen who do.

10. **Golden showers (9 percent).** The number of students participating in golden showers is greater than the number of those who fantasize about it. Heterosexual men have the most experience with golden showers (10 percent), while 9 percent of their homosexual and female classmates make up the rest. Strangely enough, when we break down the figures by class year, 13 percent of the respondents who said they've had a golden shower were freshmen, the most of any class, with sophomores close behind at 12 percent. Juniors and seniors trail at 7 percent and 4 percent, respectively. Kids these days! What can you say?

11. **Sex with violence (6 percent).** This activity was more popular with women regardless of their sexual preference than it was with straight men, and that kind of surprised us, given the impression that male sexual aggression too frequently results in violence. But that's what the numbers said. Where 5 percent of hetero men have engaged in violent sex, 6 percent of hetero women have, along with 18 percent of gay/bi women. Of gay and bisexual men, 9 percent have experienced violent sex.

12. **S&M (6 percent).** More students fantasize about this than actually do it; nevertheless, college campuses do have their share of sadomasochists—and we are not just talking about premed students. Of the heterosexual population, 6 percent of the men and 5 percent of the women indulge in S&M sex play. The gay and bisexual college men's experiences with S&M equal those of the straight women, while the gay/bi female students eclipse everyone, with 21 percent of them claiming to engage in S&M sex.

13. **Sex with a person of the same gender (5 percent).** Again, more students fantasize about this than actually do it. The heterosexual population experiencing intercourse with same-sex partners is dead even for men and women at 3 percent.

14. **Using a video camera (5 percent).** Roughly one sixth of the number of people who fantasize about videotaping their couplings actually do it. Overall, men (6 percent) do this a little more often than women (4 percent), while the gay community has a slighter higher home video production rate than the heterosexual, with 7 percent of the gay/bi men and 6 percent of the gay/bi women preparing their own skin-flick screen tests.

15. **An orgy (4 percent).** More than five times the number of those who have actually participated in an orgy fantasize about it. The numbers of heterosexual students who have been in an orgy are pretty small: 4 percent of the men and 2 percent of the women. The gay and bisexual women come out on top again in this category, with 14 percent of them reporting to have engaged in an orgy. Gay and bisexual men are close behind, with 13 percent of them having been in an orgy.

16. **Cross-dressing (4 percent).** Cross-dressing was ranked the same among fantasies of college students as it is for actual participation, although it appears that slightly more students actually cross-dress than simply fantasize about doing it. One fifth of gay and bisexual college men—20 percent—have cross-dressed and so have 15 percent of the women with nonheterosexual preferences. A very small percentage of heterosexual college students—3 percent of the Victors and 2 percent of the Victorias—has cross-dressed.

17. **Sex with the opposite gender (2 percent).** This question was posed to gay and bisexual students and, of them, 29 percent of the men and 30 percent of the women have had sex with a member of the opposite sex—considerably more have done it than fantasized about it. But because of the size of the gay and bisexual communities on college campuses, these relatively high percentages represent only 2 percent of the entire college population as a whole, and thus it ranks seventeenth.

18. **Sex with an animal (1 percent).** Well, not as many students have sex with animals as those who fantasize about having sex with animals. The percentage of heterosexual women who responded to this question was too small to tabulate. But we did come to the conclusion that 1 percent of heterosexual males in our survey have had sex with an animal, 2 percent of the gay and bisexual males have engaged in bestiality, and a rather amazing 7 percent of gay and bisexual women in our survey claimed to have had sex with a critter of some kind.

Free Willy?

Perhaps understandably, not very much research has been done to find out how many college students have performed sex acts with animals, or how often, or what kind of animal is preferred, be it mammal or (gasp!) reptile. One study that compared students' sexual practices in 1974 and 1984 revealed the following results. When asked if they had ever had sexual contact with an animal, 11 percent of the students in 1974 responded in the affirmative; 5 percent of the respondents were female and 6 percent were male. By 1984, that percentage had dropped to only 3 percent of students having had sexual contact with an animal. Again, men were in the majority with 2 percent of the affirmative responses and females with 1 percent.[2] The accuracy of these statistics is easily questioned when one stops to think about how many people would answer this question truthfully if they had, in fact, had a thing for Snoopy at some point in their college careers. In any case, the response rate to the question dropped significantly over a decade, indicating that fewer students were engaging in sex acts with animals. This implies, perhaps, that animals in the '80s simply weren't as attractive as those free-spirited quadrupeds of the swinging '70s. And no, in case you're wondering, sex with animals is not entirely safe, but condoms will prevent the spread of hoof-and-mouth disease with a 98 percent effectiveness rate.

References

1. M. D. Story, "A comparison of university student experience with various sexual outlets in 1974 and 1984," *Journal of Sex Education Therapy*, Vol. 11, No. 2 (1985).
2. Ibid.

Part Three

CHAPTER 10

Sex and Health

GOOD REPRODUCTIVE HEALTH HABITS, OR WHAT YOU DON'T KNOW *CAN* HURT YOU

We've all heard the old saying: if it ain't broke, don't fix it. This little kernel of wisdom does not, however, apply to your sex organs. For one thing, your genitals are way down between your legs or tucked up inside you, so unless you're some kind of contortionist or you have some really good mirrors, you probably aren't in the habit of checking them regularly. How would you know if they're "broke"? Many potentially fatal diseases, including cervical and testicular cancer, are initially painless and have no early symptoms that you can detect on your own.

Most diseases, if caught early, are curable—even cancer. But you must see your doctor regularly in order to be safe and stay healthy. How often is regularly? Well, for sexually nonactive men and women with no family history of serious diseases, a routine physical should be conducted every two years. Women should see a gynecologist for this exam. A gynecologist is a doctor who specializes in the female reproductive system. If you are sexually active, however, and even if you *always* practice safe sex, you should see a doctor at least once a year.

Luckily, college students generally have easy access to health care professionals—usually right at the campus infirmary. If you haven't made yourself familiar with your college health center, do so. If you can't even remember the last time you saw a doctor, call and make an appointment today. There's nothing about a visit to the doctor that should frighten you. The thing to be scared of is letting yourself become seriously ill or infertile because you were too timid or lazy or unconcerned to take care of your one-and-only body.

OK, enough preaching. Let's go over what to expect from a routine examination.

A VISIT TO THE GYNECOLOGIST (FOR WOMEN)

As a new visitor to a doctor's office, you will be asked to fill out a few forms detailing your (and your family's) medical history. Be especially careful to include information on any family history of breast, ovarian, cervical, or uterine cancer.

It is extremely important for you to be honest on these forms. Your doctor must know if you are a smoker. Why should this matter, you may ask? Some medications can become dangerous if you smoke. For example, birth control pills may not be the best choice of contraception for smokers, because they run a much higher risk of heart attack and stroke than nonsmokers. Also, your doctor should know if you have ever been pregnant or have ever contracted a sexually transmitted disease.

A gynecological exam can be a bit uncomfortable and embarrassing, especially your first time. These are normal reactions, and a good doctor will calm you, reassure you, and explain everything that he or she is doing. Bring a friend with you for moral support if you're nervous, and ask to speak with the doctor before the examination—with all your clothes on—so you can ask any questions without feeling awkward. Definitely ask *all* your questions, even if you feel silly. Your doctor will respect you for taking an interest in your health and your body.

A Note About Doctors, Your Rights, and the History of Gynecology

Shame, guilt, and fear *are not* emotions that belong in a gynecologist's office. If anything your doctor says, does, or implies offends you, frightens you, or threatens you, you should switch doctors. If your doctor refuses to answer your questions or recommends surgeries, medications, or procedures without explaining what they are and why you need them, you should switch doctors. Leave the office as soon as you can and never talk to that doctor again.

That said, here's what you can expect from a normal gynecological examination.

> **Dysmenorrhea**
>
> *Dysmenorrhea* is the fancy word for menstrual cramps. As any woman will tell you, cramps are quite real. Researchers believe they are influenced by prostaglandins, chemicals produced in the body, which, in excess, may lead to excessive cramping of the uterus. Common symptoms that go along with cramps—or sometimes appear even in the absence of cramps right before a menstrual period—are backaches, headaches, nausea, diarrhea, bloating, dizziness, irritability, fatigue, pelvic "fullness" or "heaviness." There are ways to lessen the severity of these symptoms. The week before your period begins, eat moderately and try to limit your salt, caffeine, and alcohol intake, which will reduce water retention and help you avoid bloating, puffiness, and headaches. Some women find that supplementing their diets with B-complex vitamins helps them deal with irritability and mood swings. Nonprescription pain medications such as Advil and Aleve are especially effective for cramps. If your cramps are severe or debilitating, your health care provider can discuss other treatment options with you.

Step on the Scale

Your height and weight are part of any normal medical record. You'll also have your blood pressure and pulse measured the first time you visit the gynecologist, and maybe every time.

Eyes, Ears, Nose, Throat

As part of a full checkup, your gynecologist will shine a bright light in your eyes, peek in your ears, maybe up your nose, and down your throat.

A Little Urine, a Little Blood

You'll probably have to pee in a tiny cup. The best way to do this without making a terrible mess is to start urinating first, then quickly slip the cup into your urine stream. Your urine sample can be used to check for infections or pregnancy.

You'll also have to give a blood sample. This only involves a little sting, but the syringe looks enormous. The squeamish may want to look away. Most gynecologists order standard tests for things like pregnancy, diabetes, HIV, syphilis, gonorrhea, chlamydia, cholesterol, and blood cell count. Different tests may be run, depending on your family health history and your current medical condition.

Heart and Lungs

Once you've given your bodily fluid samples to the appropriate nurse, you'll be asked to undress completely (there will be some privacy for this) and slip into a robe. You'll meet your doctor in the examining room, and he or she will ask you to sit up on the examining table. The first part of the examination will be of your heart and lungs. The doctor will use a stethoscope to make sure nothing weird, wheezy, or arhythmic is going on.

A Palpable Organ Check

The gynecologist is going to ask you to lie down so he or she can palpate your abdomen to make sure there are no swollen or enlarged organs. Palpation just means touching your belly in a kind of kneading way, sometimes pushing with both hands. There should be no pain involved (unless your doctor does discover an infected or enlarged organ). Then your doctor might press on your back to see if you have any tenderness in the kidney area (a sign of possible infection).

Breast Examination

Still using this palpating touch, your doctor will examine your breasts for lumps or cysts. Following a circular or up-and-down path, the doctor will cover the entire area around your breast from your armpit to your nipple. Then he or she will gently squeeze the nipple and check for discharge. You will, no doubt, be asked if you do monthly self-examinations. The doctor will surely explain how to do this (see also pages 188–190) and will probably have a pamphlet for you.

The Pelvic Examination

You'll notice that at the end of the examining table there are two stirrups. Your doctor will ask you to put your feet in them and slide your hips down to the end of the table. This is the part of the doctor visit that women tend to like least—not because it is painful (it shouldn't be), but because you're basically spread-eagled, with your heels high in the air, your most private regions completely exposed to a stranger. You're likely to feel pretty ridiculous, but the last thing you need to do is get upset. You might be nervous, but try to see a little humor in the situation if at all possible. If you don't see anything remotely funny about it, try to remember that it will all be over soon. If you have to use the rest room, make sure you do it before this part of the exam, because pressure will be put on your bladder.

Your gynecologist will start with an external examination of your genitals, looking for any discolorations, lesions, or irregularities. Then he or she will insert an instrument called a *speculum* into your vagina. The speculum gently spreads apart the walls of your vagina so the doctor can see your cervix. Specula can be metal or plastic, and they can be used safely and comfortably, even on virgins. It is at this point in the exam that you are likely to tense up, however. Many women have the reflex to jump, jerk, or slam their knees together as soon as the speculum touches them. Obviously, your doctor won't appreciate having his or her head crushed. A little communication is key here. Ask your doctor to let you know *exactly* when he or she is going to touch you.

All you will feel when the speculum is inserted is a little pressure. Relax your muscles, and you will be much more comfortable. The doctor will shine a bright light between your legs and examine your cervix and vaginal walls for anything unusual. (If you're curious, many doctors keep a mirror around for patients who want to see what their cervixes look like.)

The Pap Smear

Using a thin, wooden specimen collector, the doctor will gently scrape a few cells from your cervix. This is called a *Pap smear,* and it is used to detect abnormal cell growth on the cervix (a possible precursor to cancer). Your cells are put on a slide and sent to a lab for examination. The collection of the cells feels kind of weird, but it is completely painless because you have very few nerve endings in your cervix. After the Pap smear, the doctor will remove the speculum and insert a gloved finger or two into your vagina while pressing on your abdomen with the other hand. The doctor does this to make sure your uterus, ovaries, and tubes are all where they should be and to make sure there is no abnormal tenderness or any abnormal growths. They press down pretty hard to do this, but, again, it is not usually painful.

The final part of the exam will involve the insertion of one gloved finger into your rectum and one into the vagina. This should take only a few seconds and is done to make sure your organs are in proper alignment. This can be especially uncomfortable if you insist on clenching your muscles. Relax, breathe deeply, and it will be much easier. You may notice that you feel as if you need to have a bowel movement. That's because the same nerve endings that send your brain the signal that you need to move your bowels are being stimulated by your doctor's finger. As soon as the doctor removes the finger, the feeling will go away.

OK, that's it! Put on your clothes, go home, eat a pint of ice cream, and forget it ever happened.

A TRIP TO THE INTERNIST OR
UROLOGIST (FOR MEN)

An internist is a regular, all-around doctor. When you go in for a physical, an internist is the type of doctor you should see. A urologist is the male counterpart to the gynecologist for women. Urologists specialize in the male reproductive system. You should see a urologist if you think you may have been exposed to an STD (see page 75), if you have pain or discomfort in the genitals or any of the symptoms of an STD (see page 93), or if your internist refers you.

Whenever you go to a doctor for the first time, you will be asked to fill out a few forms about yourself, your family, and the medical history of your family. It may seem like a pain to spend twenty minutes filling out paperwork, but it's very important that your doctor understand your particular history and the risks you might face. Take the time to fill out these forms thoroughly—and be honest. Your doctor is not there to scold you or make value judgments about you. If you are a smoker, for example, don't lie about it. If you have been treated for sexually transmitted disease in the past, list which ones and when. These records are completely private: the only people who can look at them are you and your doctor. Unless you give permission, not even your parents can look at your medical history.

Height, Weight, Blood Pressure

The first thing the doctor will do is weigh you, measure your height, and take your blood pressure. Pretty noninvasive, huh? So far, so good.

Say "Ahh"

Here, a little poking and prodding comes in. You'll have a bright light shined in your eyes while the doctor stares deep into your pupils. Then you'll have a cone-shaped instrument stuck in your ears so your doctor can have a good look at all your earwax and that shoe from the Monopoly game you shoved in there when you were five. Next, you'll have to open wide and show off that lovely uvula of yours (that's the thing dangling in the back of your throat). That's it for your upper regions.

Breathe In, Breathe Out

Your doctor will listen to your heart and your breathing to make sure your heart isn't doing some kind of crazy mambo beat and your lungs aren't leaking. Nice doctors nowadays actually warm up their stethoscopes in their hands before slapping them on your back. Feel free to yowl if your doctor is not this considerate.

This May Sting a Bit

You're going to have to part with a little blood—one or even two syringes full, depending on what you're being checked for. Feel free to ask the doctor to explain what tests will be run. In general, you will be screened for diabetes, cholesterol level, AIDS, syphilis, gonorrhea, and chlamydia. You will not be screened for illegal drug use, and even if you were, your medical records are private, so don't worry about being arrested before you leave the doctor's office. You can have very complete bloodwork done to measure the presence of almost anything in your bloodstream, but your doctor will probably not order such complicated (and expensive) tests unless you need them.

Take Aim . . .

Very likely, especially if you are visiting a urologist, you will be asked to pee in a ridiculously small cup and proudly hand your sample to a nurse or lab technician. The challenge is to avoid spraying all over your hand and the outside of the cup in the process. (*Quick hint:* the easiest way to do this is to start your stream up, make sure it's steady, then deftly slip the cup under it.) Urine tests are usually used to detect infections.

A Big Sigh of Relief (for Now)

When you thought about this doctor's exam business, did you have terrible visions of yourself on all fours with a stranger's gloved finger somewhere it didn't belong? We're talking about a prostate examination here, and luckily you don't have to worry about that for now. The prostate examination is conducted by a doctor called a proctologist. It is recommended that every man over forty have his prostate examined by a doctor once a year. So do some quick math. You're under forty, right? Just log this information away for another couple of decades.

HEY LADIES—CHECKING YOURSELF OUT

There are a couple of easy things you should do yourself to make sure you stay healthy. We know, we know—you're busy. You don't have time for any more chores. Well, these take only a few minutes once a month, so quit whining.

Breast Self-examination

Examining your breasts takes five minutes and it could save your breasts and your life. That should be enough persuasion, but it doesn't seem to be for most women. We used up all our scare tactics in the talk about doctor visits, so let's just let the argument for self-examination rest on logic and a few simple facts. One in fourteen women will develop breast cancer at some point. The vast majority of cancerous lumps (90 percent) are discovered by the women themselves, not by doctors. A woman who conducts monthly exams is far more familiar with the feel of her breasts than even the best physician and is more likely to discover a small lump in the early stages of development. That woman has a far greater chance of keeping her breast and her life than a woman who makes do with an annual exam at the doctor's office. That's it in a nutshell.

Some doctors recommend that women begin breast self-examinations (BSEs) as soon as they have had their first period. Since breast cancer is fairly rare in women under 25, other doctors maintain that it's OK for women to put it off until they turn 25. We believe it's best to always be on the safe side. "Rare" does not mean impossible, especially if you have a family history of breast cancer or other types of cancer. No sense risking your life on the odds. Examine yourself once a month, every month, for the rest of your life.

The best time of the month for the BSE is right after your period ends and any swelling, discomfort, or tenderness has subsided. Make sure you aren't distracted or in a huge hurry. Many women find it easiest to do this right before a shower.

A BSE has two parts: looking and touching. You will find that the first few times you do this, it may take a little longer. Give yourself time to become familiar with the look and feel of your breasts. If you have questions or concerns, call your doctor.

Mirror, Mirror

First, take a good look at your breasts in a large mirror. Let your arms hang down at your sides and notice what they look like. Is one bigger than the other? (Almost all women have one breast that is larger than the other.) Is the contour smooth? Do you have any moles, birthmarks, swollen areas, or sores? Which way do your nipples point? What is the size and color of your areoles? Can you see bluish veins through your skin?

The point here is to become familiar with the look of your breasts so that you can notice any future changes. Veins, moles, and birthmarks are perfectly normal, but unexplained changes in appearance could be a problem. Areolas can be seashell pink to chocolate brown to plum-colored, or anything in between, and they can be as small as a bottle cap or as wide as a wine glass, but if you notice a different-colored patch, a dimple, or a change in shape, that also means you should see a doctor. You are looking for irregularities: if you find dimples, puckers, odd shapes, changes in the size or shape of moles, unexplained sores or rough patches, lumps, or anything out of the ordinary, you should let your doctor check it out. Remember, breast cancer is fairly rare. Abnormalities—even lumps—are not usually cancerous.

Continue to observe your breasts as you move your arms in different positions. Put your hands on your hips and squeeze your chest muscles, and look at your breasts from the front and sides. Check for any disruption of the smooth contour of your breast. Then, press your hands together in front of your chest and check yourself again. Finally, put your hands behind your head and check one more time. This may seem like a pain, but it does get easier and faster with time.

Feel Your Way

For those of you who were worried that palpation ended in the doctor's office, take heart! Now, through the miracle of BSEs, you can palpate yourself, without an appointment, in your very own home! Yes, the touching part of the BSE involves examining each breast by pressing methodically around your entire breast area.

But let's not leave out the nipple. First, squeeze each nipple gently to check for any discharge (that's any liquid). If you see discharge, *don't panic.* Lots and lots of women have it, and it's rarely a problem; however, if you do have any discharge, you *must* go to the doctor to have it checked out, just in case.

Next, go lie down somewhere comfortable. This spreads your breast tissue out so you can feel it more accurately. Put one hand behind your head (this stretches the tissue even more) and imagine there is a circle drawn around that entire breast. Then, with your other hand, start pressing firmly, moving your hand an inch at a time, around that circle (see diagram). Keep

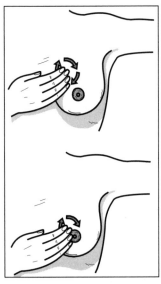

Breast self-examination.

pressing in smaller and smaller circles until you reach your nipple. Make sure you check your armpit area, too—that's where your lymph nodes are. After you are done with one breast, repeat this process on the other one.

What you are looking for is hard lumps, swollen lymph nodes, or bumps. The irritating thing is that breasts *are* lumpy. There are glands, muscle, bone, benign fibrous cysts (common, harmless lumps). How are you supposed to tell what's a bad lump and what's a regular part of your breast? Well, it may take a few months and a few visits to the doctor. Many doctors have models to help show you what a "bad" lump feels like, and all gynecologists can explain what you feel in your own breasts. If you are troubled by something you feel, have your doctor check it out. It's very unlikely that anything is wrong, and at least you'll know what's normal and what's not. After about six months of BSEs, you'll be a pro!

SELF-EXAMINATION FOR MEN

Women are not the only ones who have a responsibility to check themselves out regularly. Men must also check once a month to make sure that all is well below the belt. This is especially important for sexually active men, and even more important for men who are particularly successful at being sexually active.

First, grab a hand mirror and go somewhere where there is a good amount of light. If you are uncircumcised, pull back the foreskin. Take a close look at the head of your penis and the urinary opening. Look for roughness, redness, sores, bumps, blisters, or anything else out of the ordinary. Is there any discharge (liquid) at the urinary opening?

You'll also want to examine the shaft of your penis, looking for the same problems. The hand mirror will help you check the underside and base of the penis. Make sure to spread your pubic hairs apart and check the base of your penis thoroughly. If you do see bumps, blisters, roughness, or discharge, make an appointment with a urologist right away. These are possible symptoms of a sexually transmitted disease (see page 93 for more details), and early diagnosis is important if you want to avoid complications or possibly spreading the disease. *Do not* decide to wait and see if the problem will go away. Just because a sore goes away or your discharge disappears does not mean you're all better. It could make the problem more serious and delay an accurate diagnosis. Without an accurate diagnosis, you can't get the treatment that will make you well.

Your Testicles and You

You might hear much less about testicular self-examinations than about breast examinations, but that doesn't mean they're less important. Every postpubescent man should be examining his testicles once a month.

You need to examine them when they are relaxed, so don't go running out into a snowdrift right beforehand. The best time is right after a shower or bath (a warm shower or bath, of course), when everything is hanging loose. While standing up, reach down and gently squeeze one testicle between two fingers and your thumb, rolling it carefully to check for lumps or changes in shape or size. Your testicle should feel firm and smooth, and should be shaped kind of like an egg. After you finish, examine the other testicle. Refer to the diagram on page 65 before you begin this examination. Some men may worry that they are discovering a lump when what they are actually feeling is the epididymis on the back of the testicles.

If you feel a hard lump, or if you feel any pain during the examination (unusual pain, that is, not the kind caused by accidentally squeezing your testicle too hard), make an appointment with a urologist right away.

CHAPTER 11

Difficulties and Dysfunctions

WE ARE EXPERIENCING TECHNICAL DIFFICULTIES: SOME COMMON (AND A FEW UNCOMMON) SEXUAL PROBLEMS

Nothing ever goes wrong with Brad Pitt's sex life. He gets rock-hard erections on demand, and goes for hours and hours, no matter how tired or stressed, bringing each woman he sleeps with to new levels of ecstasy. Same thing with Pamela Anderson Lee. The words "I'm not up to it" aren't in her vocabulary. She has multiple orgasms just thinking about surfboards and bikini briefs.

Yeah, that's what we've been made to think, anyway, which makes us mere, surgically unenhanced mortals feel lousy when there's even a minor hitch with our sex lives. There's no way to prove this for sure, but we'll go out on a limb here: everybody will have some sort of sexual problem or dysfunction at some point in their sex lives—even Brad Pitt. And while we can't say that Pamela Anderson Lee has ever had trouble achieving orgasm, we can point out that she is married (for now, at least) to a has-been drummer for a rock band that reached its prime while you were in grade school. That should be some consolation.

MALE SEXUAL PROBLEMS

Performance Anxiety

Excessive worrying about whether you're good in bed afflicts both men and women. In fact, in our survey, 17 percent of men and 12 percent of women cited performance anxiety as one of the big obstacles in their sex lives. A woman, however, can go through with sex even while feeling terribly insecure, whereas a man in the grips of doubt or anxiety might find the whole thing much more difficult.

Our study shows that 33 percent of men are unsure about how to satisfy their sexual partners. A man in college who is beginning a sexual relationship with one of his classmates is likely to discover he is not her first (or second, or third) partner. This troubles some men. They worry they won't measure up to past partners—either in penis size or technical skill. They worry about not being able to please the woman. They worry about their bellies being too big. They worry about their breath. The worry about everything.

All this worrying tends to bring about the result most feared: the man gets distracted by his fears and loses his erection, either during or before sex, or he fails to reach orgasm. This can happen during casual encounters (especially if you know your partner is more experienced than you), but the upsetting thing is that it happens more with someone you care about or are very attracted to. Ironically, the more you are worried about pleasing and impressing a woman, the harder it may be to do so. This is a *very* common problem: 50 percent of the male respondents to our survey said they had trouble maintaining erections at one point or another.

What to Do About It

Performance anxiety is probably the most common sexual problem for men, and it can be very tricky if it's not handled well by both parties involved. First off, some advice to the men: sex should be good for both of you. Don't become so preoccupied with your partner's pleasure or displeasure that you lose track of your own sensations. Remember, sex does not have to end with your orgasm. If your partner has not reached orgasm by the time you do, the sex has not been a failure. There are other ways you can please her (see pages 112 and 126).

Also, remember that performance anxiety usually diminishes as you become familiar with your partner. Both of you are likely to be nervous the first time you have sex. Keep your expectations moderate your first time together, and keep your sense of humor. Even if you do panic, it's not the end of the world. Explain to your partner that the source of your problem is concern for her. Don't take it too seriously, and everything will work out fine.

Now, women, if your partner panics or otherwise gets off track during sex, the most important thing for you to do is be considerate. The problem most likely is not that he doesn't find you attractive; it's the complete opposite—you're so attractive he thinks he's not worthy of such a beautiful creature! Do not ask him to reassure you at that moment. Above all, do not become angry or say anything unkind (that is, if you ever intend to have sex with him in the future). Depending on how your partner is reacting to his difficulty, try smiling or joking mildly about it. If he's upset, let him know it's not a big deal.

Erection Problems

The failure to achieve or maintain an erection can be terrifying for men. Giant, leaping penises have been prized symbols of manhood since ancient Greek times. They even had a god, Priapus, devoted completely to the penis and usually depicted with a member the size of a small tree. Attitudes haven't changed that much in the intervening centuries. If you've ever seen a porno movie, then you know that only the most imposing and enduring of the male members are given the starring roles and this just adds to size and performance phobia. Virility is considered central to the male identity.

Almost all men experience erection problems at some point in their lives. The really frustrating thing is that, once it happens, guys tend to get upset and worry that it's going to happen again. Then it does happen again. Then their brains start whizzing and humming with doubts and fears every time they think about having sex. A whizzing brain is big trouble.

Some Common Causes

The most common reason for erectile dysfunction is alcohol or drugs. In fact, 39 percent of the men who took our survey admitted that drugs or alcohol had caused them erection problems. If you're kind of drunk, your penis is probably going to be a reluctant participant in your sexual plans. Even if you think you really, really want to have sex, you won't be able to persuade it to go along. And, if you're really trashed, your penis is likely to go into hiding completely. Not even a parade of naked showgirls could get it to emerge. However, you'll likely find that as soon as you sober up, your penis will once again become it's perky, cooperative self.

Alcohol and drugs can also impede male orgasm. You may be drunk and really, really want to have sex and have no problem getting it up, but you may have a problem getting it down because you just can't seem to achieve an orgasm. Your partner may not object to this artificially inflated staying power, but you may wonder what's going wrong. It's the booze. Relax. It can

If you're too drunk to get it up when this parades through your room, you'll hate yourself. MICHAEL S. YAMASHITA/CORBIS

be frustrating, but it's a temporary problem. Just remember, alcohol, drugs, and sex don't usually add up to two satisfied people.

Other common, temporary causes of erectile dysfunction are stress and extreme fatigue. Much as you may hate to admit it, sometimes other emotional and bodily demands take precedence over the sexual urge. Men who have experienced a recent emotional trauma (like the death of a loved one) may find themselves temporarily unable to have an erection. Men who are under a lot of stress might also experience erection problems. Also, men who are physically exhausted sometimes find that their penises are tired, too.

Prolonged erectile dysfunction, especially within the context of an established sexual relationship, can have psychological roots and can be a symptom of a deeper problem in the relationship. Erectile dysfunction of this sort can also have a physical explanation. Certain medications are known to inhibit erections. Hormonal imbalances, diabetes, urological problems, and other physical problems can also lead to erection problems.

What to Do About It

In the case of alcohol-related erectile dysfunction, the solution is obvious: don't get drunk if you want to have good sex. For tired men, the solution is to get some rest. For men under stress or emotional strain, the best advice is to go easy on yourself. Allow yourself time to come to terms with your feelings or get past a stressful period.

If you experience erection problems for more than a period of three weeks, and you are concerned about it, you might want to consider seeing a psychological counselor. Seeing a counselor is not the same as seeing a psychotherapist or psychiatrist. Counselors and psychologists, unlike psychiatrists, are not medical doctors. They will not prescribe drugs. They will not make you lie down on a couch and talk about how you were toilet trained. They are highly trained professionals who can provide you with short-term help when you are having difficulty working through a difficult situation on your own. Most likely, your college has psychologists available for you to talk with free of charge. You can call your health center to find out what your options are.

Men with prolonged erectile dysfunctions that doesn't seem to be connected with an emotional trauma should see a doctor to rule out a physical cause. If no physical cause can be found, the doctor will probably recommend that you, and possibly your partner, seek counseling to find the root of the problem.

Good Reads

New Male Sexuality (Bantam Books, 1993), by Bernie Zilbergeld, is a great reference book for guys who are either experiencing or curious about male sexual dysfunctions.
For Yourself: The Fulfillment of Female Sexuality (Doubleday, 1976), by Lonnie Barbach, is a must for women who have difficulty with orgasm, and *For Each Other: Sharing Sexual Intimacy* (Doubleday, 1983), also by Barbach, covers many other female complaints.

Premature Ejaculation

You've probably all heard the phrase "premature ejaculation." You may be surprised to know that there is no hard-and-fast clinical definition for what it means. Twenty-five or thirty years ago, arbitrary measurements such as duration of intercourse or number of strokes were used to diagnose this "disorder" (in case you're wondering, two minutes was considered the minimum required duration), but today doctors and therapists focus on the mutual satisfaction of the sexual partners as the means for determining whether ejaculation is premature. If both partners are satisfied, there is no problem.

Many men, however, report that either in the past or currently they have ejaculated more rapidly than they wanted and have applied the label "premature ejaculation" to their problem. But the definition seems to vary from man to man. For some, premature ejaculation might be any orgasm that happened "accidentally" or that wasn't fully controlled by them. Others actually set time limits on themselves and consider themselves premature if they can't last for a specific length of time. Some men consider their orgasms premature if their partners haven't reached orgasm before they do.

Some men feel that, to be a good lover, they must be able to postpone orgasm for hours and hours. Not only is this not true, it is not necessarily desirable for women. Intercourse that lasts too long can actually be downright uncomfortable for a woman, and insisting on continuing until she has her orgasm can tend to make the whole thing seem like a chore. Remember, there are many ways for both of you to be satisfied, so put your watch away.

That said, let's turn our attention to what we'll call "very rapid ejaculation." This is ejaculation that occurs within a few seconds of vaginal contact or even before penetration. Very rapid ejaculation can be very frustrating to both partners and can have a variety of causes. Luckily, almost all men who have problems with very rapid ejaculation can learn to control their responses.

Some Common Causes

Perhaps the most common causes are lack of sexual experience, extreme arousal, and long periods of sexual inactivity (sometimes termed the "dry spell"), or some combination of these three factors. These are problems that plague college students: 23 percent reported experiencing a three-month dry spell, 23 percent more reported that they had gone six months with no sex, and 34 percent said that they had gone more than a year without sex at some point. Many men recall ejaculating very quickly during their first sexual encounter, probably because of the combination of nervousness and excitement. The same factors exist for a man who has not had sex in a long time. Unfortunately, many men find this anticlimactic (excuse the pun): after waiting for sex for so long, they find it's over practically before it begins.

What to Do About It

Very rapid ejaculation is not necessarily a problem, especially if it occurs infrequently. For example, some men find that they ejaculate quickly with a new partner because of extreme arousal, but that doesn't mean the sex is over. You can continue to stimulate your partner, either orally or manually. It's likely you will develop another erection, and by that time you will have settled down enough to enjoy more leisurely intercourse.

However, if very rapid ejaculation continues to be a problem after your first encounter with someone, you may need to go into "orgasm training."

The first thing you must do is get to know your own sexual responses. The best way to do this is through masturbation. There will come a point when you feel orgasm is about to occur, but you could still stop it. Train yourself to recognize this feeling. During masturbation, bring yourself to this peak, then stop whatever stimulation you are using and wait for the feeling of impending orgasm to go away. Then continue the stimulation again, stopping again when you feel on the brink. Do this three times before allowing yourself to have an orgasm. There are worse forms of physical training.

If you can't get the kind of control over your ejaculation that you want, you should see a sex therapist. Almost all men who experience very rapid ejaculation for nonmedical reasons can solve their problem through therapy.

Painful Sex

Pain is nature's way of telling you something is wrong. If you or your partner experiences unexplained pain during, before, or after sex, you should see a doctor. There are many different disorders that can cause pain in the genitals, and most are easy to fix, so don't put up with it!

FEMALE SEXUAL PROBLEMS

Lack of Orgasm and Sexual Inhibition

Even now, nearly thirty years after the sexual revolution, women are being brought up to feel ambivalent about their sexuality. We may talk about sexual freedom being the right of all women, but scratch the surface and you'll find that even educated young people still have hang-ups about female sexuality. The old rule that "nice girls don't" is even more complicated now: nice girls might, but only in some circumstances.

Our survey shows that the old sexual double standard might be giving way at least a little—or at least the same moral code is being applied equally.

It is considered almost as bad for a man to have multiple sexual partners as it is for a woman: 77 percent said it was not fine for a man to sleep around, and 79 percent said women shouldn't either.

The most unfortunate effect of the stigmatization of female sexuality is that it keeps women from enjoying sex fully. This problem can manifest itself in several ways, from failure to become aroused to reluctance to perform certain sex acts, but the roots are the same: somewhere along the line, the woman developed negative feelings about her sexuality. What makes matters worse is that today, while there is still a double standard, women are supposed to be erotic dynamos capable of dazzling sexual acrobatics and countless orgasms. If they aren't, they have some kind of hang-up. In effect, they are stigmatized for being stigmatized.

We can trace the problem in part to the fact that, before the 1960s, few people realized the important role of the clitoris in arousal and orgasm. Yes, Freud strikes again. Doctors (who were mostly men) accepted the pronouncement of the father of psychotherapy that "real" orgasms came from vaginal stimulation, and the clitoral orgasms were the product of an immature sexuality. We now know that the clitoris is in some way involved in all female orgasms, and many women need direct stimulation of the clitoris to achieve orgasms at all (see Chapter 5). Unfortunately, misconceptions about the all-important clitoris left countless women unaroused and unsatisfied. Thankfully, this term isn't bandied about the way it used to be. If a woman isn't enjoying sex, it's generally considered a case of miscommunication that can be rectified if she explains her likes and dislikes and her partner listens.

There are, however, many psychological factors that can lead a woman to react negatively toward sex, and these are much harder to address. A woman with such psychological blocks may not show any interest in sex whatsoever. If she has a boyfriend or husband, she may try to avoid sex and put off her partner's advance. She often finds it extremely difficult to communicate about sex, and if she participates in intercourse at all, she may find herself hoping for the act to end as quickly as possible.

Past sexual, physical, or emotional abuse can definitely cause problems, especially if the woman was abused as a child by a family member. Rape or date rape (see Chapter 12) can also deeply traumatize a woman. Even an overly repressive or punitive upbringing can form negative attitudes toward sex. Talking about these issues with your partner may take a long time and require more help than you alone are able to provide, but one thing should be understood: if you know your partner has experienced some form of sexual trauma, don't push the subject of sex (you'll just reinforce the barriers

But could he always keep his cigar up?
LIBRARY OF CONGRESS/CORBIS-BETTMAN

that are already there) and don't feel rejected, because it isn't your fault nor is your desirability at stake. Be as understanding as you possibly can. Trust, especially sexual trust, comes even harder than normal for anyone who's been a victim.

Lack of Orgasm

Among respondents to our survey, 13 percent of the women reported that they had never had an orgasm by any means. Lack of orgasm is a problem that can be attributed either to the misconceptions and miscommunication we talked about above or to deeper psychological reasons we just described. Almost all women can learn to have orgasms, both alone and with a partner. See Chapter 5 for more information about the female orgasm.

Sexual Inhibitions

"Inhibition" is another slippery term that means widely different things to different people. Women who refuse to have sex with the lights on might be described as sexually inhibited. (Interestingly enough, 64 percent of the women we surveyed said they would prefer to keep the lights out during sex, because they are embarrassed.) So might women who refuse to perform oral sex. Or those who refuse to have anal sex, or sex in a certain position, or sex outside. The problem is, all these things are relative.

A woman is perfectly within her rights not to want to have intercourse at all. If she feels she is leading a happy, full, satisfying life without sex, great. If she doesn't like performing fellatio or having anal sex, and her partner feels satisfied, that's not a problem either. The difficulty arises when one partner wants to do something and the other doesn't.

Such "inhibitions" can be a matter of personal preference (a woman might simply dislike the way a certain sex act feels) or moral or religious beliefs, the result of negative attitudes toward sex (as described above), fear, or lack of trust. Because of this, any disagreement over sexual practices must be approached with great consideration and respect.

What to Do About It

If your partner wants to do something that you're uncomfortable with, by all means do not feel obliged to do it. Think carefully, however, about why you object. Shutting yourself off to new sexual acts definitely limits the types of pleasure you and your partner can share. If you are frightened or uncertain about something, tell your partner about it. He might be able to give you the reassurances you need or clear up some misunderstandings you might have. (A prerequisite here is that your partner is someone you trust. If you think your partner would do something that might hurt you or would ignore your feelings, you should dump him or her pronto, or at least seriously rethink getting naked with that person.)

If you're still not sure, do a little research on the topic. Ask some close friends, read relevant parts of this book. Don't be afraid to try new things, but not if you find them upsetting. Don't force yourself—some ideas need to germinate for a while before they bloom, and some sexual acts are much more enjoyable within the context of a strong, established relationship than they are in the early stages of a romance. Put the issue on a back burner, and return to it later.

Uncertainty isn't the only reason you might refuse some form of sex. Say you tried having sex with your knees up around your ears (this is only an example, by the way) and it was downright uncomfortable. Well, one bad experience doesn't necessarily mean the whole idea is out of the question. Consider giving it a second chance. If you are absolutely certain that you hate it, however, your partner is just going to have to deal with it. We can't all like everything.

If you are troubled by strong negative feelings about sex, a caring, patient partner is very important, but usually not nearly enough to fully address the problem. You should see a counselor or psychologist, even if you can't think of any reason for your feelings. In fact, it's precisely because you might not be able to figure out why you feel the way you do that you should seek professional help. Painful memories and feelings are often pushed away deep down inside. It may be more comfortable in the short run to leave those feelings alone, but you will be hampered by them throughout your life unless you get the help you need and work through them.

Vaginismus

Vaginismus describes acute pain felt during any penetration of the vagina, whether by a penis, a tampon, a finger, or a medical instrument. The muscles around the opening of the vagina contract involuntarily, making penetration impossible or very painful.

It's been estimated that from 2 to 9 percent of women experience vaginismus. The cause is psychological, but the symptoms are very real and physical. Because of strong negative feelings or past trauma, the body reacts to the prospect of penetration with this protective reflex. It is very important to note that vaginismus is an unconscious reaction—it's not something you can be coaxed or argued out of. You may even feel you want to have sex, but your body will not cooperate.

What to Do About It

The good news is that vaginismus is almost always curable, although you'll need to see a sex therapist or psychotherapist to get the help you need. A combination of counseling and special exercises usually does the trick. Ask your gynecologist (or a doctor at your college health facility) for a referral.

Know Your Body, Know Your Options

The female reproductive system is very complicated. The disorders and issues that we mention here and in Chapter 4 are only the most common. It's very important that you understand how your body works, and a book on women's health issues is a good place to start. Most bookstore chains now have a women's health or women's issues section, where you'll find several books on this topic. We highly recommend *The New Our Bodies, Ourselves: A Book By Women For Women,* written by the Boston Women's Health Book Collective (Simon & Schuster, 1992). It's extremely thorough and friendly.

Vaginitis and Yeast Infections

Vaginitis is the general term to describe any infection of the vagina. All healthy women have certain bacteria present in their vaginas. These bacteria perform useful functions, such as destroying harmful organisms and maintaining the proper acidity. The vagina is a moist area of the body, and most women will notice this moisture around the opening of their vaginas or on their underwear. This is what is referred to as "discharge," and in a healthy woman it can be slick and clear, milky and sticky, or even kind of thick, depending on where she is in her menstrual cycle. This discharge is virtually odorless, and it is completely normal.

The yeast fungus may also be present in the vagina. This isn't necessarily bad, unless the yeast organisms start to reproduce or get out of control and cause a yeast infection (also known as candida). A yeast infection creates a clumpy, thick discharge with a strong yeasty smell, kind of like bread (only not as nice). An itching or burning sensation in the vagina accompanies this discharge. Most women will get a yeast infection at some point in their lives. They are generally brought on by stress, illness, bad diet, or prolonged use of an antibiotic (the antibiotic kills the bacteria in the vagina that stave off the yeast explosion). For some women, yeast infections are a frequent and particularly annoying problem.

If you notice you have a grayish, foamy discharge that is especially foul smelling (like a fish gone wrong), that's the sign of another sort of common vaginal infection: trichomoniasis (commonly known as "trich") or bacterial vaginosis. Both these infections can be transmitted sexually, but they can also be contracted through contact with contaminated washcloths, towels, and even wet toilet seats. Your mother was right after all! You shouldn't sit on public toilet seats. Men can also be affected by these infections and will experience similar discharge from their urinary openings. Sometimes, the man will have symptoms before the woman, because the infection in the woman is dormant. If this happens, please be communicative; otherwise, the problem will just go on repeating itself.

Women who have or suspect they have a vaginal infection should not have unprotected sex until they are cured. Women with vaginal infections—yeast infections especially—usually don't feel very much like having sex anyway.

What to Do About It

You may have seen a lot of advertisements on television and in magazines for over-the-counter cures for yeast infections. These treatments are very effective and useful for women who have problems with recurring yeast infections. However, only women who have been diagnosed by a doctor in the past and are absolutely sure that they are suffering from another yeast infection should use these treatments. If you've never had a yeast infection before or are unsure about your symptoms, do not treat yourself. Let your gynecologist check you out first. Any medication you apply might only mask your symptoms, making a diagnosis and cure more difficult.

Yeast infections and other vaginal infections are cured with vaginal suppositories, oral medication, or both. It can take a few days to a week to clear up the problem, but relief from itching and pain often takes just a day or two. As we just pointed out, even though vaginal infections aren't usually listed as sexually transmitted diseases, you can transmit these problems to your partner through sex. Avoid intercourse or use a condom.

You can help prevent these and other vaginal infections by making sure you keep the vaginal area clean and dry. Wash with warm water daily. Wear comfortably loose cotton underwear (cotton does not trap moisture). Wash your underwear with hot water and soap. After using the rest room, wipe yourself from front to back, not back to front. Don't share underwear or washcloths. Pretty much common hygiene sense, right?

Too much alcohol, caffeine, and sugar leave some women open to these infections, so practice moderation. Get plenty of sleep and exercise to keep stress levels low. Some women also swear by unsweetened cranberry juice (taken orally, that is). Cranberry juice makes the pH level of your urine more acidic, which alleviates some of the pain felt during infection (see the section on urinary tract infections below). As a preventative measure, it is unclear exactly how cranberry juice works, but doctors recommend it, many women are convinced, it's a great source of vitamin C, and it certainly doesn't hurt, so why not drink a glass a day?

Urinary Tract Infections and Cystitis

Urinary tract infections (UTIs) are another very common problem that most women experience at least once. A UTI is, quite simply, an infection of the urinary tract. The most common form is cystitis, an infection of the bladder. The infection or irritation can be caused by a whole host of things: bacteria in the urethra, lowered resistance due to stress or illness, irritation from soap or bubble bath, too much caffeine or alcohol, a sudden increase in sexual activity, careless hygiene. Cystitis is not a serious condition if treated promptly. If you do not seek treatment, the infection can spread to your kidneys, which is a serious problem. Luckily (or unluckily, you may decide) the symptoms of a urinary tract infection are almost impossible to ignore and usually send even the bravest of women scampering to the doctor.

The first symptom of a UTI you might encounter is the sensation that you need to urinate every couple of minutes, but when you try, it stings or burns and almost nothing comes out. The pain seems to increase every time you try to urinate. You may also feel a dull pain near your pubic bone. The symptom that freaks most women out (aside from the intense pain) is the appearance of blood or pus in the urine (this doesn't always happen).

UTIs have quite a range of severity. Some are just irritations, not bacterial infections, and can be taken care of at home. Luckily, this is usually the case. But if a bacterial infection is involved, especially if accompanied by fever or vomiting, you must see a doctor quickly.

What to Do About It

When in doubt, it's always best to go to the gynecologist. If you've never had a UTI before, even a mild case will be distressing. Go get a definitive diagnosis. If you see blood or pus, you've got a whopping case of cystitis, so definitely see a doctor right away. If your symptoms persist for more than a day or two (and we'd err on the earlier side), go to the doctor.

Your doctor will ask you for a urine sample and will conduct a pelvic exam to rule out other problems. Then, he or she will give you what you need: the magical drugs to take that nasty pain away. Usually, you will be given some type of antibiotic, which you may have to take for several days. In the case of extreme pain, there is a drug called Pyridium that does an effective job at anesthetizing the urinary tract quickly. If your doctor gives it to you in the office, you will probably feel better before you get home. Pyridium does not do anything for the infection, but at that point, pain is your primary problem. Pyridium also dyes your urine a bright, glowing orange that can stain clothing.

If you've had a UTI before, you know the only thing you care about, once the symptoms start, is making the pain stop. There is now an over-the-counter version of Pyridium you can take to relieve the pain while you make arrangements to see the doctor. It is called Uristat;tm. Remember, even though it makes you feel better, you are not cured. You must go to the doctor. The medicine just lets you sit in the doctor's office more comfortably.

Once you've had a UTI, you will never forget the symptoms. There are several things you can do to try to nip the problem in the bud if you feel the beginnings of an infection or irritation. First, get yourself a big bottle of cranberry juice (unsweetened is better because sugar can be irritating, but sweetened will do in a pinch). Drink a couple of glasses and follow it up with as much water as you can force into yourself. Cranberry juice (as we pointed out above) makes the pH level of your urine more acidic, which alleviates the pain and makes your urethra less friendly to bacteria. Drinking plenty of water is always a good idea, but it's especially important when you have a UTI. You have to flush yourself out. Taking a warm bath—without soap bubbles or soap—can also relieve your discomfort.

There are several things you can do to cut your chances of developing a UTI. Drink at least eight big glasses of water a day, for one thing. Don't overdo the coffee, soda, tea, or alcohol. Don't hold your urine in—urinate whenever you feel the need. If you wear sanitary pads during your period, change them frequently. Avoid using strongly perfumed soaps on your genitals—they can cause irritation.

Douching Is Dumb

Unless your doctor specifically tells you to douche for some reason, do not. Your vagina does not need cleaning. It has its own highly refined cleansing process and a delicate pH balance. Douching messes up the acidity level of the vagina, can irritate the tissue of the vaginal walls, and can bring on yeast infections and urinary tract infections faster than you can say "ouch."

A healthy vagina does not smell bad. If you notice a strong, bad odor, it is the sign of a health problem that should be treated by a doctor. Douching will not help and it definitely could hurt. Why anyone ever thought that a woman's vagina should smell like "Garden of the Ocean Mist" or "Sunny Tulip Breeze" or "Enchanted April" is a mystery. You'd never catch a man spritzing cologne on his penis. While we're on the subject, keep those feminine deodorant sprays far, far away from your genitals. They contain harsh chemicals that can irritate that very sensitive area.

Sexually active women should make sure their partner's hands and genitals are clean before having sex. Be careful to avoid spreading any bacteria from the anus to the vaginal area (whether on a condom or through manual contact). Also, try to urinate just before sex and always urinate just after sex. This can clear out anything that's liable to cause an infection. It may not be particularly romantic to hop right out of bed and head for the bathroom, but a UTI is not particularly romantic either.

The disorders we've mentioned are only common examples of those problems that might throw a hitch in your sex life. Good sexual health depends on good information, however, and men and women both should become familiar with the workings of their own bodies and their partners' bodies. There are other problems that can foul up your sex life, some of them for your entire life. These are not dysfunctions or infections, but serious diseases, such as syphilis, herpes, and the HIV virus. You do not want to get any of these or their lesser cousins, and you can make sure that you don't. Yes, it's scary, it's pretty grim, and it's a serious concern, so read Chapter 4 now that we're on the subject.

CHAPTER 12 # Rape and Date Rape

The number of women on college campuses who experience some form of sexual coercion and/or rape is alarming. College should be a time and a place where students can explore and learn about anything they wish, including sex, in a healthy, safe, and communicative environment. Sadly, this is not the case on America's campuses today, despite the best efforts of students and administrators to educate and intervene. With this chapter we hope to show you the reality of the danger of these abuses on campus, how to protect yourself, and how to keep yourself and others from ever going through such an experience, one that should never have to be associated with sex.

There are many forms of sexual coercion, from taking advantage of someone whose judgment is impaired due to alcohol or other substances to aggressive verbal coercion and, worst of all, rape. The past few years have seen much debate on the definition of rape, as opposed to date rape, and the subject is so sensitive that there is always the risk that it will be talked right over and ignored. That won't happen here. We'll start with clear definitions of terms. These terms are derived from the wording of federal statutes that legally define rape and sexual coercion.

 *Why all these terms?*

With the possible exception of abortion, rape and its definition will be the most sensitive issue you and your classmates will ever face, especially on a

Rape   The legal definition according to federal law is: physically forcing an unwilling person to perform sexual acts, by physically restraining them, assaulting them, threatening them with a weapon (including fists), or otherwise threatening their physical well-being in some way.

Date or acquaintance rape   Same as above, only the assailant is someone the victim knows, possibly even someone the victim has had some sort of physical or sexual contact with before.

Aggressive verbal coercion   The act of compelling an unwilling person to perform sexual acts through verbal threats, intimidation, or the exploitation of fears and anxieties.

Sexual coercion   The broad term we will use to cover rape, date rape, aggressive verbal coercion, and any other form of nonconsensual sex.

campus where it is not unlikely that students will know both a victim and her attacker, and partisan lines will be drawn across campus when supporters of the innocence of one or the credibility of the other take their sides. In fact, the term "date rape" became necessary because of the public reluctance to accept the label of "rape" to describe an act involving two people who know each other socially. When people—even within our court system—heard "rape," it conjured up the image of an unknown male assailant who used potentially deadly force that resulted in observable physical injuries to force a woman into performing a sexual act. This image obviously doesn't fit the experience of some of the thousands of women who will have unwanted sex this year. The plain fact is that the majority of rape victims know their attackers.

The original common-law definition of rape deems it "unlawful sexual intercourse with a female without her consent." What, exactly, is unlawful sexual intercourse?, you might ask. There used to be some strange loopholes for married couples on the books (who could only have *lawful* sexual intercourse in the eyes of the court), but those have since been removed. The common-law definition has since been replaced by federal law, which states that it is against the law to knowingly cause another person to engage in a sexual act by force or threat. The federal law has been adopted by most of the states in their sexual assault statutes and has also been rendered non-gender-specific. Where forced penetration was an essential part of meeting the common-law definition, the federal law makes no such limitation, although to prove a rape in court, evidence of penetration can still be a crucial factor. The legal issues are complicated and if you want to know more, please visit your college's health center, where they should be able to provide you with litera-ture and references that will help you answer your questions.

? Have you ever been stalked or harassed with obscene phone calls?

In the first incidence of what you will see in this chapter as a grim trend, nearly twice the number of female students than males can answer yes to this question: 45 percent of the women and 25 percent of the men said yes.

? Has there ever been anything that someone wanted you to do that you wouldn't do?

We didn't ask for specifics about what activity was being proposed by their partners, but 70 percent of the women said that there have been activities they did not want to do, although their partners did. Only 30 percent of the men had encountered the same problem.

? Have you ever said no to someone's advances?

The overwhelming majority of women, 92 percent, have rejected someone's sexual advances, while 68 percent of the men also have. Read from this sta-tistic what you will, but it is clear that women are more often exposed to this kind of sexual pressure than men are.

? Has a date, sexual partner, or friend ever physically forced you into a sexual act?

Eleven percent of college men say they have been forced into a sexual act by an acquaintance, whereas 29 percent of our female respondents have expe-rienced this. That is close to one third of college women who have been forced into a sexual act by someone they know and probably trusted. It is worth noting that 40 percent of our gay and bisexual female respondents answered yes to this question, the highest percentage of the college popula-tion to experience this form of coercion.

? If forced into a sexual act by a date, sex partner, or friend, did you consider it rape?

As an objective reader, you might think the answer to this question is obvi-ous, but that is far from the truth. Of the women who had experienced sex-

> ### Acquaintance Rape
>
> A 1993 study of women at three midwestern universities showed that, of all the women surveyed, 42 percent had been victims of some sort of sexual coercion in dating situations while in college. Of these women, 70 percent had engaged in sexual intercourse as a result of feeling overwhelmed by a date's constant pressuring and arguments, a situation that can be legally defined as date rape. Further, of the 42 percent of women who had experienced some form of coercion, 39 percent had experienced a situation legally defined as rape at the hands of an acquaintance or date.[1]
>
> If you assumed that the majority of these cases occur in the freshmen and sophomore years when students are not as aware of the dangers of certain aspects of campus life (Greek parties, effects of alcohol and drugs), think again. In the 1993 study, the majority of victims were juniors and seniors who dated often.
>
> A study conducted at a southern state university revealed that 9.8 percent of female undergraduates had experienced a forced sexual encounter in the previous year, with 4.9 percent of these victims having been forced into either oral sex or sexual intercourse. Both of these acts meet Florida's legal definition of felonious sexual battery punishable by forty years to life imprisonment. The study projected that, if the percentages were accurate, 494 women out of the 10,087 students at the university were victims of sexual battery in a given year on campus.[2]

ual coercion at the hands of a friend, lover, or dating partner, 51 percent considered it rape, while the remaining 49 percent did not. The men were even more lenient: only 11 percent of them considered it rape. And, while only 33 percent of the freshmen respondents considered this experience rape, 60 percent of the seniors did.

> ### What Percentage of Female Students Lose Their Virginity Due to Some Form of Sex Crime in College?
>
> A study done at a midwestern university researching the first sexual experiences of college students revealed that 14 percent of the women surveyed had their first experience with sexual intercourse against their will. The nature of the offense was not made clear—whether it was a date rape or a rape by a stranger—but the percentage is still high enough to be quite disturbing. Interestingly enough, 1 percent of the women in the study reported having their first sexual intercourse experience against the will of their partners, the male being the victim of unwanted sexual activity. Of the men in the study, 2 percent admitted that their first sexual intercourse experience was against the will of their partners.[3]

? *Have you ever tried to get someone drunk or high to get them into bed?*

Of the college students answering that they've done this, 30 percent were men and 14 percent were women, accounting for 21 percent of the overall college population who have tried to use drugs and alcohol to get someone to submit to sexual activity they might not otherwise consent to. That is a fifth of the college population, so it is safe to say that this practice is not uncommon. Of the students who have used this tactic, 6 percent of the men and 3 percent of the women say they would do it again. You must be careful when you're partying—a subject we'll further discuss later in the chapter.

? *Have you ever had sex with someone who was drunk or high?*

The majority of college students, 76 percent of them, have had sex with a partner who was drunk or high. While 73 percent of the men have had a partner under the influence of drugs or alcohol, 77 percent of the women had. This is not so strange when you consider how many students experiment with drugs and alcohol during sexual encounters (see Chapter 7 for more on this).

Sex, Drugs, and Alcohol

Studies show that in instances of forced sexual behavior, involving either verbal or physical coercion, nearly all incidents occur when either the victim, the perpetrator, or both are using drugs and/or alcohol. According to a 1986 study of undergraduate women, 25.9 percent report having experienced acquaintances trying to force themselves on them sexually when they were under the influence of alcohol or drugs. Another 31.3 percent of the women report having had unwanted sex when under the influence of drugs or alcohol that the man had provided. Clearly, the presence of mind-altering substances can lead some women into places of extreme jeopardy and can lead men into taking advantage of acquaintances.[4]

? *Have you ever had sex with an incoherently drunk or unconscious partner?*

This is not very common on campus: 7 percent of college men have had sex with partners who were unaware of what was going on and 3 percent of

> **Alcohol, Fraternities, and Rape**
>
> In her terrifying book, *Fraternity Gang Rape* (New York University Press, 1990), Peggy Reeves Sanday documents three case studies of gang rape performed by members of fraternities, although she points out that gang rape also occurs in association with athletic teams (another form of fraternity) as well as in residence halls. Drugs and alcohol were *always* present, and the gang bangs or "pulling train" generally occurred during or after a party. The victim was invariably a female student who was not in control of her faculties due to drugs or alcohol. You may hear stories of women who supposedly consented to this activity, but such tales are usually lies.
>
> Sanday documents one case in which a female in one of her classes had taken four hits of the powerful hallucinogen LSD before attending a fraternity party, at which she also drank and eventually passed out. When she awoke, she was half dressed on a couch in the main room of the fraternity, at which point one of the brothers dressed her, picked her up, and brought her upstairs to a bedroom where she was raped by several men. She was barely conscious and unable to push them off. The perpetrators of this crime were not convicted and the incident was largely ignored by the school.

women have also. Still, this activity does occur and is something to be aware of, especially when you are partying hard on campus.

? Has a partner ever physically resisted your attempts to have sex with him or her?

It will probably come as no surprise to anyone that men are in the majority here. According to our respondents, 17 percent of college men report that they have had partners who have resisted their attempts at sex, while 9 percent of the women can say the same of their partners. After resistance was met, 47 percent of the men went through with intercourse in spite of their partners' physical resistance, as did 39 percent of the women. The only encouraging thing about these statistics is that a lot of students are less likely to ignore their partner's physical resistance to sex than to ignore it. Of the overall college population, only 56 percent didn't go through with intercourse after their partners had resisted them physically.

? In your opinion, if two people are having intercourse and one asks the other to stop and the person doesn't stop, is that rape?

This is a question that has haunted victims, accused attackers, courts, and college students. It is a difficult question to answer since the scenario indicated makes the label "rape" hard to assign for many people. You will get no consensus on the answer to this question, since people have a hard time agreeing on what constitutes rape. Here's how our respondents answered:

Answer	% Overall	% Men	% Women
Yes, it is rape.	67	58	74
No, it is not rape.	9	11	6
It is unclear.	25	30	20

While the majority thought it was rape (notably a significantly higher number of women thought it was rape), a full quarter of the college population couldn't make a judgment call because, in the context of the scenario, it was too unclear for them to decide.

When Is It Rape?

You will not get a definite answer to this question simply because people will disagree about what defines rape. A study on college student attitudes toward forcible date rape posed this hypothetical date rape scenario: "A male and female college student go out on a date. Afterward, they go to his apartment and sit in front of the fireplace for a while and sip a glass of wine. He kisses her and, even though she resists his advances, he uses his superior strength to force her to have sexual intercourse." After reading the scenario, students were given a set of nine circumstances to consider (such as "If she had let him touch her breasts," "If they had dated for a long time," "If she was drunk or stoned") and then asked "Is it rape?" Of the students responding to this survey, 18 percent maintained that the male's activity in the scenario was definitely unacceptable under any of the circumstances, while 11 percent did not consider the male's behavior definitely unacceptable under any of the circumstances. Bear in mind that there were women among the 11 percent, even though the majority were male. The remaining 71 percent fell between these polar opposites.[5]

Have you ever been the victim of a forcible rape by a stranger?

Overall, 2 percent of the college population has had to endure this terrible experience. Of that 2 percent, 1 percent were men and 3 percent were women. Projecting from this statistic, if you attend a middle- to large-size university with a student population of 10,000 students, 300 women have been raped by strangers.

We asked the respondents to this question where they went for help. Here are their answers:

Source of help	% Overall	% Men	% Women
Parents	63	32	74
Professional counselor	53	65	49
College or other health center	53	35	60
Church	5	0	7
Police	4	0	5
Rape crisis center	34	25	38
Support group	10	0	13
Other	17	0	23

If you are ever the victim of a rape, we strongly encourage you to seek help and guidance. Going to any of the options listed above is a good idea. However, first let's talk about how to avoid ever being put into a sexually coercive situation.

YES AND NO—TWO VERY IMPORTANT WORDS

As a rule, no means no, case closed, end of story. Then why does this question always come up? Does no ever mean yes? Can you say, "Open a can of worms?" Well, that's what you are doing when you ask this question, but the answer here may surprise you. If you are with someone you want to have sex with and the person returns the feeling, but, for whatever reason, you said no even when you fully intended to have sexual relations, then you have said no when meaning yes.

This is known as "token resistance" to sexual intercourse and plenty of people do it. A study of college students at five different universities across the United States revealed that 38 percent of women had said no when meaning yes and 47 percent of the men had also done so. That's right, men were found to be in the majority. Of the subjects reporting token resistance to sex (both men and women), 44 percent reported doing it only once during the course of the encounter, 41 percent reported doing it two to three times, and 15 percent reported having done it four or more times. So, indeed, no sometimes does mean yes.[6]

But be careful with that knowledge, because there is a flip side to it. Sometimes yes can mean no (as if English and sexual communication weren't hard enough to understand already). If you are with someone who wishes to have sex with you when you do not, but for some reason you indicate that you want to, then that is saying yes when you mean no. Consent to unwanted sex happens for many reasons (and it is this very issue that is the cause of much debate on defining rape), such as peer pressure or intoxication, which we will discuss in more depth below. The same study (this time using only the nonvirigins surveyed) revealed that 35 percent of male and 55 percent of female undergrads had consented to unwanted sex. Of the respondents, 45 percent reported an occurrence of unwanted sex only once, while 45 percent said it had happened twice, 39 percent indicated it had happened two or three times, and 16 percent reported a frequency of four or more times.

When No Doesn't Work

Many types of coercion are used by men when attempting to convince a woman who doesn't want to have sex to engage in sex. They range from verbal coercion to threats of violence to actual physical injury. In a study taking a sample of 77 university females, 46 of them had experienced verbal persuasion and 11 percent had experienced verbal threats. Out of the 77 women, 12 had experienced physical intimidation, while 14 had been subject to physical abuse such as pushing and slapping.

Five of the women had been severely abused by being choked or beaten, and one had experienced assault with a weapon.[7] Keep in mind that these offenses occurred on college campuses, not on big city streets. The problem is very real and it is most likely that in four years of college you will know at least one person who has been the victim of a rape. Remember, for every victim there is at least one assailant, so you will probably also know at least one rapist, whether you realize it or not.

The yes and no issues, and the fact that they can be interchanged, may make you wonder if you're ever safe assuming what the other person wants. Well, as we have been stressing throughout this book, talk to your partner! Talk about anything and everything that bothers you, especially when it comes to your sex life. Sexual hang-ups and dissatisfactions that aren't talked about can lead to a lot of things, few of them good. In fact, lack of honest communication about sex is one reason the yeses and nos often get mixed up.

It is absolutely essential that you work to understand what your partner means, whether your partner is your longtime girlfriend or someone you just met. When in doubt, the best rule of thumb on a no response is to accept it at face value.

The Pavlov Syndrome—Expected Social Response

Nice women don't say yes and real men never say no. That is how our society has been trying to condition us for years and years, and even though this convention has been bucked hard in the last few decades, all you need to do is watch some television commercials to see how preconceived conceptions of gender are still ingrained in our society. It is precisely this bit of socialization that often results in token resistance to sex. Researchers Muelhlenhard and Hollabaugh reported that women may engage in token resistance for three major reasons:

- Practical reasons, such as fear of being labeled promiscuous—another socially gender-biased definition. Men don't seem particularly concerned about being labeled promiscuous.
- Moral or religious concerns about the repercussions of their actions—again, something that is reinforced by traditional societal or religious values.
- The desire to be in control of the sex in the relationship. People are still often taught that men should be the initiators of sexual activity. Women react by trying to take some control for themselves, and one socially acceptable control is saying no, even if they mean yes.[8]

As these three reasons demonstrate, token resistance is often related to deeply held sexual attitudes and beliefs. Women who exhibit token resistance usually accept various traditional ideas: that romantic relationships are often adversarial, that men are entitled to get what they want and may use force to do it, that women like men to overpower them, and that resisting sex is something nice girls must do. The basic idea is that, if a woman puts up some sort of fight, then she's not a tramp for having sex—she just gave in to the man's overwhelming sexuality. Women aren't the only ones acting out this script. These social myths also affect male sexual response.

For males, however, the stereotype works the opposite way, causing them to say yes when they mean no. Would a real man ever decline an opportunity to show himself as the sexual tyrannosaurus he really is? Of course not! It is just this sort of thinking that can cause men to consent to unwanted sex. Some studies have shown that more men have consented to unwanted sex than women, by a majority of 63 percent to 46 percent[9] in one study and 49 percent to 40 percent[10] in another. In the latter study, other reasons for men consenting to unwanted sex were enticement, altruism (which, as we saw in Chapter 7, is a factor in intercourse), inexperience, and intoxication.

It may be difficult to change something you've been socialized to do, but try your hardest to be honest in your words and actions. Do not, above all, twist this knowledge of token resistance to rationalize any form of sexual coercion. The idea that no always means yes and that a woman who resists a man's sexual advances just wants him to try harder is absolutely, positively not true. To be safe, you should always assume that no means no, and stop your sexual advances in the face of any resistance. If your partner was just putting up token resistance, she's likely to change her game plan and become much more straightforward when she realizes you intend to take her at her word.

The lesson to be learned here? Be aware of stereotypes and don't accept them as truths. Nice girls do say yes and real men do say no.

PREVENTION AND AVOIDANCE: SITUATIONS TO AVOID

Intoxication: Know When to Say No

Drugs and alcohol often play a significant role in date rape cases. The issue of consent becomes blurry when the judgment of the partners is impaired. Say, for instance, there is a couple in which the partners have mutually consented to having sex, but both are intoxicated. When they begin having sex, both are conscious, but during the act, the woman passes out. If the man continues to have sex with his unconscious partner, is that to be considered a rape? Probably not. But what if, upon waking the next day, the now-sober woman begins to regret the previous night's actions and *then* decides she didn't want to have sex. Now is it rape?

Muddled scenarios like these happen frequently on college campuses. Sometimes charges of rape are brought up. This is an unfortunate problem—for men as well as women—due solely to two things: drugs and alcohol. College students tend to unthinkingly act on sexual impulses when drunk, often with disastrous results.

Don't let yourself become incoherent or out of control on alcohol or other illicit substances. We're not saying you shouldn't have a good time. Partying is integral to much of college life. Just learn how to do it responsibly. An intoxicated person is an easy target for all sorts of criminals, rapists included. Never become so drunk that you become unaware of your actions and your surroundings. If you do intend to go out and party hearty on a given night, make sure you do so with several good friends so that you can all keep tabs on each other.

How Much Is Too Much?

As a college student, chances are you aren't an experienced drinker. In a way, this can be dangerous for you. If you do intend to drink while in college, you should familiarize yourself with a few guidelines—you don't want to put yourself in a dangerous situation.

- Don't drink and drive. Even if you have only a couple of drinks, your judgment and reflexes are impaired. Don't let someone who has been drinking drive you anywhere either. Call a cab. Many campuses also have chaperones you can call, where sober students escort drunk students home safe and sound.

- Eat something before you start drinking—preferably a cheeseburger or some pizza, or something with a lot of protein. Drinking on an empty stomach is the quickest way to wind up passed out in a gutter. Food slows the absorption of alcohol into your bloodstream.

- Say no to chugging, shotgunning, funneling, tubing, doing shots, or other drinking games or races. Sip your drink slowly. It's more fun to watch a bunch of idiots wind up with beer-soaked clothes than it is to join them.

- Don't drink the punch (or any unrecognizable liquid being served out of a tub or vat). Most punches served at college parties are liberally spiked with more than one potent alcohol, even (state law permitting) pure grain alcohol, which is twice as powerful as regular liquors and has almost no taste or smell. That sticky red/green/purple stuff may taste like candy going down, but . . . well, you get the picture.

- Pace yourself. Most women need two whole hours to metabolize one drink (a can of beer, a glass of wine, a regular-sized cocktail). That means if you want to stay sober, have one drink every other hour. Most men need one hour to metabolize one drink. If you drink more than this, you are going to get drunk. If you drink a lot more than this, you are going to get very drunk. Keep track of how much you've had to drink (take a pen with you and keep a tally on your arm, if necessary) and gauge your level of drunkenness periodically.

- Switch to water or soda. If you start to feel pretty drunk, you don't necessarily have to go home. Just stop drinking. Drink water or soda until you feel in control of yourself again.

- Keep in mind that 80 percent of the alcohol you drink is absorbed into your bloodstream immediately upon contact with your stomach, so even if you stop drinking or puke, you're not anywhere near being in the clear.

- Coffee doesn't help anyone get sober. If you are really drunk, drink water, not coffee. Water replenishes the liquid your body needs to get sober again and prevents you from dehydrating yourself. Coffee will only make you an awake drunk.

Studies have shown that drugs and/or alcohol were used by either the victim or perpetrator or both in nearly all incidents of sexual coercion and rape. You can avoid this situation by being responsible to yourself and not getting so wasted that you are incoherent or incapable of making decisions. We cannot stress this point enough. If you find that you frequently attend parties where you drink or do drugs to excess, to the extent that you have blackouts or trouble recalling any part of the evening or have found yourself vomiting due to excessive drinking, you should alter your behavior or see a counselor about your drinking. Intoxicated people are easy victims. Intoxicated people are also more willing perpetrators and may do things while they are inebriated that they would not do if they were sober. In either case, it's no excuse. Partying can be fun, but there are many dangers to consider.

Potential Trouble Spots: The Woman Alone

Being the only woman, or an unaccompanied woman, at a fraternity party or another mostly male function can be dangerous, even if you are friends with a lot of the men present. The danger increases in the presence of alcohol and/or drugs. People get out of control and being the lone female in a room full of drunken men is also probably not that much fun anyway. We're not saying that fraternities or other male-dominated organizations are bastions of evil or that fraternity members are more predisposed to rape than those who are not fraternity members. It's just not a good idea to put yourself in a situation in which you don't have control over what happens to you.

We're also not saying you shouldn't go to these parties. Just bring some friends with you. If you begin to feel threatened or notice that the party is getting destructive or violent, leave. You won't be offending anyone. In fact, the guys will probably be relieved that they can go on being howling idiots without any female witnesses.

Walking home alone from a party can also be worrisome, particularly on large metropolitan campuses. Some colleges offer escorts, either by a campus security officer or a student volunteer group (see more under "Services and Resources" later in this chapter), for people who do not want to go home alone. Use these services, particularly if you are intoxicated or feel hesitant about the walk. It's always better to be safe.

It is not advisable to walk to your home with a drunk acquaintance or someone you have just met. Incidents of sexual coercion and rape on campuses are most likely to occur in the man's apartment or room, with the next likely place being the woman's apartment or room. A very small proportion of attacks occur in a car or outside. Walk home with a friend you trust and know well. Stay out of strangers' rooms and don't invite a stranger into your room (even if he is really cute), *especially* when one or both of you is intoxicated.

SEXUAL COERCION

Many forms of sexual coercion exist, from verbal pressure to rape. These are hard topics to read about and harder topics to confront, but your best defense against experiencing (or perpetrating) these coercive acts is to understand what they are and what factors lead up to them. One of the best ways to protect yourself is to learn how to recognize the early warning signs of sexual coercion and take steps to stop it or avoid it—usually by physically removing yourself from a potentially dangerous situation.

Of course, as we all know, coercion can sometimes be sudden, physically overwhelming, and terrifying. If you ever find yourself in a physically coercive situation, we have one bit of advice: fight back. In a survey of college women, of whom 22 percent reported having been forced to engage in some form of sexual activity, 14 percent of those attacked successfully prevented rape by saying no, crying or screaming, talking the attacker out of it, or physically resisting.[11] After we've discussed the behaviors, we'll tell you how to fight back through assertiveness training, self-esteem, and self defense.

Fight Back

A cross section and representative sample of college men revealed that 5.7 percent had forced a female date to engage in sexual activity within the previous year. According to that estimate, then, in any one year at the college where this study was conducted, as many as 588 college men forced their dates into sexual activity despite the women's protests. This does not mean that protesting is ever in vain and, if you find yourself in a position where you are being pressured to have sex against your will, by all means, protest in any way you can. The same study revealed that 11 out of 77 women being forced into sexual acts against their will were able to fend off their attackers by saying no, crying, screaming, reasoning with the assailant, or physically resisting.[12]

Verbal Coercion and How to Confront It

Pressure from a Date

Sexual coercion comes in many forms, the most common of which is verbal coercion. Studies have shown that the number of college men using verbal coercion (such as saying things that were not true, making false promises, or simply talking the woman into it) is as high as 42 percent. Additionally, another study showed that 69.8 percent[13] of undergraduate women surveyed had given in to intercourse when they didn't want to because they were overwhelmed by a man's continual arguments and pressure. Of the forms of sexual coercion examined in this study, the majority of women had experienced unwanted intercourse due to verbal coercion.

Sweet Talk?

College men who have lied about themselves to get someone in bed: 29 percent.

College men who would do it again: 7 percent.

College women who have lied about themselves to get someone in bed: 14 percent.

College women who would do it again: 2 percent.

Sexual Harassment or Pressure from an Authority Figure

Certain people may try to pressure you to have sex with them by using their position of authority over you (someone like a professor or boss). They may threaten to fire you or give you bad grades if you don't accept their advances, but more often the pressure is less direct and hard to define. You may even be made to feel that you are somehow responsible for this unwanted attention.

These are examples of sexual harassment, an act almost as hard to define as date rape. Make no mistake, however: if you are being pressured to have sex, even in a subtle way, by someone with power over you, you are being sexually harassed. If you find this happening to you, remove yourself from the situation and tell someone about it—a friend, if you like—or report it to the authorities: the school administration, campus security, the police, or all of them. If the situation arises again, you *must* report the incident to the proper authorities. On a college campus the best place to go is your health services department or the dean's office. Explain the problem and name the offender. It might be tough, but it will protect you, stop the problem, and, we hope, prevent the offender from attempting to intimidate or coerce somebody else.

Pressure or Harassment from a Stranger

Verbal coercion can also come from a stranger. If it does, your best bet is to simply ignore the offender unless you feel threatened or see him often and he repeatedly accosts you. If a stranger is verbally accosting you with any level of frequency, immediately file a complaint with campus security and the dean's office. This will send a clear message to the person that you are not a victim and will stand up for yourself. It will also be good for your self-esteem.

Pressure from a Girlfriend or Boyfriend

Things get tougher when the coercion comes from a familiar or even friendly face. The reported percentage of college women who have experienced verbal coercion while in dating relationships ranges from 15 percent to 48 percent.[14] Making someone consent to unwanted sex through verbal coercion may not seem so bad because no overt force or violence is used, but the effects of such an experience can still be very debilitating to the victim. Extreme cases of this type of coercion, which we can call *aggressive verbal coercion*, go beyond pleading and persuading and can even be considered rape if they involve verbal threats. These cases can leave victims feeling just as traumatized as victims of physical coercion. Most often, verbal coercion leaves the person who was coerced feeling cheated and disrespected.

If you're being verbally coerced, confront it immediately, as it's happening. Point out exactly what sorts of behavior are making you uncomfortable, and give examples of the things he or she says or does that put unwanted pressure on you. Your partner should be understanding and respectful. If he or she reacts with hostility to your discussion, take a moment to look closely at your friendship. If your boyfriend's or girlfriend's reaction to your complaints of verbal coercion is overly negative or downright angry, you should consider talking to someone else about this problem. A friend is a good person to start with, but if the problem persists, you should seek professional assistance (again, the health service at your college is a great place to go to find out how to get help) and consider getting out of the relationship.

Also, be aware of any progression of the verbal coercion. Is it always the same or does its intensity increase? Are there ever threats involved, such as ending the relationship or finding someone else to have sex with? Are there ever physical threats involved? These are all red flags. A persistent and annoying nagging is one thing, but threats, either emotional or physical, are another altogether. This is aggressive verbal coercion.

If you are experiencing aggressive verbal coercion, you should seek professional help and seriously consider ending the relationship. Being threatened into sex is different from being talked into it. It indicates that whoever is threatening you doesn't respect you for your feelings. Lack of respect and consideration are not things you should expect from a friend or lover. Even if you believe that you are somehow responsible, remember what is really at stake. It's not just sex anymore, but your mental health. If you are enduring threats like this, you are not being fair to yourself. Be in touch with your own feelings before you worry that you are the cause of someone else's feelings. Remember: friendship and sexual relationships are two-way streets. Don't let someone manipulate you, under the auspices of friendship, into something you don't want to do.

Physical Coercion and How to Confront It

The laws against rape are very clear about physical coercion. If you've ever been physically forced into a sexual act, whoever did it broke the law. One study shows that 38.5 percent of college women have had a man attempt unwanted sexual intercourse with them by using physical force, 25.9 percent experienced unwanted intercourse in conjunction with the use of force, and 12.9 percent experienced unwanted sexual acts by men who used force to make them.[15] The first case is considered attempted rape and the latter two are rape.

More Partners, More Risk

Women who have had a greater number of sex partners tend to have had more experiences with sexual coercion than those with fewer sex partners. Here is the breakdown of our respondents:

Experience	% Women who have had more than 6 sex partners	% Women who have had less than 6 partners
Stalked or harassed with phone calls	53	44
Date, sex partner, or friend physically forced you into a sexual act	50	27
Victim of forcible rape by a stranger	7	2

It should go without saying that physical force should never be used to compel someone to have sex. It is not only against the law, it is morally reprehensible by most standards across most cultures. If you experience rape or attempted rape by a stranger, you should:

- Go to a hospital immediately for a complete examination. Even if you don't think you've been seriously hurt, you may have sustained injuries that need treatment. Make it clear when arriving at the hospital that you have been raped or assaulted. It's important that you not change clothes or bathe before going to the hospital. Proving rape in court can be difficult, but it is much easier if conclusive medical evidence can be provided.

- Call the police, or ask the doctor or nurse to call the police for you.

- Seek professional counseling. Rape is one of the most traumatic experiences a woman can encounter. Don't try to just forget about it or deal with it on your own. A trained psychologist can help you work through your feelings, and the sooner you seek help in trying to get past such a horrible experience, the better off you'll be.

Physical Coercion from Someone You Know

Dealing with physical abuse from a friend or lover is something that one out of two college students has experienced at some point in life. A full 30 percent of these students are still currently involved in unsafe relationships.[16]

If an acquaintance, friend, or romantic partner hits or slaps you, shoves you, restrains you, or physically forces you into having sex against your will, you should leave the scene where it occurred as soon as you can get away and go somewhere you know you are safe, whether that is a friend's house or a public place. This will allow you to think clearly and reinforce your feeling of safety. If you have been raped, the best place to go is your campus health service facility or a hospital. A doctor should examine you to determine whether you suffered any internal injuries. You should then contact the police, campus security, or the National Domestic Violence Hotline (1-800-333-7233). Do not wait for an apology or an explanation. Take immediate measures to protect yourself.

Unfortunately, humans can be extremely illogical. People indeed go back to someone who has hurt them or threatened to hurt them, thinking that everything will be all right, that the problems in the relationship can be overcome no matter how dire the situation might be. This is where friends come in. If you suspect that a friend of yours is involved in an abusive relationship, where physical or verbal coercion is involved, try to help. Gently confront your friend and offer to help in any way. Encourage her to talk not only to you, but to a professional. You may be what your friend needs to find the strength to break free of a dangerous relationship.

How to Spot a Friend in Trouble

The following is adapted from *"It Won't Happen Again, I Promise": Is Your Relationship Abusive?*, a pamphlet published by Healthwise of Columbia University.

If you are concerned about a friend's relationship, here are some things to look for when deciding whether to become involved. If you can answer yes to a lot of these, then take some action.

- Have you noticed any personality changes?

    Frequent outbursts of emotion.

    Frequently avoids conflict and will not engage in class discussions.

    Has become invisible and tries to escape notice by anyone.

- Have you noticed any behavioral changes?

    Your friend has become a loner and doesn't interact with others.

    No longer has time for friends and other activities since he or she started the relationship.

    Has frequently demonstrated urgency to meet with the person she or he is seeing.

    Has begun drinking, smoking, or sleeping more than usual.

    Has continually spoken of breaking off the relationship but hasn't done so.

- Have you noticed physical change?

    Attire has changed drastically, either to cover up or draw attention.

    Has had bruises on arms or neck; wears heavy eye makeup to conceal bruises or crying.

    Has become more unkempt than usual.

- Have you noticed any changes in your friend's attitudes toward school?

    Grades have dropped.

    Has dropped from extracurricular activities.

    Panics over necessity to stay late after classes or organized events.

If you find yourself, or a friend, in a situation where physical abuse or threats are present, seek help or encourage the other person to seek help. If you have experienced rape or know someone who has, seek help or encourage the victim to seek help.

Seeking Help

Feelings of guilt or shame prevent many from even talking about an abusive experience. One study showed that, of a population of college women who had experienced sexual coercion, 72 percent did not seek help from anyone after the incident. Of the 28 percent who did seek help, 75 percent went to friends, 9 percent sought help from a counselor or therapist, 6 percent contacted the police, and the remaining 9 percent depended on a parent, another relative, a rape crisis center, a physician, or a hospital. Of the 28 percent who sought help, 58 percent did so within two weeks of the incident, while 13 percent waited until more than a year had passed. The fact that a significant number of victims waited so long is an indication of just how hard it can be to reach out for support.[17]

Researchers have found that the better acquainted a victim is with the offender, the less likely she is to seek help. There are several powerful emotions that can prevent victims from reporting or discussing date rape. Shame or guilt may make a woman think that somehow she brought on the attack herself or allowed it to happen, and she might feel "unclean" or "dirty." Another feeling is fear—the simple fear that the attacker might hurt them again. There is often also a desire to protect the attacker. If a friend or a boyfriend committed rape, the victim might not want to get him in trouble simply because they had been close, they trusted each other, and they even loved each other at one point.

If someone assaults you, that person is not your friend and certainly doesn't deserve your love. By seeking help for yourself, you may even indirectly cause the offender to receive professional counseling, which is what he needs. If you still care for the person who assaulted you, the best thing you can do for both yourself and him is get the help you need.

A victim of rape by a stranger is more likely to seek help than victims of date or acquaintance rape, because there are none of the friendship and trust issues to work through. Still, feelings of fear and shame may keep any rape victim from seeing a counselor. Again, it's important not to let these emotions fester. A professional counselor can help you overcome the feelings of anger, fear, or guilt you might have if you've experienced any form of sexual coercion.

The majority of rape and date rape victims seek help from friends, which is fine. Friends are a great source of comfort and support. However, your friends do not have the training or skills to help you make a full emotional recovery. Counselors and staff at your college's health service facility are there to provide help with these problems. There are also many support groups and organizations that offer professional advice and counseling. See the list of telephone numbers at the end of this chapter.

Medical Options

If you are a victim of rape, date rape, or acquaintance rape, and you are unsure if any type of birth control was used, you should allow for the possibility of pregnancy or sexually transmitted diseases. Go immediately to your campus health facility and tell them what happened. A doctor can usually prescribe a "morning-after" pill to prevent an unwanted pregnancy and antibiotics to prevent infections. Even if you think protection was used (which would be unusual in a case of coercive sex), you should go to health services anyway and have yourself checked out.

What If You're Unsure?

If, when you've talked with a friend and a counselor, they tell you that your experience was sexual coercion, then let the professional counselor inform you about what to do next. It is important that you trust this person completely. If you don't like a particular counselor that you talk with, get another.

You might be unclear in your own mind about a sexual experience—unable to definitely decide if what occurred constituted something more than just an unpleasant sexual experience. If you are worried that you were coerced or that you were in a situation that might be considered rape, ask for a second opinion. Tell a friend about the experience (or what you remember about the experience, if you were intoxicated) and see what the friend has to say. Talk to a professional at your campus health service facility as well. When you are recounting the event, make sure to recount it as accurately as possible. Sometimes victims are not clear about the experience they just had because they are trying to deny that it occurred, protecting themselves from a painful memory.

PREVENTION AND THERAPY

There are services offered for victims of sexual coercion and those who wish to learn how to avoid these situations. Many college health services offer assertiveness training. This training consists of classes that teach you methods of improving your assertive powers (which is a good set of skills to have, not only to prevent sexual coercion, but to succeed in all of your goals) through role-playing and discussing hypothetical situations.

In role-playing, you might be put into an uncomfortable situation with another member of the group. One of you will play the dominant role and the other will play the passive party—the victim. The instructor coaches you on how to deal with this situation. You will learn strategies and methods for dealing with coercive tactics. Check with your health services or women's resource center and find out what type of assertiveness training or rape prevention seminars they offer. Keep in mind that these are not only for women, but for men, too, and both sexes can learn from these seminars.

One thing these classes try to do is boost your self-esteem. Women (and men) with low self-esteem tend to feel that they deserve the bad treatment they receive, or they may feel that they are incapable of improving the situation.

Self-Defense

Self-defense classes are great ways to fulfill your physical education credits, enhance your performance in sports, boost your self-esteem and self-image, improve your physical condition and reflexes, and learn how to protect yourself. Self-defense classes may be offered through your college's women's resource center or the physical education program. There are many methods of self-defense, from karate, to judo, to boxing. Check them out and find one that suits you. Just knowing how to defend yourself is a great way to improve your confidence and your safety. If you know how to defend yourself physically, you are much less likely to be a victim. It's nice to know you can kick some ass if you have to.

Knowing how to kick ass is not only helpful, but good for your health and self-esteem as well. UPI/Corbis-Bettmann

There are other methods of self-defense, such as carrying a can of spray mace (tear gas—not legal in all states), pepper spray, and noisemakers. While these are widely used in large metropolitan areas, we still do not advise that you rely on them. A noisemaker can be easily stolen by an attacker larger than yourself and spray mace can be used against you if it is wrestled away. Of course, if carrying these items makes you feel safer, then by all means use them. However, learning an actual method of self-defense is much more effective, both mentally and physically.

The best way to defend yourself, however, is to avoid having to defend yourself. Be smart. You should avoid walking alone late at night (especially if you attend an urban college), but if you have to, stay on well-populated, well-lighted streets. Constantly scan the area in front of you and think ahead about where a potential attacker might conceal himself. Be aware of who else is on the street, and walk briskly and purposefully. Cross the street well in advance of any large group of men or any person you find intimidating. If you think someone is following you, step into a store or another public place and wait for that person to pass.

If you have to walk through a parking lot at night, walk down the center of the lanes. Always have your keys out and ready before your reach your car so you don't have to fumble through your pockets or handbag. Check the backseat of your car before getting in, and always drive with the doors locked.

Don't live in constant fear: just be cautious.

Services and Resources

No, this is not a dating service. Many colleges or student unions offer sober escorts (they have different names at different campuses) for people who want to be walked home. Some colleges offer escorts through the campus security department—all you have to do is call from where you are and an escort will meet you outside and take you home. Other forms of escort services are provided by groups of volunteering students who refrain from any intoxicants during large party weekends or party nights and keep themselves available to walk people home. People may want escorts for any number of reasons, but if you don't feel like walking home alone after a party or feel like losing a person who has been hounding you all night, get one of these escorts. They take you from the door of the party to the door of your home. If your college doesn't offer one of these services, consider starting one through a student organization. It's a great service, plus it's fun see all of your friends inebriated while you remain sober. At the very least, it will give you a different perspective and allow you to help anyone who feels the need for an escort.

Get the Numbers

Finally, you should have some important phone numbers around to get help, treatment, counseling, or training for yourself or a friend. See the list below for some of these numbers, and also stop by your campus health services facility—it probably puts out a pamphlet of important numbers to call for problems ranging from accidental poisoning to assault and rape. Take advantage of what the campus offers you to prevent yourself from becoming a victim. And, if you are a victim, reach out to those on campus who can help you. They are there, and they are there to help.

Here's a list of other, important numbers that are national. If you find yourself in some sort of trouble and for any reason feel uncomfortable or are unable to contact organizations on campus that can help, use the numbers below. They are national hotlines and are available twenty-four hours a day, seven days a week. Also, check for the local numbers of these organizations in your area.

National Clearinghouse on Marital and Date Rape (NCOMDR) *415-524-1582*
Rape Crisis Network *800-491-RAPE*
The Rape Crisis Center 24-hour hotline *210-349-7273*
National Rape Crisis Hotline *800-656-4673*
Gay Men's Health Crisis (GMHC) *212-807-6655*
National Domestic Violence Hotline *800-333-7233*

References

1. R. J. Ogletree, "Sexual coercion experience and help-seeking behavior of college women," *Journal of American College Health*, Vol. 41 (January 1993).
2. B. L. Yegidis, "Date rape and other forced sexual encounters among college students," *Journal of Sex Education Therapy*, Vol. 20, No. 2 (1990).
3. S. M. Bajracharya, P. S. Sarvela, and F. R. Isberner, "A retrospective study of first sexual intercourse experiences among undergraduates," *Journal of American College Health*, Vol. 43 (January 1995).
4. Yegidis, loc. cit.
5. Gloria J. Fischer, "College student attitudes toward forcible date rape: Cognitive predictors," *Archives of Sexual Behavior* Vol. 15, No. 6 (1986).

6. C. L. Muehlenhard, and L. C. Hollabaugh, "Do women sometimes say no when they mean yes? The prevalence and correlates of women's token resistance to sex," *Journal of Personality and Social Psychology*, Vol. 54 (1988), pp. 872–879.

7. Yegidis, loc. cit.

8. Muehlenhard and Hollabaugh, loc. cit.

9. C. L. Muehlenhard, and S. W. Cook, "Men's self-reports of unwanted sexual activity," *The Journal of Sex Research*, Vol. 24 (1988), pp. 58–72.

10. C. L. Muehlenhard, and P. J. Long, "Men's versus women's reports of pressure to engage in unwanted sexual intercourse," *paper presented at the Western region meeting of the Society for the Scientific Study of Sex*, 1988.

11. Yegidis, loc. cit.

12. Ibid.

13. R. J. Ogletree, "Sexual coercion experience and help-seeking behavior of college women," *Journal of American College Health*, Vol. 41 (January 1993).

14. M. E. Craig, K. C. Seth, and D. R. Follingstad, "Verbal coercive sexual behavior among college students," *Archives of Sexual Behavior*, Vol. 18, No. 5 (1989).

15. Ogletree, loc. cit.

16. M. A. Pirog-Good, and J. E. Stets, *Violence in Dating Relationships* (New York: Praeger, 1989).

17. Ogletree, loc. cit.

The Big Picture

If our survey showed us anything, it was that college students see sex as part of the "big picture": just one part of what it takes to have a happy life. Long-term commitment to a partner was high on the list of life goals. Overwhelmingly, the students we surveyed affirmed that they want to get married some day: 70 percent said they love the idea of marriage, while 26 percent admitted marriage might be difficult, but definitely worth the effort.

Is sex the most important part of marriage or a long-term commitment? Not according to the students we surveyed. When asked what they would do if the frequency of sex began to decline while they were in a long-term relationship, did they opt to bail out? No! Most of them, 67 percent, realize that a relationship takes work. They favored confronting the problem and fighting to keep the fire alive. Even the lazy ones, the 31 percent who said you should just make do with a drop in sexual activity, said that there is more to a relationship than sex.

No doubt about it, though, college students are looking for great sex lives. Eighty-four percent believe that there is such a thing as "perfect sex," and they want to find it. What do they think is the most important part of great sex? Love, love, love. That's right, even in the final years of the twentieth century, love is the thing—54 percent listed it as the most important part of a good sex life. Believe it or not, good communication, at 19 percent, comes in second on the list of keys to good sex—five percentage points ahead of physical attraction at 14 percent.

On the downside, we learned that students are either reluctant or careless about protecting themselves from the hazardous side of sex. Less than half practice safe sex all the time. And women must still contend with partners who violently assert their sexual will: 21 percent reported being physically forced by an acquaintance to have sex. Clearly, there are some serious problems that must be resolved to make the world a better place for sex.

Overall, it looks like college students know what they want and know how to get it. And they are happy with where they are heading. Although 21 percent of the students we asked felt that their parents' generation had better romantic relationships, 36 percent felt that love and sex are better now than they used to be.

Looks like the twenty-first century is going to be one big love-in.

Glossary

Here's every word (or almost every word) that you won't learn in class, but that you've probably heard and used. Some of these words may have meanings you didn't even know about. Did you know what a "hot plate" was before you read this? In some cases, the number of slang terms for any one actual word is tremendous. We've listed 21 common slang terms for the pudendum, 31 for the penis, and 45 for sexual intercourse. Of course, we're sure there are even more out there—some more creative, most surely less creative—than the common ones we've accumulated.

The glossary is organized by synonyms. The headings are the technical/medical terms for various things, and the colloquial equivalents and related terms follow. Where clarification was warranted or an interesting tidbit of etymology arose, we've included it.

Anal Sex

backdoor

butt fuck—The slang word *butt* has been around in print since the 1720s, and *fuck* is one of the oldest, most versatile words in English, so how come it took until the 1960s for the term *butt fuck* to enter the popular printed lexicon? Maybe we'll never know.

fudge packing—Also a derogatory term used against male homosexuals, as in *fudge packers.*

Greek-style

rim

Breasts

bazooms

boobs—This was originally the word *bub*, which surfaced in the 1820s. Bub was derived from *bubby*, which made its slang debut in the 1650s.

gazongas

hooters

jugs

melons

pair/set—As in "She has a nice pair on her."

rack

tits—Not as slangy as one might imagine, deriving straight from the technical term *teat* or *teats*, but simply derogatory most of the time.

yabos

yams

Condom

glove

jimmy hat

party hat

protection

raincoat

rubber

sheath

skins

Cunnilingus

box licking

donning the beard

eating out—Variations of this have been around in print since 1916.

eating pussy

going down on

muff diving

rug munching

Dating Scene (related terms)

beer goggles—Ever get so drunk that the couch starts looking good—not just for sleeping on? Then you've been wearing a pair of these.

coyote/wolf morning—When you'd chew your arm off to get away from the person lying next to you, who is usually considered to be coyote-ugly.

jailbait—Like Lolita: a minor, usually female, usually quite sexually desirable, for those of you who don't know.

hit on—To try to attract the attention of someone for sexual purposes, put the moves on someone ("to hit on them").

macking—See *scamming*.

scamming—Usually in reference to guys who are trying out their newest pickup lines on numerous women in the same vicinity and then focusing on one to *scam on*, but women can scam, too. See *hit on*.

six-pack chick/guy—A relative of *beer goggles*, the six-pack chick or guy is someone you would be attracted to only after you had downed at least six beers.

tonsil hockey—Especially energetic making out that inspires people to shout "get a room!"

trolling for cock—Women who get all gussied up in their sexiest outfits and head out to the bars, alone or in groups, with the sole purpose of getting some, are *trolling for cock*.

Ejaculate

cum (as a noun, can also mean semen; see below)

gizz/jizz (a noun and a verb)

shoot/blow a load

shoot/blow a wad

spew

Fellatio

blow job—This term popped up sometime in the twentieth century, apparently. It has a second definition that is kind of funny and seems to have been largely forgotten: an unpleasant experience or bad turn of events. Example: "That was a real blow job," meaning it really sucked (figuratively, not literally) or was a real bummer.

deep throat—This came into the popular lexicon in 1973, with the release of the infamous pornographic film of the same name.

going down on

hose beast

hummer

schmoke/smoking the bologna

smoothy

sucking off

Female Sexual Juices

honey

jam

juice

soup

Intercourse

bang—The exact date for the first time "bang" was used in print to mean copulation is unknown due to the uncertainty of the date of publication of the manuscript it was included in, a book entitled *Pills*—the title an odd foreshadowing of the birth control method that would later come to prevent big bangs.

bump

bumping uglies

doing it

doing the nasty

doing the wild thing

doggie style—a favored sexual position that is self-explanatory, if you've ever seen dogs have sex.

dogging/dogged

drill

dry humping—Wildly passionate making out, in which people keep their clothes on but go through all the bumping and grinding of real sex.

fucking—Ever wondered how long this word's been around? In 1680 it was first listed in a supplement to the *Oxford English Dictionary*, but it isn't originally of English origin. It comes from Germanic roots—the word *fokken*, meaning "to thrust, copulate with," from the Swiss *focka*, meaning "to strike, push, copulate" and *fock*, meaning "penis"; also from Norwegian *fukka*, meaning "to copulate." Think those old Norwegians ever used to go around saying *mutha fukka?*

getting busy

getting some

home run

humping

jamming

knocking boots

laying pipe

making the beast with two backs

nailing

playing hide the salami

screwing

strapping

Masturbation and Manual Stimulation

abusing yourself

beating off

giving yourself a hand

jerking off
making soup—Pertains only to female masturbation.
self-love
slapping your meat
spanking the monkey
stroking it
turning Japanese
wanking
whacking off

Penis (erect and otherwise)

boner/bone
cock—This is an oldie that first appeared in a Middle English Dictionary in 1325.
dick—Another classic, first appearing in print in the 1880s as slang for the penis, as opposed to its other slang definition ("a peculiar man").
dong
dork
hard-on
johnson
member
mojo
one-eyed wonder worm
pecker
pitching a tent—To have an erection that causes a tentlike formation, i.e., an erection that is visible through your pants.
pole
poll
prick
rod
schlong
stiffy
third leg
tool
wanker
willy
woody

Semen

cum/come—Apparently, this word first appeared in print in a book called *Le Slang* back in 1923 as a synonym for "sperm." Nowadays, it can also mean "to orgasm" in men or women, as in "Donnie and Marie came simultaneously" or "He/she came all over the sheets."

gizz/jizz/jism

seed

spoo

spunk

Testicles

balls

blue balls—This supposedly refers to testicles that are uncomfortable because of vascular constriction brought on by lack of sexual release. Believe it or not, this is a complaint many men use to try to get their girlfriends to comply with their sexual desires. There is no discomfort in the testicles that cannot be relieved through simple masturbation, so don't fall for it, girls.

cajones—From Spanish, it can mean a scrotum and its contents, but it tends to imply machismo, much the same way as "You must have some pretty big *balls* to challenge me" implies courage and guts.

family jewels—Doesn't this term sound as old and sweet as your grandfather? That's because it is, first appearing in print between 1916 and 1922.

huevos—Taken quite literally from Spanish, meaning "eggs," it is also Spanish slang for testicles.

nuts

sack

Vulva

beaver—Honestly, we've never really understood why this particular animal (sure it's a hairy animal, but so is a possum) became associated with the pudendum, but it has, in print as early as 1927.

booty

box—This term goes all the way back to the Bard himself. Check out *All's Well That End's Well*, Act II, scene iii, line 275, if you don't believe us.

clam/bearded clam

cunt—Uniformly thought of as the worst curse word one can use, the word originates from Middle English and has appeared in texts dating back to 1230. Geoffrey Chaucer even uses a form of it in *The Canterbury Tales*. Check out the prologue to the "Wife of Bath's Tale."

hair pie

hole

muff

piece of ass

poontang/tang
pussy
quim
slash/gash
snatch
tail
trim

Miscellaneous

felch—First defined in the book, *The Queen's Vernacular,* published in 1972, and defined as: "complicated erotic process of sucking the come one has ejaculated into an ass and returning it orally."

golden showers—If you don't know already or can't figure it out, then you probably don't need or want to know. Think urine.

grudge fuck—When you sleep with someone you actively dislike, for whatever reason.

hot plate/plating—An activity in which one's partner squats over the other's face, or nearby, and has a bowel movement onto a clear plate placed either directly over the face of the observer or another part of the body.

pity fuck—This is usually a female province: a woman takes pity on an abjectly pathetic guy and has sex with him just because she thinks it might help his self-confidence, or maybe so he'll quit whining about what a loser he is.

rodeo—Largely, a term related to a sad fraternity practice in which the male is having intercourse with a women doggie-style, says something intended to offend her immensely, and then grabs her hair while trying to maintain penetration with his penis for eight seconds before she can "buck him off." We're not making this up. There are still Neanderthals among us.

shrimping—Toe sucking for sexual pleasure

snowballing—A distant cousin of the *felch,* this is when the ejaculate one has released into the mouth of the other is returned orally through French kisses directly after fellatio.

tea bagging—Having one's scrotum placed entirely inside the partner's mouth and held there for a period of time while it is suckled.

water sports—See *golden showers.* Watch for this when reading personal ads in the backs of newspapers. Ever wonder why "water sports" pops up as a hobby so often, even in landlocked, lakeless areas?

About the Authors

Leland Elliott is a writer and has worked in publishing since 1992. He attended Dartmouth College, where he was an English and Film major and where he also had and enjoyed sex. He now lives in New York City, where he has found that being the author of this book is both a curse and a blessing when it comes to meeting women. He continues to write fiction and screenplays, although not all of them are about sex.

Cynthia Brantley is a writer who is currently getting her M.A. in Literature from the University of Texas at Austin. Cynthia attended Tulane University as an undergraduate, where she also had and enjoyed sex. She currently lives in Austin, Texas, with her husband, so she has not been able to fully experience the repercussions, both good and bad, that authoring a sex book can have on one's social life.